Beadwork

Learning Off-Loom Beading Techniques One Stitch at a Time

Visual®

by Chris Franchetti Michaels

WILEY

Wiley Publishing, Inc.

Praise for the
Teach Yourself VISUALLY Series

I just had to let you and your company know how great I think your books are. I just purchased my third Visual book (my first two are dog-eared now!) and, once again, your product has surpassed my expectations. The expertise, thought, and effort that go into each book are obvious, and I sincerely appreciate your efforts. Keep up the wonderful work!

—*Tracey Moore (Memphis, TN)*

I have several books from the Visual series and have always found them to be valuable resources.

—*Stephen P. Miller (Ballston Spa, NY)*

Thank you for the wonderful books you produce. It wasn't until I was an adult that I discovered how I learn—visually. Although a few publishers out there claim to present the material visually, nothing compares to Visual books. I love the simple layout. Everything is easy to follow. And I understand the material! You really know the way I think and learn. Thanks so much!

—*Stacey Han (Avondale, AZ)*

Like a lot of other people, I understand things best when I see them visually. Your books really make learning easy and life more fun.

—*John T. Frey (Cadillac, MI)*

I am an avid fan of your Visual books. If I need to learn anything, I just buy one of your books and learn the topic in no time. Wonders! I have even trained my friends to give me Visual books as gifts.

—*Illona Bergstrom (Aventura, FL)*

I write to extend my thanks and appreciation for your books. They are clear, easy to follow, and straight to the point. Keep up the good work! I bought several of your books and they are just right! No regrets! I will always buy your books because they are the best.

—*Seward Kollie (Dakar, Senegal)*

Credits

Acquisitions Editor
Pam Mourouzis

Project Editor
Donna Wright

Copy Editor
Lynn Northrup

Editorial Manager
Christina Stambaugh

Publisher
Cindy Kitchel

Vice President and Executive Publisher
Kathy Nebenhaus

Interior Design
Kathie Rickard
Elizabeth Brooks

Photography
Matt Bowen

About the Author

Chris Franchetti Michaels is a writer and jewelry artisan specializing in beaded designs, wirework, and metal fabrication. She has written extensively about jewelry and jewelry making on the Internet since 2003, and she is the author of *Teach Yourself Visually Jewelry Making & Beading, Beading Visual Quick Tips,* and *Wire Jewelry Visual Quick Tips.* Chris has also appeared on several episodes of the DIY Network television show *Jewelry Making,* and her designs have been featured in popular jewelry project books. Visit her Web site www.beadjewelry.net for more help and inspiration.

Acknowledgments

No books about bead weaving would exist if artisans all over the world had not been willing to pass down their knowledge and skills to future generations for thousands of years. Many contemporary instructors and authors have made important strides in continuing that tradition, and it's because of their efforts that I've embraced bead weaving and am now able to help new beaders explore the craft. Of those wonderful teachers, I'd especially like to thank Carol Wilcox Wells whose work has been a great inspiration to me.

I also thank my agent, Marilyn Allen, for all of her help and encouragement, and fellow designer Shari Bonnin, who believed from the start that I was up to the task of writing jewelry books. Donna Wright, Pam Mourouzis, and Lynn Northrup all devoted many hours of work to make this book a useful resource, which still wouldn't have happened if not for the excellent photography of Matt Bowen and the artistic skills of the Wiley graphics department. I owe a debt of gratitude to SK, VK, BH, and ETC, for their patience during my absence in Eldre'Thalas as I worked on this book, and to my husband, Dennis, who not only made Thanksgiving dinner by himself but also managed to keep three computers, two printers, and a scanner running during the entire writing process.

Online Appendix

An Appendix to this book is available online at www.wiley.com/go/tyvbeadwork. Titled "Reference Materials," it contains lists of helpful Web sites (including online suppliers of materials used in the projects), useful bead size charts, beads-per-unit estimates, hints for coating beads with protective spray, and troubleshooting tips.

Table of Contents

 **chapter 1** **Introduction to Beadwork**

 **chapter 2** **Essential Skills and Techniques**

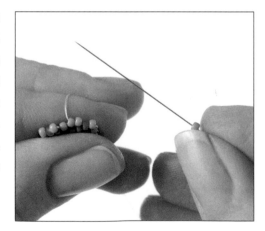

chapter 3 Peyote Stitch

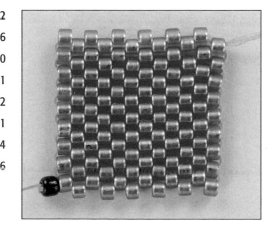

chapter 4 Beaded Netting

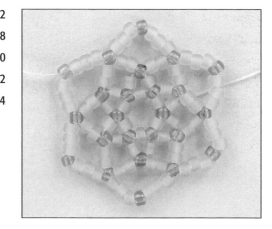

chapter 5 Ladder Stitch and Brick Stitch

chapter 6 Square Stitch and Spiral Rope

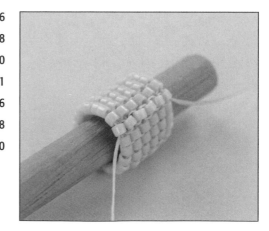

chapter 7 Right-Angle Weave

 chapter 8 Herringbone Stitch

chapter 9 Details and Jewelry Finishing Techniques

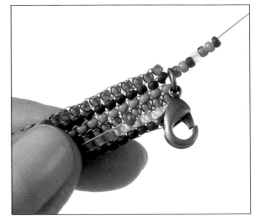

chapter 10 Beginner Projects

chapter **11** **Intermediate Projects**

chapter 1

Introduction to Beadwork

Have you admired intricately woven, colorful beadwork, but assumed that you could never make it yourself? Perhaps you were intimidated by the tiny dimensions and sheer number of the beads, or maybe you felt overwhelmed by the complex project instructions in a book or magazine. Put your worries aside, and allow this book to guide you, step by step, through the most popular contemporary beadwork techniques. You will discover that bead weaving is not overly difficult, and that it is more rewarding than you may have imagined.

Bead weaving is the process of stitching beads together using a needle and thread. With *off-loom bead weaving*, you stitch beads while holding the beaded fabric—called *beadwork*—in your hands, rather than using a loom to support it. You can use off-loom bead-weaving techniques to create jewelry, artwork, and items of décor for your home.

This book covers introductory off-loom bead weaving for beginners, but it also includes some intermediate techniques that you can learn over time as your skills develop. As you progress, remember that successful bead weaving takes lots of practice, and your initial swatches and projects will not be perfect. Be patient, and enjoy the process of watching your skills improve. Below is an overview of how this book is organized and how you can use it to get started.

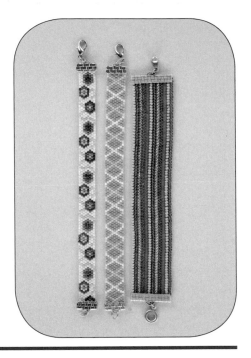

Learn the Basics of Bead Weaving

Begin by reading the sections on beads, needles, thread, tools, and supplies in this chapter. They contain important terminology that is used in bead-weaving project instructions and will help you set up a work area stocked with essential materials.

After you finish Chapter 1, look over all of the sections in Chapter 2. They explain the basic techniques required to start and complete most bead-weaving projects. Pay especially close attention to the final section, which defines essential terms that are used throughout the rest of the book. Keep in mind that you can return to Chapter 2 anytime, and you do not need to learn all of the techniques covered there at once.

EXPERIMENT WITH OFF-LOOM STITCHES

Chapters 3 through 8 demonstrate how to perform the most popular off-loom bead-weaving *stitches*, which are ways that you can weave beads together. Each stitch has a unique name and produces beadwork with a distinct look and feel. You can use most stitches to create beadwork that is flat, tubular, or circular in shape.

Many new beaders begin with peyote stitch, featured in Chapter 3, but you are free to try any stitch that interests you. To learn a new stitch, begin with its flat version and make a practice swatch: Prepare an initial length of thread (see Chapter 2), and then follow the steps for that stitch until you have a length of beadwork. You can use practice swatches to improve your overall skills, and to test alternative methods for beginning and ending thread. Once you feel comfortable with the flat version of a stitch, you can move on to its tubular or circular version, or you can try a flat-beadwork project (see the next section). Later, you can return to that stitch's chapter to learn how to add shape and dimension to your beadwork using increases and decreases.

TRY THE EXAMPLE PROJECTS

Once you feel comfortable performing a stitch in swatches, you can make one of the beginner-level projects in Chapter 10 that uses that stitch. When you're ready to attempt more complex projects, try those in Chapter 11. Both chapters give you an opportunity to practice following project instructions, reading patterns, using stitches in interesting ways, and adding the decorative details and clasps that are covered in Chapter 9.

Beads Used for Bead Weaving

Small, glass beads called *seed beads* are most commonly used for bead weaving. They are available in many sizes and shapes, and in hundreds of colors and finishes.

Varieties of Seed Beads

TRUE SEED BEADS

True seed beads (sometimes called *rocailles, E-beads, round seed beads,* or simply "seed beads") are tiny, slightly cylindrical glass beads that have rounded edges, like doughnuts. The highest-quality modern seed beads are made in Japan, the Czech Republic, and France. Many beaders use only Japanese beads, which tend to be very consistent in size. You can also find *vintage seed beads* in some bead shops and on the Internet. These are typically extra-small beads that were once made in Europe, but are no longer manufactured.

You can use true seed beads for any type of bead-weaving stitch. They produce a textural, flowing style of beaded fabric.

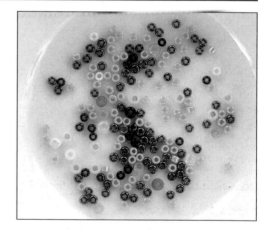

FAQ

My local bead shop sells beads labeled "Rocaille," which seem different from regular seed beads, and I have some project instructions that call for "E-beads," but they do not specify a shape or size. Do these terms refer to special kinds of seed beads?

Yes, in these instances, "rocaille" and "E-bead" have more specific meanings than the general term "seed bead." The Miyuki company of Japan adopted the name Rocaille for its specialty line of tiny (size 15/0), very evenly shaped, rounded seed beads. "E-beads" sometimes refer specifically to large (size 5/0 or 6/0) seed beads. (To learn about sizing, see "Bead Sizes" on page 8.) When your project instructions or patterns call for E-beads, without providing any other size information, you can normally use seed beads that are either size 5/0 or size 6/0.

CONTINUED ON NEXT PAGE

CYLINDER BEADS

Cylinder beads are small glass beads made exclusively in Japan. They are manufactured by a special process that gives them a pronounced cylindrical, or tubular, shape with straight edges (unlike true seed beads, which are only slightly cylindrical and have rounded edges). Cylinder beads are extremely uniform in size and shape, and they have especially large holes to accommodate multiple passes with a needle and thread. Currently, most cylinder beads are produced by two Japanese companies, Miyuki and Toho. You may find these beads for sale under the brand names Delica, Treasure, and Aiko.

Use cylinder beads when you want your beadwork to have a very dense look and smooth feel. They work best with flat or tubular peyote, brick, and square stitches; and they are rarely recommended for loosely woven, or *open*, stitches, such as right-angle weave, netting, and circular stitches.

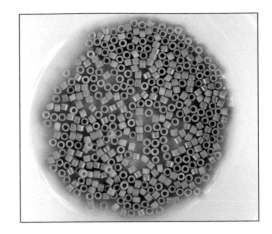

BUGLE BEADS

Bugle beads are narrow glass tubes that are longer and less uniform than cylinder beads. Standard bugle beads are straight, but you can also find ornate *twisted bugle beads*.

Some bugle beads have unpolished, jagged edges that can cut through thread and damage your beadwork. Look for high-quality, Japanese versions of these beads (which may have polished ends), or "buffer" them by stringing a smooth bead immediately in front of and behind each one, as shown on the far right.

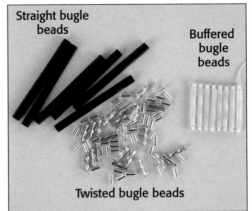

Straight bugle beads

Buffered bugle beads

Twisted bugle beads

TIP

Purchasing Seed Beads by the Unit

Seed beads are usually sold in bulk units rather than by the number of beads in a container or bag. Sometimes these are units of weight. For example, most Japanese seed beads and all cylinder beads are sold by the gram, and French seed beads are usually sold by the ounce. In contrast, many Czech seed beads are sold per 10- to 20-inch strand, or by the *hank*, which is a bundle of between 8 and 14 strands. Project instructions normally indicate how many grams, ounces, strands, or hanks of beads are required, and over time you should develop a feel for how many beads it takes to complete a given type of design. See the online Appendix (www.wiley.com/go/tyvbeadwork) for some typical beads-per-gram, beads-per-ounce, and beads-per-hank estimates.

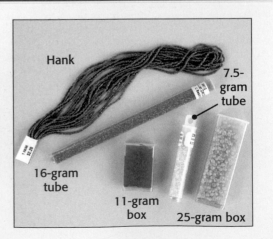

Hank

7.5-gram tube

16-gram tube

11-gram box

25-gram box

CUT SEED BEADS

Cut seed beads are seed beads with one or more flat edges, which create *facets*. Here are the three most common types:

- *Two-cuts* (also called *hex-cuts*) are similar to very short bugle beads, but have six relatively even facets that run lengthwise.
- *Three-cuts* are two-cuts with extra facets at the ends.
- *Charlottes* (also called *one-cuts*) are true seed beads with a single facet.

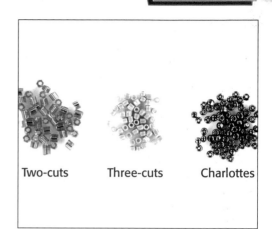

Two-cuts   Three-cuts   Charlottes

SHAPED SEED BEADS

Shaped seed beads are manufactured in different shapes than true seed beads. Here are the most popular:

- *Triangle beads* have three equal sides and ends that are shaped like triangles.
- *Drop beads* (also called *fringe beads*) are tiny, broad, teardrop-shaped beads used to create texture or to accent the ends of fringe. (These include Magatamas, which are manufactured by the Toho company.)
- *Cube beads* (also called *square beads*) have four equal sides and ends that are shaped like squares.

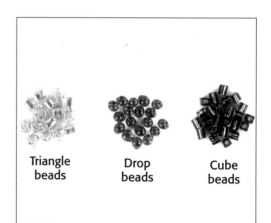

Triangle beads   Drop beads   Cube beads

TIP

Using Larger Beads for Bead Weaving
You can use larger glass beads as accents with many bead-weaving stitches. *Czech fire-polished beads* and *Austrian crystal beads* are two popular varieties. With beads made from other materials, check to ensure that the holes are large enough to accommodate multiple passes with a needle and thread—and that they are free from sharp edges that may damage thread—before using those beads in a project.

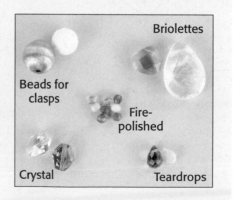

Beads for clasps

Briolettes

Fire-polished

Crystal

Teardrops

CONTINUED ON NEXT PAGE

Bead Sizes

The sizes of true seed beads, cylinder beads, charlottes, two-cuts, three-cuts, and some triangle beads are denoted by numbers called *aught sizes.* Historically, aught sizes may have corresponded to the number of beads that made up 1 inch of beads stacked side by side (not strung end to end). Accordingly, a larger aught number refers to a smaller bead, and a smaller aught number to a larger bead. (See the online Appendix, at www.wiley.com/go/tyvbeadwork, for a chart that compares aught sizes with their approximate lengths in millimeters.)

Note: *Because bead size standards have changed over time, aught sizes are not a good indicator of how many beads make up 1 inch of side-by-side beads in your beadwork. To determine that number accurately, create a test swatch (see page 49 in Chapter 2).*

An aught size may be written as a fraction (11/0), as a number followed by a degree symbol (11°), or simply as a number (11). Seed beads range in size from about 24/0 (smallest) to about 5/0 (largest). Originally, cylinder beads were only manufactured in size 11/0, but some are now produced in sizes 15/0, 10/0, and 8/0. Be aware that different manufacturers may size their beads slightly differently. For example, a size 8/0 Czech seed bead may not have exactly the same dimensions as a size 8/0 Japanese bead. For this reason, it's a good idea to use beads from a single manufacturer for a given project.

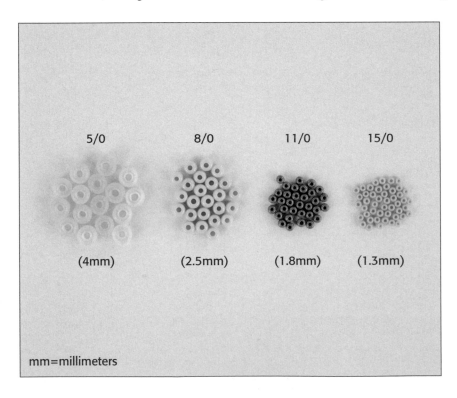

5/0   8/0   11/0   15/0

(4mm)   (2.5mm)   (1.8mm)   (1.3mm)

mm=millimeters

Note: *These images are not shown to scale; the actual measurements of the beads are provided.*

Cube beads, drop beads, some bugle beads, some triangle beads, and most beads that are larger than seed beads are sized in millimeters rather than in aught sizes. These beads are usually measured lengthwise end to end (hole opening to hole opening), with the exception of drop beads, which are often measured top to bottom.

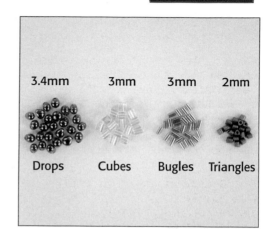

3.4mm   3mm   3mm   2mm

Drops   Cubes   Bugles   Triangles

Some Japanese and Czech bugle beads have their own sizing systems. Their sizes are denoted by a pound sign followed by a fraction or a whole number (such as #1 or #2). These beads are available in a more limited range of sizes than other seed beads. (See the online Appendix [www.wiley.com/go/tyvbeadwork] for a chart that matches typical bugle bead sizes with their approximate lengths in millimeters.)

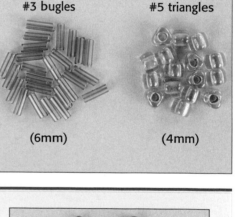

#3 bugles   #5 triangles

(6mm)   (4mm)

TIP

Culling Beads

The bead-manufacturing process results in beads that have slightly different dimensions, even among beads of the same "size." Occasionally, you may come across a bead that is noticeably smaller or larger than the others, a bead that appears misshapen, or a bead that is chipped or otherwise damaged. To keep your beadwork looking smooth and even, you should *cull*, or remove, those beads from your supply. An easy way to cull beads is to examine the beads in your bead dish or on your mat (see page 16) and use a needle to pick them up and set them aside. You can either discard culled beads or keep them for possible future use. For example, extra-narrow and extra-wide beads are useful for making certain increases and decreases in peyote stitch (see Chapter 3).

CONTINUED ON NEXT PAGE

Seed Bead Colors and Finishes

Seed beads are available in an enormous array of colors and with many kinds of treatments, called *finishes*. Here are the most common types of colors and finishes, and what you should know about them.

OPAQUE, TRANSPARENT, AND TRANSLUCENT COLORS

These are basic bead colors, with no special finishes applied. *Opaque colors* are solid; they absorb light and very little light passes through them. *Transparent colors* allow much light to pass through. As a result, you can see through most transparent beads, which makes thread color an especially important choice when using them. *Translucent colors* are very similar to transparent colors, but they allow slightly less light to pass through. When you use opaque and transparent or translucent colors together in a design, the opaque colors usually appear to come forward, or be slightly raised, and the transparent or translucent colors seem to fade into the background.

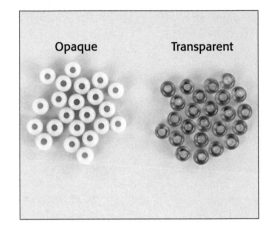

Opaque   Transparent

Whether a bead is opaque, transparent, or translucent is usually indicated in its name, often by an abbreviation such as "Opq" for opaque or "Tr" for transparent or translucent (ask your bead supplier for a key to their abbreviations). If a color is a light or dark version of a standard color, the name may also include an abbreviation such as "Lt" for light or "Dk" for dark.

TIP

Using Manufacturers' Numbers to Identify Beads

Some major seed bead manufacturers assign numbers to their beads, rather than (or in addition to) naming them with descriptive terms. (For example, Miyuki assigns the number "DB0875" to its opaque, mauve Delica beads that have a matte aurora borealis finish.) Some online bead suppliers provide the option to shop for beads using these numbers, in addition to the beads' descriptive names. This is a valuable service, because some patterns use manufacturers' numbers to identify the beads required for a design. Some suppliers also use the numbers to create lists or charts of matching beads in different shapes and sizes, which can help you to develop your own designs.

SPECIAL FINISHES

- *Aurora borealis* is a multicolored, reflective finish. It is commonly indicated by the letters "AB" in bead names, but it may also be called *iris, iridescent, rainbow,* or *oil slick.*

- *Dyed beads* are colored at the surface and not all the way through, which makes them prone to losing their color over time. You should coat them with a clear protective spray before using them (see "Apply a Protective Coating to Beads" in the online Appendix [www.wiley.com/go/tyvbeadwork]).

- *Color-lined beads* have a colored finish on the inside surfaces of their holes. Be careful not to scratch these linings with your needle, and be aware that beads lined with metallic colors may darken over time as their linings *tarnish* from exposure to air. Lined beads are usually labeled with an abbreviation such as "S/L" for silver lined or "G/L" for gold lined.

- *Matte* and *frosted* beads have a lightly etched surface, which gives them a soft, less reflective appearance than other beads.

- *Satin* beads are manufactured to have numerous tiny bubbles that create a reflective sheen that glistens in different directions.

- *Metallic beads* are finished to look like metal. Lower-quality metallic beads are painted with metal-colored paint and are likely to chip or wear over time.

- *Galvanized* beads and *plated* beads are coated with metal in a process called *electroplating*, which uses an electrical current. Although plating is more durable than paint, it may also wear off or change color by tarnishing.

- *Luster finishes* are transparent surface treatments that add shine to beads. They include *pearl luster*, which has a pearly sheen, and *gold luster*, which reflects a shimmer of metallic gold. *Ceylon* is a special finish that is usually applied to pastel-colored beads to make them look like tiny pearls.

- *Two-tone* beads are made with two distinct colors of glass, where one side of the bead is the first color and the other side is the second color.

- *Combination beads* have two or more special finishes. For example, a "matte galvanized silver" bead is silver-colored with a matte and galvanized finish.

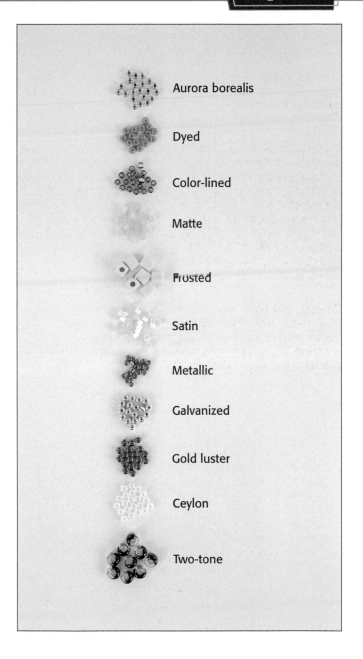

Aurora borealis

Dyed

Color-lined

Matte

Frosted

Satin

Metallic

Galvanized

Gold luster

Ceylon

Two-tone

Beading Needles and Thread

Beading needles, which are the most common needles used for bead weaving, look like sewing needles with especially narrow eyes. *Beading thread* is a sturdy, smooth thread that is intended for use with beads. You can find beading thread and beading needles at bead stores and on the Internet. Be aware that different brands of needles and thread have slightly different characteristics. You may want to experiment to determine which you like best.

Types and Sizes of Beading Needles

TYPES OF BEADING NEEDLES

Most beading needles are manufactured in England or Japan, and they often include the country of origin in their names—such as *English beading needles* or *Japanese beading needles*. Some manufacturers produce beading needles that are stiff and remain relatively straight while you stitch beads, and others produce softer needles that can become curved. Stiff needles are usually easier to work with, but they may be more prone to breaking than softer needles.

SIZES OF BEADING NEEDLES

English beading needles have a traditional sizing system that uses numbers to indicate needle thickness. These range from #16 (thinnest) to #10 (thickest), with #12 the most versatile. The size numbers approximate the sizes of seed beads that you should use them with (see the Needle and Thread Size Recommendations chart on page 15). English beading needles are also available in different lengths: *short beading needles* (also called *sharps*) are usually 1 inch to 1¼ inches long, and *long beading needles* (also called *normal beading needles*) are about 2-inches long. The length of needle you use is typically a matter of personal preference.

With needles made in different countries, such as Japan, ask your supplier how their sizes compare to the traditional English sizes.

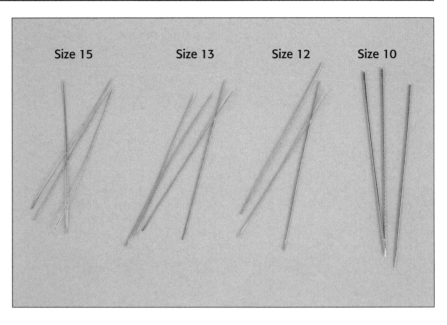

Size 15   Size 13   Size 12   Size 10

FAQ

What are *twisted wire needles* and *big-eye needles*?

These needles are commonly used for stringing beads, rather than for bead weaving. Twisted wire needles have soft wire eyes that you can collapse with your fingers to fit them through bead holes. Big eye needles are slit vertically down the middle so that you can use them with wide stringing materials, like ribbon.

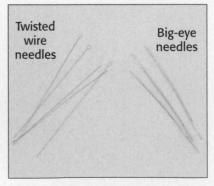

Twisted wire needles

Big-eye needles

Types of Beading Thread

NYLON THREAD

Nylon thread, which is available in a wide variety of colors and sizes, is one of the most popular types of beading thread. It consists of many thin strands of nylon plastic, which are either stacked and bonded together, or twisted together like tiny rope. Untreated nylon thread may stretch out over time, so you should treat it with beeswax or thread conditioner and pre-stretch it before use (see the section "Prepare a Length of Thread" in Chapter 2). Popular brands of nylon thread include Nymo, C-Lon, and Silamide.

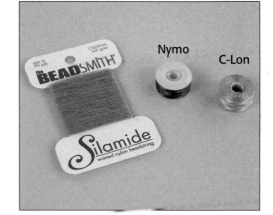

GEL-SPUN POLYETHYLENE THREAD

Gel-spun polyethylene thread, or *GSP thread,* has some benefits over nylon thread in that it is stronger, isn't as prone to stretching, and is less likely to fray at the ends. However, it is available in a more-limited range of colors and sizes than nylon thread. You can use a "plied" variety such as Power Pro or DandyLine to stitch larger glass beads, crystal beads, or non-glass beads. The brands Fireline and Wildfire work well for beadwoven designs that may experience extra wear, such as finger rings.

TIP

Beading Wire as an Alternative to Beading Thread

It is possible to perform some bead-weaving stitches using stringing materials other than beading thread. The most common alternative is size .010 (very thin) *beading wire* (also called *bead stringing wire*). Beading wire is composed of many tiny metal strands that are woven or wound together, and then covered with a thin layer of nylon. Popular brands of beading wire include SoftFlex and Beadalon. You can make knots with .010 beading wire, but it does not work with a regular beading needle. You must use it without a needle (it is stiffer than beading thread), or use a special needle made by the beading-wire manufacturer.

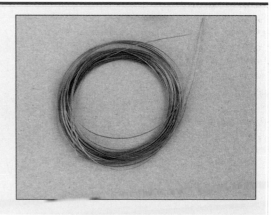

CONTINUED ON NEXT PAGE

Beading Needles and Thread *(continued)*

Sizes of Beading Thread

Beading thread is available in a range of thicknesses, also called *weights*. The thicker (or "heavier") a thread is, the stronger it tends to be. Most nylon thread weights are denoted by letters, with the very thinnest threads denoted by zeros, as noted in the following chart.

Thinner	→	→	→	→	→	→	→	→	*Thicker*
000	0	A	AA	B	C	D	E	EE	F

Gel-spun polyethylene thread may be sized based on its actual thickness in fractions of inches or millimeters, or by its strength, as determined by strength tests performed by its manufacturers. The larger a thread's *pound test number*, the strong and thicker it is. For instance, thread labeled "30 pound test" (or "30#") is stronger and thicker than thread labeled "8 pound test" (or "8#").

You should use the thickest thread that is reasonable for your project, both for strength and to ensure that the beads lie properly. After you select the type and size of beads to use, try to determine the maximum number of times you need to pass the needle through any bead in your design. All stitches require you to pass through some beads twice, and most require at least three passes. Factor in any thread ends that need to be woven in, whether you need to attach fringe or findings, and whether you have increases or decreases that require weaving through the beadwork extra times. Use that number as the basis for determining which thread to use. For example, if you need to pass through some beads four times, test to make sure that the thread (and needle) you choose can do this without the needle becoming stuck in a bead. You can use the chart on the next page to narrow your options of thread sizes to try.

FAQ

How should I select a color of beading thread?

When you use nylon beading thread, you have a large variety of colors to choose from. Here are some things to consider when making your selection:

- Typically, your thread should be as invisible as possible within your beadwork, and you should therefore select a color that matches (or nearly matches) the most prominent beads in your design, or a slightly darker color that will blend in.

- When you perform a stitch where some thread always shows (like right-angle weave), you can either use a matching color to disguise it, or break the rules by using a coordinating color that becomes part of the design.

- If your design will ultimately lie on top of another material, use a thread color that matches the color of that material if you would like the thread to "disappear" into the background. For instance, use black thread for a beaded tube that you plan to string onto black cord.

Gel-spun polyethylene thread is typically available in neutral colors like black, white, gray, and olive green. You should experiment to determine which color you prefer to use with various bead colors and stitches.

Needle and Thread Size Recommendations			
	Bead Size	*Needle Size*	*Thread Size*
Larger	5/0 and 6/0	#10	F or FF
	8/0	#10	E, F, or FF
	9/0	#10	D, E, or F
	10/0	#10	B or D
	11/0	#10	A or B
	12/0	#11	A or B
	13/0	#12	A or 0
	14/0	#13	A or 0
Smaller	15/0	#13 or #15	0, 00, or 000

TIP

Bead Size Versus Bead Hole Size

Logically, it is a bead's hole size—not its overall size—that affects the size of thread and needle that you can use for a project. Keep in mind that not all beads of the same size have the same size holes. For example, Japanese seed beads may have slightly larger holes than the same size Czech seed beads. For this reason, it is always a good idea to experiment with different needle sizes, and sometimes different thread sizes, before you begin a project using unfamiliar beads. If a needle starts to become stuck in beadwork that you are stitching with single-strand thread (see the section "Prepare a Length of Thread" in Chapter 2), you can try switching to a smaller size needle mid-way through the project.

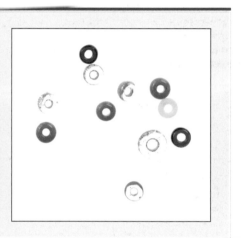

More Tools and Supplies

Here are some other tools and supplies useful for bead weaving. All of these materials are sold at most beading and craft stores. You will learn how to use them in the following chapters.

Essential Tools and Supplies

These items are required for most bead-weaving projects.

- *Beading scissors* are small, sharp scissors that you use to cut soft beading thread, such as Nymo and C-lon. To cut stiffer thread, such as FireLine and PowerPro, you should use children's craft scissors instead.

- *Beeswax* and *thread conditioner* are products that you apply to nylon thread to make it easier to work with and less likely to tangle and stretch. Because beeswax is thick and somewhat sticky, many beaders prefer to use a thread conditioner, like Thread Heaven, instead.

- A *bead dish* is a small plate, bowl, or tray that you fill with beads so that you can easily pick them up and stitch them into your bead-work. Many beaders use smooth white porcelain bead dishes that are available at some bead stores. Alternatively, you can use condiment dishes, like the dish shown on the right. You can keep larger beads in piles on a *bead mat*. The most popular bead mats are sheets of a soft material called Vellux. (Gray Vellux is shown as a background in the photo.)

- Keep a ruler or measuring tape on hand for measuring beadwork and sizing jewelry.

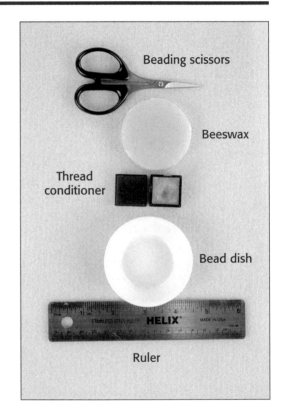

Beading scissors

Beeswax

Thread conditioner

Bead dish

Ruler

Optional Tools and Supplies

Many of these items can help you complete bead-weaving projects more easily. Others allow you to create beadwork of a certain type or style.

- A *form* is any cylindrical object used to support tubular beadwork as you stitch beads. Wooden dowels and metal tubes from hardware stores work well, but you can also use household items such as pencils and knitting needles.

- You can use a *beading awl* to undo knots in beading thread and to unstitch beads to correct a mistake.

- *Clear nail polish* is useful for tacking the ends of thread inside of beadwork when you end a thread or begin a new one.

- You can use *masking tape* or small, coiled clamps called *Mini Bead Stoppers* to prevent beads from falling off of loose ends of thread. These are alternatives to using stop beads, which are defined in Chapter 2.

- A *thread burner* cuts thread close to beadwork and shrinks the end of a thread so that it seems to disappear. You can use it as an alternative to scissors and clear nail polish when ending a thread or beginning a new one.

- *Bead scoops* are small metal shovels that you use to quickly pick up beads. You can use them to transfer beads from a bead dish to a storage container, or to gather spilled beads.

- A *pincushion* or *magnetic pin holder* (not shown) is useful for temporary placement of needles while you work.

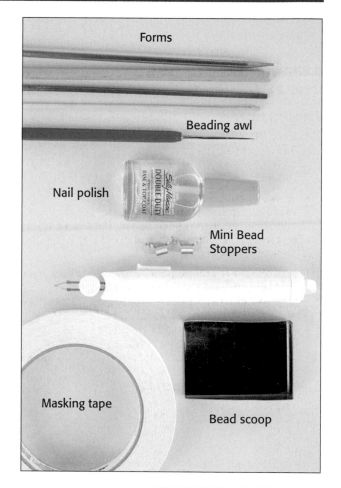

Forms

Beading awl

Nail polish

Mini Bead Stoppers

Masking tape

Bead scoop

CONTINUED ON NEXT PAGE

- If you plan to design your own beadwork patterns, you can use *colored pencils* to plot color schemes on graph paper.

- *EZ Bob bobbins* come in handy when you need to contain a long length of thread and keep it tangle-free. They have soft-plastic tops that flip open and closed, and they stack together for storage.

- *Jewelry findings* are components that serve practical purposes in jewelry. The most common jewelry findings used in beadwork designs include *jump rings*, *clasps*, *clamp ends* (also called *ribbon clamps*), and *ear wires*. *Crimp ends* are also sometimes used.

- To attach jewelry findings to your beadwork, you can use *chain nose pliers,* which are short needle-nose pliers with flat, smooth jaws. You need two pairs of these pliers for opening and closing jump rings (see page 174). For some applications (like securing clamp ends to beadwork) you can also use *flat nose pliers,* which look like chain nose pliers with broad, flat tips.

- Use a *craft glue*, like E6000 or G-S Hypo Cement, to attach findings that can be glued, such as clamp ends. It's a good idea to use a toothpick to apply small amounts of glue to your beadwork. Waxed paper is a good surface to work on when you apply glue, and paper towels come in handy for cleaning up.

- Cloth or fabric *first-aid tape* can serve as a cushion between beadwork and larger findings, such as clamp ends.

- *Cabochons* are jewelry stones that are flat on the bottom and domed on the top. You can bead around them to create *beaded bezels*.

- You can use *buttons* to create certain types of beaded clasps.

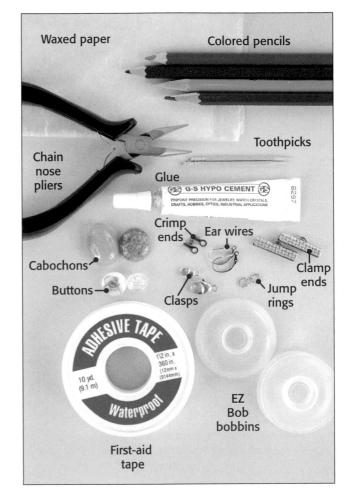

Storage and Organization

You should store your beads, thread, tools, and supplies in a way that keeps them organized and accessible. Seed beads are sold in small plastic bags or clear plastic tubes or boxes. *Flip-top boxes* are excellent containers for beads, because you can open and close them without spilling beads. (You can purchase them online and at some bead stores.) Tubes are also useful, but you should remove their tops slowly to avoid spills, especially with full tubes. If you purchase beads in bags (which is how most Czech seed beads are sold), it's a good idea to transfer them to boxes, tubes, or jars for storage. Always label your bead containers with the beads' size, color, and finish (or with the manufacturers' numbers).

Store needles in their original packages, or in labeled containers called *needle cases*. Some needle cases have magnets to keep needles secure until you need them.

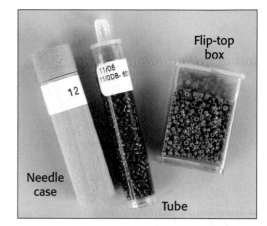

Flip-top box

Needle case

Tube

TIP

Setting Up a Bead-Weaving Work Area

Your *work area* is the space you use to perform beadwork. It should include a place for bead dishes, a clear area over which you can hold your beadwork, and space for other essential tools and supplies.

Many beaders prefer to anchor their work area with a bead mat. You can place your bead dishes on top of the mat, or just to the side. At the edges of the mat, you may place needles, a spool of thread, beeswax or thread conditioner, a ruler, and any findings or jewelry components that you plan to use.

Make sure you also have a good-quality task light, and consider investing in a magnifier (one attached to a headband, or a desk-top model) to help you see intricate beadwork. Use a chair that allows you to sit upright while you work, with your hands and wrists in a comfortable, supported position. Avoid working in a cluttered space or at a table or desk that has protruding knobs that may catch your thread as you work. Finally, if you have children or pets, designate a secure container for storing scrap thread that you plan to discard or use later, because it can cause serious health problems if swallowed.

2

Essential Skills and Techniques

This chapter covers the essential skills and techniques that apply to all bead weaving, regardless of the type of stitch you use. They include preparing and using a beading needle and thread, holding your beadwork and stitching beads, and ending an old thread and beginning a new one. You will also learn how to correct a mistake, secure thread and beads using knots, create professional-looking beadwork, and read project instructions and patterns.

Keep in mind that you do not need to master all of these skills at once. You can return to this chapter anytime while you work on new stitches, beginning with peyote stitch in Chapter 3.

Prepare a Length of Thread

After you select a needle, thread, and beads for a project, you can prepare a length of thread and start beading. Preparing the thread involves pulling and cutting a length of thread from its spool, waxing or conditioning it as needed, threading the needle, and devising a way to keep beads from falling off of the end.

How to Get Started with Thread and Needle

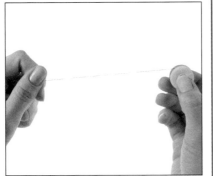

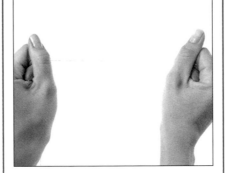

PULLING AND CUTTING THREAD

Begin by holding the spool gently in one hand and the end of the thread in the other. Pull the end of the thread and the spool away from each other as far as your arms reach, allowing the spool to spin and release the thread. If you plan to use a doubled strand of thread (see "Positioning the Needle" on the next page), then pull another arms' span of thread. Use beading scissors to cut the thread close to the spool. (You can always use a longer length of thread if you'd like; see the FAQ on page 24.)

PRE-STRETCHING NYLON THREAD

Because nylon thread is prone to stretching, it's a good idea to pre-stretch it before you begin beading. Working in sections, hold the thread with your hands about 1 foot apart, and gently tug the thread in opposite directions. Do this for the entire length of thread. This minimizes the risk that your completed design will stretch out over time.

WAXING OR CONDITIONING NYLON THREAD

When you use untreated nylon beading thread, you should treat it with beeswax or thread conditioner to strengthen it, protect it from moisture, and make it less prone to tangling and stretching.

To apply wax or conditioner, hold one end of the thread against the surface of the product, and slowly pull the entire length of thread through the product until the thread is fully coated. Go back and pull the thread between your finger and thumb to even-out the coating. You can repeat this process as you stitch beads, whenever it feels like the coating has worn off.

THREADING THE NEEDLE

You can thread a beading needle the same way you thread a sewing needle. For best results, always trim the end of your thread with very sharp beading scissors (straight across with nylon thread, and at a slight angle with other threads). It also helps to press the end of nylon thread between your fingers to slightly flatten it.

To pass the thread through the eye of the needle, hold the thread between the finger and thumb of your non-dominant hand, and use your dominant hand to slide the needle onto the thread. (For example, if you are right-handed, hold the thread in your left hand and the needle in your right.)

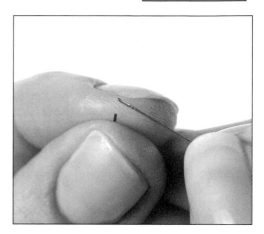

POSITIONING THE NEEDLE

Most woven beadwork is performed using *single-strand thread* (a), with the needle positioned several inches from the end of the thread, and with the thread tail folded over. As you work with single-strand thread, keep the eye of the needle pressed between your finger and thumb to keep the thread from slipping out.

For *double-strand thread*, you usually position the needle at the center point of the thread, and then bring the ends of the thread together so that the entire length of thread is doubled (b). Another option is to pass both ends of the thread through the eye of the needle, and then use the doubled thread as if it were a single-strand (c). A drawback to this method, however, is that it can be difficult to pass two ends of thread through a very-small needle eye.

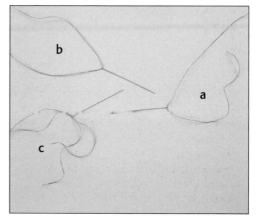

FAQ

When should I use double-strand thread?

Only use double-strand thread when project instructions call for it, or when you create a very small design or work with beads with large holes. (In that case, a double strand may add extra bulk to help you keep proper tension.) Keep in mind that it is difficult to correct mistakes using double-strand thread; you may need to cut the thread to remove the needle, and then remove all of the beads on that length of thread, one by one. Double-strand thread can also tangle more easily than single-strand thread, and it leaves two tails to weave-in instead of one. As an alternative, you can use single-strand thread and stitch through each bead twice as you work. This adds bulk and strength to your stitches while avoiding the drawbacks of double-strand thread.

CONTINUED ON NEXT PAGE

How to Create a Bead Stop

Most projects require the use of a *bead stop*, which is any method or device that keeps beads from falling off the end of the thread as you string them. In some instances, a bead stop can also help you keep proper thread tension.

ATTACHING A STOP BEAD

The most common bead stop device is a *stop bead* (sometimes called a *tension bead*). This bead is usually not part of your design, and you remove it when it's no longer needed. Here's how to attach one.

1. Select a small, round bead that is a different color than the beads in your first row of beadwork.

2. String the bead and position it about 6–8 inches from the long end of the thread (or about 12–14 inches from the end, if you plan to use the tail to attach jewelry findings; see the section "Attach Findings" in Chapter 9).

3. Holding the bead in place with one hand, use your other hand to pass the needle through the bead again, in the same direction that you passed it through the first time.

4. Pull the thread taut.

5. **Optional:** Repeat Steps 3 and 4 one more time. (Do this especially if the bead feels very loose on the thread.)

Later, when you're ready to remove the stop bead (see the section "End a Thread by Weaving-In"), use the needle or a beading awl to gently loosen the thread around the stop bead (a), and then slide the stop bead off of the thread tail.

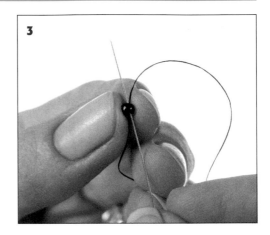

3

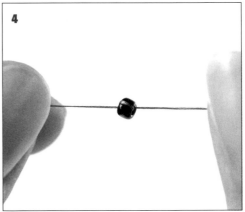

4

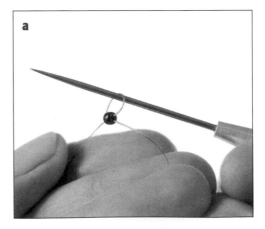

a

FAQ

Can I use an extra-long length of thread to reduce the number of times I run out of thread before completing a project?

Yes. The precise length of thread that you work with is a matter of personal preference, and some beaders use lengths up to 3 yards long for single-strand beading. However, longer lengths are more likely to tangle and snag, and they make stitching more cumbersome.

For some projects, you can reduce the number of times you need to change thread by beginning at the middle of a pattern instead of at one end. With this technique, you use a long length of thread and position the bead stop at its center point. You then stitch the first half of the pattern, from the middle to the end, before going back and using the long tail to stitch the second half.

USING A MINI BEAD STOPPER

As an alternative to using a stop bead, you can use a Mini Bead Stopper as a bead stop. The Mini Bead Stopper is a small metal spring with a loop of wire on each end. You squeeze the loops together using your finger and thumb to open the spaces in the spring, slip the thread into one of the spaces, and then release. The Mini Bead Stopper should remain attached to the thread until you're ready to remove it by squeezing the loops again to release it.

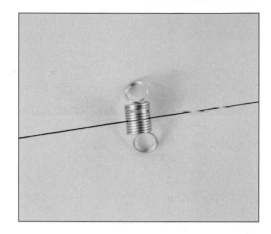

USING TAPE AS A BEAD STOP

Some beaders use a small piece of masking tape as a bead stop. Simply fold the tape in half over the thread, and then press the tape between your finger and thumb to secure it. To remove the tape, slowly pull the folded tape along the thread tail until it slides off.

USING A KNOT AS A BEAD STOP

Tubular and circular stitches typically begin with a short length of strung beads that you pull into a ring by passing the needle through the first bead a second time. It's sometimes helpful to make a square knot or a surgeon's knot (see the section "Learn the Knots Used in Beadwork") just before making that second pass. This eliminates the need for a traditional bead stop and holds the thread tension; however, keep in mind that if you need to correct a mistake later, undoing that area of beadwork will be difficult if it contains a knot.

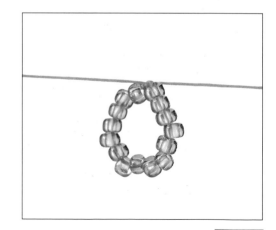

Stitch Beads Together

Once you have prepared your thread, you can begin stitching beads. Stitching beads together with a needle and thread is different than sewing with cloth because you create the beaded fabric as you work. You usually stitch beads in rows—either back and forth (for flat stitches), or in rounds (for tubular and circular stitches). As you work each row, you add one bead or set of beads at a time, attaching them to one or more beads that you previously stitched-in.

Select a Stitch

There are many different types of bead-weaving stitches, the most popular of which are covered in Chapters 3 through 8. (A good place to begin is the even-count flat peyote stitch in Chapter 3.) You should experiment with lots of stitches to discover which you like best and how you can use them in your designs. Here are some examples of the stitches covered in this book. You can use the Table of Contents to locate the instructions for each one.

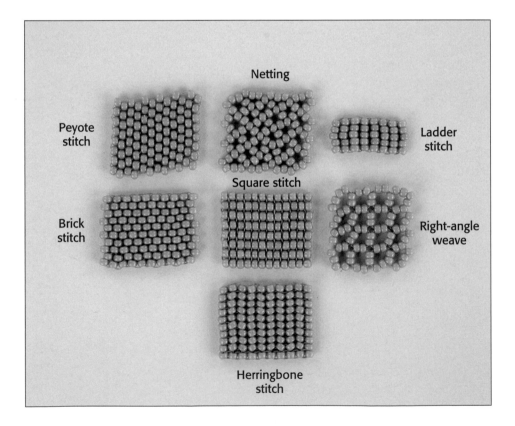

Peyote stitch

Netting

Ladder stitch

Square stitch

Brick stitch

Right-angle weave

Herringbone stitch

How to Hold Beadwork

When you stitch beads together, you should always hold your beadwork in a way that is comfortable and that grants you easy access to the row being stitched. This section provides some strategies for getting started, but feel free to modify them as you discover your own preferences.

As a general rule, always hold the needle and thread in your dominant hand and the beadwork in your non-dominant hand. Keep in mind that the first few rows of any stitch are the most challenging, and they require that you hold the beadwork very securely.

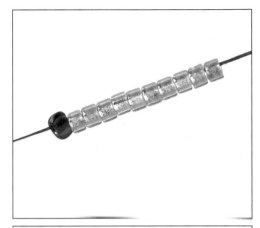

HOLDING FLAT AND CIRCULAR BEADWORK

① String the first set of beads and slide them against the bead stop. (The number of beads will depend on the type of stitch and the design of the project.)

② Position them in the proper configuration for the first stitch, based on the type of stitch. (The example is for the flat peyote stitch, where the beads are simply aligned end to end.)

③ Gently squeeze the beads between the pads of your finger and thumb, leaving the edges of the beads exposed so that you can stitch new beads onto them.

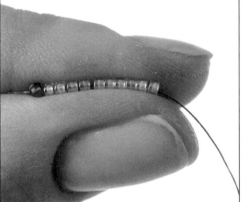

FAQ

In which direction should I stitch beads for each row of flat beadwork?

You can begin stitching beads either right to left or left to right, whichever you find most comfortable. The example above shows the thread emerging toward the right, which allows you to stitch the next row from right to left. If you prefer to work left to right, then you should position your initial beads with the thread emerging toward the left, as shown on the right.

For subsequent rows, some beaders prefer to turn their beadwork around at the end of each row, so that that they can continue to work in the most comfortable direction.

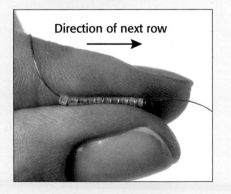

Direction of next row →

CONTINUED ON NEXT PAGE

HOLDING TUBULAR BEADWORK

You can stitch tubular beadwork by holding the developing tube in your fingers by itself, but it's often easier to use a form (see page 17 in Chapter 1). This is the same method you can use to bead around a decorative object, like a vase or a round trinket box.

1 Following the directions for the type of stitch you are making, slip the initial ring of beads onto the form.

2 Use your finger and thumb to press the thread tail firmly against the form, just below the ring of beads.

3 Keep the thread tail pressed down as you stitch new beads, rotating the form slowly as you work.

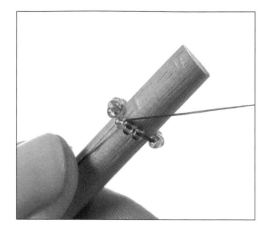

4 When the beaded tube becomes long enough to hold its shape, you can move your finger and thumb onto the beadwork, closer to where you are stitching new beads. (Alternatively, you can remove the tube from the form and hold the beadwork gently between your finger and thumb as you work.) The photo on the right shows what a beaded tube looks like when it starts to develop.

TIP

Choose a Direction to Stitch Beads Around the Form

With most tubular stitches, you may stitch either clockwise or counterclockwise, whichever direction you find most comfortable. (One exception is the tubular square stitch, where you change direction with each round.) The examples above show beads stitched counterclockwise. To stitch clockwise, place the initial loop of beads onto the form in the opposite direction, as shown on the right.

How to Pick Up and Stitch Beads

PICKING UP BEADS

The easiest way to place a small bead on a needle is to use the needle to spear and *pick up* the bead. You can either pick up beads from a bead mat or from a bead dish. Porcelain bead dishes with rounded inside corners are especially helpful, because you can slide the tip of the needle along the side of the dish as you pick up the bead, without the bead falling off. You can then allow the bead to slide toward the eye of the needle, and hold it there between or against your finger and thumb. If a stitch requires that you pick up more than one bead at a time, you can pick them up one by one and hold them together as a group on the needle.

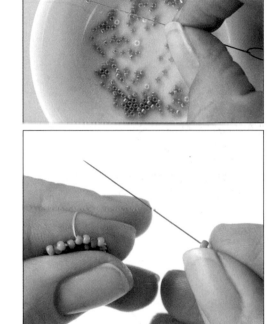

STITCHING BEADS: FLAT AND CIRCULAR BEADWORK

You can use the following basic method to stitch both flat and circular beadwork. With flat beadwork (shown in the example) you stitch the beads back and forth, and with circular beadwork, you stitch them around in circles. In the example, a single bead is stitched onto another single bead in the previous row; however, with some stitches you will stitch sets of multiple beads instead.

1 With a bead on the needle, bring the needle up to your beadwork, which is in your other hand. (With circular beadwork, it's a good idea to hold the end of the thread securely with the fingers of that hand.)

2 If the thread below the needle is draping down and blocking your view of the beadwork, take a moment to wrap the thread up over the index finger of your hand that is holding the beadwork, and bring down your middle finger to hold the thread in place, as shown.

3 Guide the tip of the needle into the hole of the bead that you need to stitch into, as called for by the type of stitch. Position the needle as close to the inside upper edge of the bead hole as possible (to avoid hitting and splitting the existing thread), and do your best to keep the needle parallel to the top edge of the previous row or round (that is, avoid entering the bead at a sharp diagonal, which can cause tension problems or twisting in some stitches).

Note: If you are using lined beads, be careful not to scratch off the color on the inside of a bead with the tip of the needle.

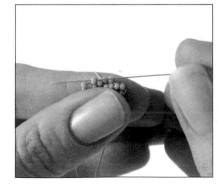

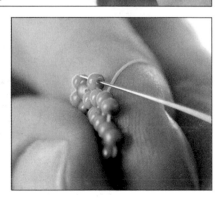

CONTINUED ON NEXT PAGE

④ With the hand that is holding the beadwork, gently roll the tips of your index finger and thumb slightly toward one another to catch the bead that is on the needle. (In the photo on the right, that bead is marked by an arrow.)

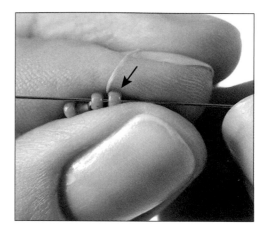

⑤ While still holding the beadwork between your index finger and thumb, use your other hand to *slowly* pull the needle and thread until the thread passes completely through both the new bead and the existing bead in the beadwork. (Release the thread from beneath your middle finger if it was held there during Step 2).

Note: If you are using thread that is longer than an arms' span, you may need to put down the needle and pull the thread directly one or more times to bring it all the way through the beads. The photo on the right shows the last bit of thread being pulled through.

⑥ If the thread begins to twist or tangle, stop right away and use the needle to free it before it creates a permanent knot.

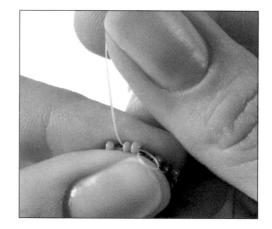

⑦ Using your dominant hand, grasp the thread a couple of inches away from the beadwork and tug it gently to pull the thread taut.

The new bead is now stitched into the beadwork (a).

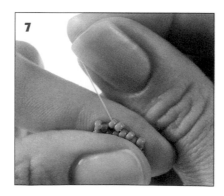

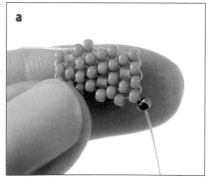

STITCHING BEADS: TUBULAR BEADWORK

In this example, a single bead is stitched onto another single bead in the previous round. Some stitches call for stitching sets of multiple beads instead.

1 Perform Steps 1 and 2 of "Holding Tubular Beadwork," on page 28.

2 Guide the tip of the needle into the hole of the bead that you would like to stitch into, as called for by the stitch. Position the needle as close to the inside upper edge of the bead hole as possible (to avoid hitting and splitting the existing thread), and do your best to keep the needle parallel to the top edge of the previous round of beadwork, and tangent to the form.

Note: As always, if you are using lined beads, be careful not to scratch off the color on the inside of a bead with the tip of the needle.

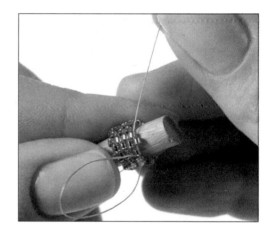

3 Slowly pull the needle and thread until the thread has passed completely through both the new bead and the existing bead in the beadwork.

4 If the thread begins to twist or tangle, stop right away and use the needle to free it before it creates a permanent knot.

5 Using your dominant hand, grasp the thread a couple of inches away from the beadwork and tug gently to pull the thread taut.

The new bead is now stitched into the beadwork.

End a Thread by Weaving-In

Weaving-in is the technique used to secure and hide a thread tail within an area of beadwork. After you stitch at least several rows of beadwork with a new length of thread, you can go back and *end* the thread tail by weaving-in. Later, weave-in any other thread tails that emerge from the beadwork where you ended an old thread or began a new one.

Weave-In a Thread Tail

You can weave-in thread with or without using knots. Whenever possible, use the following "with-knots" technique; use the "without-knots" technique only when your beads are too close together to tie knots between them.

Be sure to always select the best path for weaving thread into existing beadwork. See the section "Keys to Successful Bead Weaving" on page 43 for some guidelines.

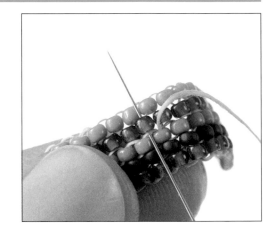

WEAVING-IN WITH KNOTS

1. Thread a needle onto the thread tail and position it for single-strand weaving (see "Positioning the Needle" on page 23).

2. Make sure that the thread is pulled taut (but not too tight; see the tip on the next page). Give the thread tail a few gentle tugs to close any unwanted spaces between beads in the surrounding beadwork.

3. Pass the needle through the next two adjacent beads.

4. Again, gently pull the thread taut.

5. Tie a half-hitch or overhand knot over and around the thread that runs between the last bead passed through and the very next bead (see the section "Learn the Knots Used in Beadwork" on page 40).

● = Knot

6 Pass the needle through two or three more adjacent beads, passing through no more than two beads at a time.

7 Gently pull the thread taut, sliding the knot (from Step 5) into the next bead.

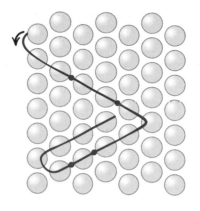

8 Tie another knot around the thread.

9 With most projects, you should repeat Steps 5–7 at least once more, to ensure that the thread is secure. If you are working on flat beadwork, you may change direction one or more times, as shown (also see "Navigating Through Beadwork" on page 43). With tubular beadwork, you can take a spiral path around the tube.

10 Pass the needle through a few more adjacent beads.

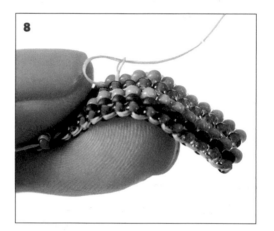

TIP

Keep Beadwork from Puckering While Weaving-In

If you pull the thread too tight as you weave-in, your beadwork may pucker from the heightened tension. To keep this from happening, only pull the thread gently taut, so that its tension matches that of the surrounding beadwork.

Puckered beadwork

CONTINUED ON NEXT PAGE

⓫ Optional: Instead of pulling the thread taut; pull it gently until it forms a tiny loop between the beads, as shown, and then apply a small drop of clear nail polish to the loop. This helps to keep the end of the thread from coming loose and protruding from the beadwork. Only perform this step if you plan to trim the thread later with scissors, rather than with a thread burner (see the tip below).

 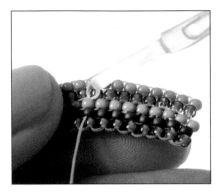

⓬ Now pull the thread taut. (If you performed Step 11, the loop should disappear inside of the last bead that the needle passed through.)

⓭ While still holding the thread taut with one hand, use your other hand to trim the thread tail as close to the last bead as possible, using either scissors or a thread burner.

TIP

Use a Thread Burner to Trim Thread After Weaving-In

You can use a thread burner to trim thread close to beadwork as an alternative to using beading scissors. The thread burner has a heating element that cuts through thread on contact and slightly shrinks the thread so that it seems to disappear within the beadwork. If you use this device, be sure to follow all of the safety precautions provided by the manufacturer, and never allow the heating element to touch your skin or any threads that you do not wish to cut through. Also avoid using a thread burner on beadwork that you have dabbed with nail polish.

WEAVING-IN WITHOUT KNOTS

In some designs, the beads may be so close together that it is nearly impossible to make knots between them. When this happens, you can weave-in without using knots, as long as you take care to maintain the tension of the thread and to weave it in securely.

One approach is to weave the thread down, over, up, and back over again in a circular path (a). Another method is to weave through a set of two beads diagonally (b) or horizontally (c), depending on the stitch, then skip down to the previous row and weave back in the opposite direction. Continue weaving back and forth through the fabric for several rows before trimming off any extra thread. You can also use a combination of these two techniques.

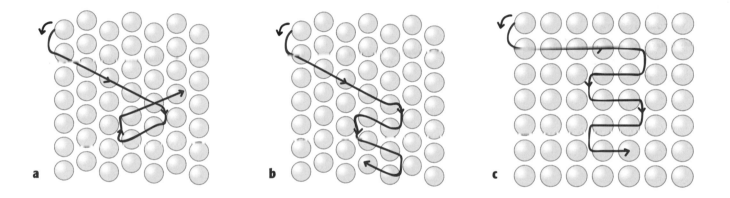

a   b   c

TIP

Avoid Splitting Thread

Thread splitting occurs when the needle catches on and passes through the thread. If you split a thread while stitching beads, the next stitched bead often appears crooked in the beadwork, as shown in this example. Thread splitting may not be as obvious during weaving-in, but you should still work to avoid it. To learn how to correct a split thread, see the section "Correct a Mistake" on page 44.

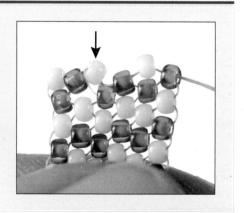

Begin a New Length of Thread

Most projects require more than one length of thread; when your first thread begins to run out, you stop and begin a new one. The best way to transition from an old thread to a new thread is to stop stitching, begin the new thread, and then, after stitching several more rows, go back and weave-in the tail of the old thread. You may begin a new thread by weaving-in, or you may wait to weave it in after stitching several rows.

BEGINNING A NEW THREAD BY WEAVING-IN

1 Stop stitching when you have 6–8 inches of thread remaining and have not yet completed your project.

2 Preserve the tension in the old thread by making a half-hitch knot over the nearest thread running between two beads in the beadwork, and then remove the needle. (See the section "Learn the Knots Used in Beadwork" on page 40 to review knots.)

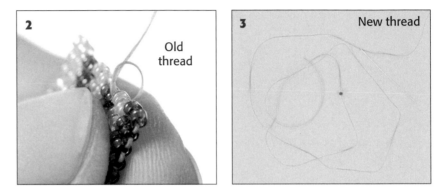

3 Prepare a new length of thread, using the same technique you used to prepare the first thread, but leave a tail of only 3 or 4 inches at the end (rather than the usual 6–8 inches).

4 Pick up the beadwork and press the tail of the old thread down using your thumb.

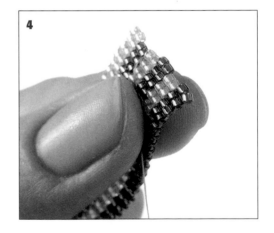

5 With the new length of thread, pass the needle through two beads in the beadwork that are about nine beads away from where the old thread emerges.

6 **Optional:** Pull the thread taut, pass through an adjacent bead in the bead-work, and then pull the needle and thread until a small loop forms on the beadwork. Apply a drop of nail polish to the loop. Only perform this step if you are going to trim the thread with scissors, rather than with a thread burner (see the tip on page 34).

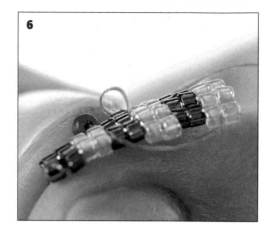

7 Pull the thread taut, and then tie a half-hitch or overhand knot over and around the thread that runs between the last bead passed through and the very next bead.

8 Pass the needle through two or three more adjacent beads, moving toward the bead that the old thread is emerging from, and then make another knot.

9 Continue passing through beads and knotting (weaving-in), working your way toward the bead that the old thread is emerging from, and taking a route that will result in the new thread exiting that same bead, in the same direction. Try to make a total of at least three knots.

10 Pass the needle through the bead that the old thread is emerging from. Both the old thread and the new thread should now be emerging together from the same bead.

11 Resume beading, stitching-in beads using the new thread.

12 When you have completed at least several more rows of beadwork, go back to the end of the old thread and thread-on a needle.

13 Gently pull the old thread taut.

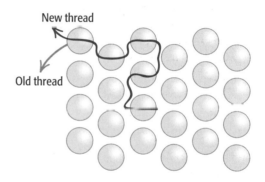

New thread

Old thread

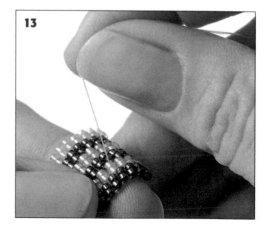

CONTINUED ON NEXT PAGE

⑭ End the old thread by weaving-in. For best results, weave the old thread into the beadwork that you stitched using the new thread.

⑮ Pull on the short tail of the new thread, and trim it as close to the beadwork as possible.

⑯ Return the needle to the new thread, and resume stitching.

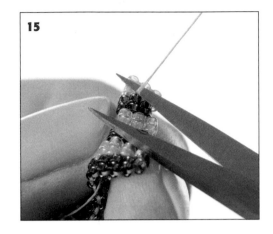

15

AVOID TENSION PROBLEMS IN THREAD TRANSITION ZONES

Before you weave-in the tail of an old thread, make sure that its tension matches that of the rest of the beadwork (even if you have already anchored it with a half-hitch knot). If the tension appears too loose, tug gently on the thread to correct it. This is especially important for tubular stitches, like the tubular peyote shown here, where you need to keep the tension even all the way around the tube. Also be careful not to make the tension too tight in these transition zones, to avoid the puckering that can occur any time you weave-in a thread too tightly.

Area of loose tension

FAQ

Can I weave-in to begin a new thread without using knots?

If the beads in your beadwork are so close together that you are unable to make knots, you can weave-in without using knots, using the technique described under "Weaving-In Without Knots" on page 35. Just be sure to weave-in as securely as possible, switching directions often.

BEGINNING A NEW THREAD WITHOUT WEAVING-IN

Some beaders prefer to wait to weave-in the tail of a new thread until they have stitched several rows or rounds and are ready to go back and weave-in the tail of the old thread.

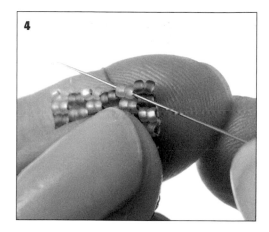

① Stop stitching with the old thread, knot it, and hold it down just as you would before beginning a new thread by weaving-in.

② Prepare the new thread using the same technique that you used to prepare the first thread, leaving a tail of 6–8 inches.

③ Pass the needle through one or two beads adjacent to the bead that the old thread is emerging from, following the path of the old thread.

④ Now pass the needle through the same bead that the old thread is exiting. Both threads should now emerge together from the same bead.

⑤ Pull the new thread taut. (The red bead in the photo is a stop bead.)

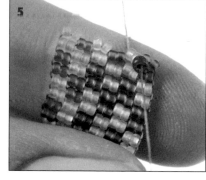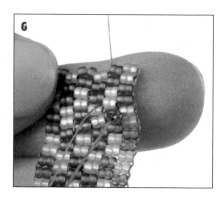

⑥ Resume stitching beads until you have at least several more rows of beadwork completed.

⑦ Go back to the tail of the old thread and weave it into the beadwork that you just created using the new thread.

⑧ Now go back to the tail of the new thread and weave it into the beadwork that you stitched using the old thread.

Learn the Knots Used in Beadwork

As described in the previous sections, knots are used to secure thread within beadwork. The type of knot you make depends on your personal preference, how secure you want the thread to be, and how much space is available between beads. The most popular knots used in bead weaving are illustrated below.

Knots Used for Weaving-In a Thread

THE HALF-HITCH KNOT

This is not a very secure knot, but it takes up little space, is easy to hide inside of beads, and is usually enough to hold thread when used in multiples.

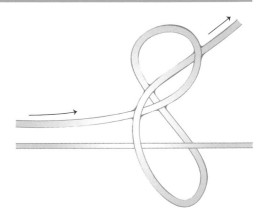

① Pass the needle beneath the thread that you plan to make the half-hitch knot around.

② Gently pull the needle until its thread creates a tiny loop just above the surface of the beadwork.

③ Bring the needle behind the loop, and then pass it through the loop.

④ **Optional:** For added security, repeat Step 3 one more time.

⑤ Pull the thread taut.

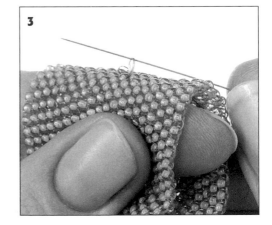

FAQ

Are the "weaving-in" versions of knots the same as the standard, or macramé, versions of those knots?

Not exactly. Both the half-hitch knot and the overhand knot are usually performed a little differently for weaving-in than they are in other applications. To learn how to make these knots for macramé work, see the book *Teach Yourself Visually Jewelry Making & Beading*.

chapter 2

THE OVERHAND KNOT

This knot is slightly more secure than the half-hitch knot, but it also takes up more space and may be more difficult to hide within a bead. Consider using it with beads that have larger holes.

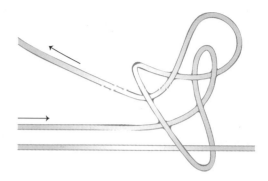

1 Perform Steps 1 and 2 on the previous page.

2 Bring the needle behind the loop, and then pass it through the loop, but do *not* pull the thread taut.

3 Gently pull the needle until the thread forms another small loop.

4 Pass the needle through the second loop.

5 Pull the thread taut.

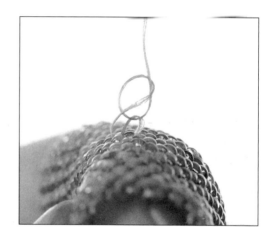

TIP

Be Aware of Conflicts in Knot Terminology

Beading instructors, books, and magazine articles may use different names for the same type of knot used for weaving-in. For example, some use "overhand knot" to describe what others call a "half-hitch knot." When you're unsure which knot is intended, use the one that you feel is both adequately secure and easy to hide within your beadwork given the size of the beads, the bulk of the thread, and the stitch.

CONTINUED ON NEXT PAGE

Multi-Purpose Knots

There are two knots used for securely attaching two threads, or two ends of the same thread, together. The *square knot* is the basic knot, and the *surgeon's knot* is a square knot with an extra wrap for better durability. Some projects use a third knot, the *double overhand knot*, to loop a thread and tie it back onto itself.

SQUARE KNOT

1. Beginning with one strand in each hand, wrap the left strand around the right strand to twist the strands around each other.
2. Now wrap the right strand over and around the left strand, creating a second twist.
3. Pull down the second twist snugly onto the first twist.
4. Pull the two strand ends to tighten the knot.

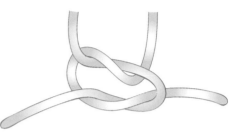

SURGEON'S KNOT

1. Perform Step 1 of "Square Knot."
2. Now wrap the right strand over and around the left strand *twice*.
3. Pull down the twists you made in Step 2 snugly onto the twist from Step 1.
4. Pull the two strand ends to tighten the knot.

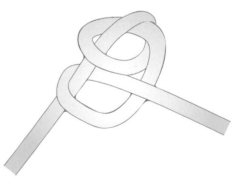

DOUBLE-OVERHAND KNOT

1. Pull the end of the strand back up and over itself to form a loop.
2. Pass the strand end through the loop.
3. Pull the strand end to tighten the knot. You now have a *single-overhand knot*.
4. Repeat Steps 1–3 to complete the double-overhand knot.

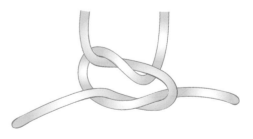

This section covers some important strategies for making your beadwork as beautiful, durable, and functional as possible. Keep them in mind as you practice new stitches. Before long, your artisanship and attention to detail will show in all of your designs.

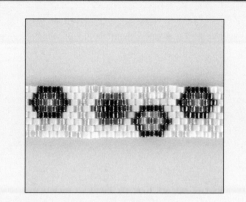

MONITORING THREAD TENSION

Always be aware of your thread's tension as you stitch beads. For most projects, you should keep the tension uniform throughout the design. The "correct" tension is usually one that keeps as little thread showing as possible, while allowing the beadwork to drape or lie flat without unsightly puckering. To keep the thread taut and the beads in alignment, give the thread a gentle tug after stitching each bead or set of beads.

HIDING THREAD AND KNOTS

Your designs will look more professional if you do a good job of hiding the thread within your beadwork. Avoid any maneuver that results in thread wrapping around the outside of a bead, and keep the thread taut to minimize the visibility of thread between beads. Hide all knots by sliding them into the hole of the next adjacent bead.

NAVIGATING THROUGH BEADWORK

Your ability to keep proper thread tension and hide thread and knots depends in part on the path you take through beadwork when you weave-in. Here are some strategies for best results:

- Before you weave-in a thread, plan a general path to take. Try to avoid areas where other thread is already woven-in, or needs to be woven-in later.

- When possible, make knots around thread that runs horizontally or diagonally—rather than vertically—between two beads. This makes it easier to pull knots into the holes of adjacent beads.

- Whenever thread is likely to show between beads (such as in open stitches like right-angle weave), follow the path of an existing thread as much as possible. If a weaving-in thread passes between beads in a way that is inconsistent with how the stitch is performed, then the thread is more likely to show, and the beadwork may even become distorted.

Correct a Mistake

All beaders occasionally make mistakes, such as stitching-in the wrong color of bead, splitting a thread, or passing thread through the wrong bead. To correct most mistakes, you need to undo at least a portion of your beadwork using a procedure called *ripping*. To reduce the amount of beadwork that you need to rip, always try to catch mistakes as quickly as possible.

RIPPING A SINGLE-STRAND THREAD

Ripping is especially easy when you stitch with single-strand thread.

1 Remove the needle from the thread.

2 Use the needle or a beading awl (shown in the example) along with your fingers to gently pull out each bead, in reverse order that you stitched it in, until you reach the last stitch that you made before the mistake occurred. (To review the definition of a beading awl, see the section "Optional Tools and Supplies" on page 17 in Chapter 1.) Be sure to remove beads slowly so that they do not scrape the thread and damage it.

3 Re-thread the needle.

4 Resume stitching.

RIPPING A DOUBLE-STRAND THREAD

When you work with a thread that is doubled-over with the needle at the center, you cannot remove the needle without first cutting the thread. This means that you must rip all of the beadwork that you stitched using that length of thread.

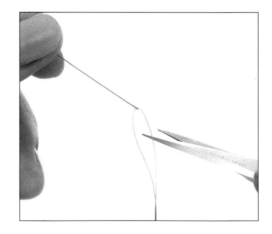

1 Cut the thread and remove the needle.

2 Use the needle and your fingers to gently pull out each bead, in reverse order that you stitched it in, until you reach the end of the current length of thread.

3 Completely remove the thread and thread tail from the beadwork.

4 Prepare and weave-in a new length of thread, and then resume stitching.

IDENTIFYING HOW MISTAKES HAPPEN

The causes of some mistakes may be obvious, such as when you stitch the wrong color or size bead for a pattern. Other mistakes, like those which cause your beadwork to pucker or a bead to appear crooked, may be more difficult to identify. The Troubleshooting chart in the online Appendix (www.wiley.com/go/tyvbeadwork) provides examples of many common beadwork mistakes and lists their potential causes. It can help you to determine what caused a mistake so that you can avoid that problem in the future.

STARTING OVER WHEN RIPPING FAILS

With some stitches, ripping is difficult because the thread follows a complex path through the beadwork, which serves to "lock" the thread in place and prevent you from removing beads. Ripping may also fail if the beadwork contains a knot or a split thread. If you are unable to rip an area of beadwork, you may need to either start over from the beginning of the pattern or allow the mistake to remain in the beadwork. If a mistake occurs early in a design, or if you plan to sell your beadwork, starting over is the better option.

FAQ

If I catch a mistake quickly, can I pass the needle back through a bead to "unstitch" and remove it?

Unfortunately, "unstitching" is rarely successful, especially with very small beads, because the needle usually catches and splits existing thread inside of the bead. However, there are two situations when you may want to attempt unstitching. One is when the bead you pass back through is a size 8 seed bead or larger, because the hole may be large enough that you can avoid splitting existing thread. The second is when you have stitched a significant amount of beadwork using double-strand thread, and you know that your only other option is to rip all of the beadwork that uses that thread and start again.

Beading Instructions and Patterns

Most bead-weaving projects that you find in books and magazines include a supplies list, a series of numbered instructions, and diagrams to illustrate the instructions. Some also provide colored patterns called *graph patterns*. This section covers some important terms that are used in bead-weaving instructions and provides an overview of how to use a pattern. Patterns for individual stitches are covered in more detail in Chapters 3 through 8.

Terms Used in Project Instructions

Here are some terms that are commonly used in bead-weaving project instructions. Their basic definitions are given below; detailed examples of each are provided throughout this book.

Go through	See *pass through*, which is the more common term.
High bead	In beadwork with an uneven edge, the bead that protrudes the farthest from that edge; or one of several beads that protrude to the same degree from surrounding beads. (Also see *low bead*.)
Link bead(s)	One or more beads that you pass back through after picking up additional beads. These are used to make netting (Chapter 4) and some styles of fringe (Chapter 9).
Low bead	In beadwork with an uneven edge, the bead that is recessed the farthest from that edge; or one of several beads that are recessed to the same degree. (Also see *high bead*.)
Pass back through	Bring the needle through one or more beads in the beadwork in the *opposite* direction that you went through the bead(s) previously.
Pass through	Bring the needle through one or more beads in the beadwork in the *same* direction that you went through the bead(s) previously.
Pick up	Use the needle to pick up one or more beads, using the tip of the needle to spear the beads through their holes.
Step up	From a low bead, pass through one or more adjacent high beads; or pass from a previous row up into the current row.
Sew through	See *pass through*, which is the more common term.
Skip	Skip over one or more beads, usually in the same row or round, before passing the needle into the beadwork to complete a stitch.
String	Pick up one or more beads with the needle and slide them down onto the thread.
Tail	The unbeaded loose end of a length of thread.
Turn	Perform the next stitch or stitches in the opposite direction, usually to begin the next row or round. *Turn* does not mean that you must physically turn the beadwork around in your hands, although this is optional with many stitches.
Turning bead(s)	A bead (or beads) that you pick up before you reverse direction and pass back through the previous bead, or before you turn and begin stitching the next row of beadwork.
Turning chain	A set of beads that are picked up before you turn and pass back through a previous bead. (Also called a *turning picot*.)

Number-Letter Combinations

Project instructions for simple designs such as stripes or checks often assign a capital letter to each color of bead used. The pattern may suggest a specific set of colors for the design, or it may invite you to substitute the colors of your choice. Here is an example:

Use four colors of size 11/0 cylinder beads (A, B, C, and D).

An easy way to remember which color is which is to pour beads of the same color into a beading dish or dish compartment, and then use a sticky note to label the dish or compartment with the letter that corresponds to that color.

In project steps, a number is placed in front of each letter to indicate how many of that color of bead you should use. For example, in the written instructions for a flat peyote stitch project, the first step might be to pick up two each of beads A through D, in that order, as shown in the photo on the right. These instructions might read:

Pick up 2A, 2B, 2C, and 2D, and position them against the stop bead.

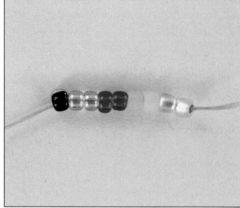

With peyote stitch, these initial beads are for the first two rows of beadwork (see Chapter 3). The next several steps, which add the third row and pull the second row into alignment, might read:

Pick up 1D, turn, skip a bead, and pass through the next bead.
Pick up 1C, skip a bead, and pass through the next bead.
Pick up 1B, skip a bead, and pass through the next bead.
Pick up 1A, skip a bead, and pass through the next bead.

These steps have been completed in the photo on the right.

CONTINUED ON NEXT PAGE

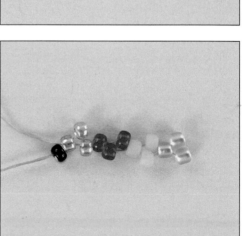

Graph Patterns

GRAPH PATTERN BASICS

Graph patterns are printed arrangements of units, or *cells*, which can be squares, rectangles, circles, or ovals. Each cell represents one bead in the design. Colored cells indicate which colors of beads make up each row.

When you read a graph pattern, you typically begin at one corner and then follow the first row of the pattern horizontally, either right to left or left to right. The corner that you choose to start from depends on the type of stitch and on your personal preference. (You will learn how to select a starting corner for each type of stitch in Chapters 3 through 8.) When you follow a graph pattern, it helps to use the edge of a sheet of paper or a ruler to mark the row you are stitching.

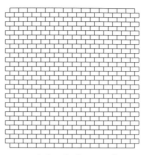

Brick stitch graph

The cells in graph patterns are arranged according to how the beads align in a particular stitch. For example, the cells in a brick stitch graph pattern are offset like bricks, while the cells in a square stitch graph pattern are aligned in a true grid.

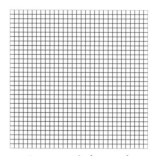

Square stitch graph

FAQ

I have a graph pattern that did not come with instructions. Which size of beads should I use?

Highly detailed or pictorial peyote, brick stitch, and square stitch patterns are usually designed for size 11/0 cylinder beads. Cylinder beads create smooth, tightly woven beadwork that allows for higher-resolution designs, and most cylinder beads are size 11/0.

With less-detailed patterns, or for open stitches like netting and right-angle weave, you can use just about any size of bead you like. Keep in mind that larger beads produce a wider and longer piece of beadwork, and smaller beads produce a narrower and shorter one.

MAKING YOUR OWN GRAPH PATTERNS

You can find printable, blank graph patterns for all types of stitches on the Internet, or you can photocopy blank patterns from some beading books and magazines. (See the online Appendix [www.wiley.com/go/tyvbeadwork] for some recommended resources.) Use colored pencils to color in your designs.

As you progress into more intricate designs, you may want to create patterns on a computer using bead-design software. Some applications even allow you to scan pictures and convert them into graph patterns, which you can then print out.

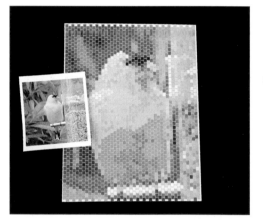

TIP

How to Make a Pattern for Sized Beadwork

Graph patterns are usually longer and/or wider than the actual beadwork. To design a pattern for beadwork of a certain size or length, begin by making a *test swatch*. One way to do this is to stitch one square inch of flat beadwork (or an inch of tubular beadwork), and then count the number of beads both vertically and horizontally (or, for tubular beadwork, just vertically). Those numbers are the horizontal and vertical beads-per-inch for your design. If your design includes some beads of different sizes, you can either estimate the effect they may have on the size of the beadwork, or create another test swatch that includes those beads.

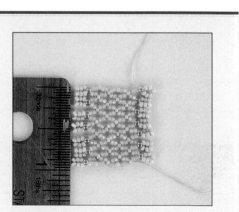

To make your project a certain width in inches, divide that width by your horizontal beads-per-inch; this is the approximate number of bead columns your pattern should have. To make a project a certain length, divide that length by your vertical beads-per-inch; this is the approximate number of bead rows your pattern should have.

chapter 3

Peyote Stitch

Peyote stitch, also called *gourd stitch*, is one of the oldest and most popular bead-weaving stitches. Its beads are each offset by one half, so that the beadwork looks like a brick wall turned on its side. The basic peyote technique involves stitching a bead, skipping the next bead in the previous row, and then stitching another bead. Keep in mind that the first few rows are the most challenging, and that your technique will improve with practice.

You can use *flat peyote stitch* to create a sheet or band of beadwork. To try a beginning-level peyote stitch project after reading this section, see "Patterned Flat Peyote Bracelets" on page 184.

Flat Peyote Stitch Rows and Columns

Before you attempt a new stitch, it is a good idea to familiarize yourself with the alignment of its rows and columns of beads. In flat peyote stitch, beads are tightly stacked and offset by half of a bead. On the top and bottom ends of peyote beadwork, every other bead protrudes outward like a tooth. The sides, however, are relatively straight because those beads are aligned end to end.

When you perform flat peyote stitch, you begin with the first two horizontal *rows*, and then stitch additional rows one by one to create beaded fabric. Just as the beads are offset by one half in peyote stitch, the rows are also offset. Vertical peyote *columns* are aligned side by side.

In the diagram on the right, the first row, "R1," is shown as the lowest row, with additional rows worked in an upward direction. Keep in mind that in some graph patterns, the "first" row may be the topmost row in the graph instead. (See the section "Flat Peyote Stitch Graph Patterns" on page 76.)

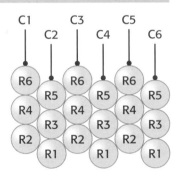

C = Column
R = Row

TIP

Row and Column Terminology
Not all project instructions use the same terminology to describe rows and columns of beads. For example, some projects refer to columns as "vertical rows." Most projects, however, are accompanied by diagrams or grid patterns that clarify the written instructions.

Flat Peyote Stitch

EVEN-COUNT FLAT PEYOTE

The even-count flat peyote stitch has an even number of columns and creates flat beadwork. Remember that, as with most stitches, the first few rows are the most challenging, and they take more time to stitch than subsequent rows. You need to hold the beads securely while you slowly build each new row, making sure that the developing beadwork remains flat between your finger and thumb.

1 After preparing your thread (see Chapter 2), pick up an even number of beads to equal the width that you'd like the beadwork to have.

2 Move the beads away from the bead stop to create a space that is about two or three beads wide. (This frees some thread that will be taken up again in the following steps.)

3 Pick up another bead (bead 7 in the diagrams). This is a high bead (see the section "Beading Instructions and Patterns" on page 46 in Chapter 2 to review this and other important bead-weaving terms).

4 Pass back through the second to last bead that you picked up in Step 1 (bead 5 in the diagram).

5 Gently pull the thread taut.

6 Turn, and pick up another bead (bead 8 in the diagram below). This is also a high bead.

7 Gently pull the thread taut. Be sure to hold this bead in position against the beadwork as you pull the thread, to avoid the appearance of loose thread along the edges of your beadwork.

8 Pass back through the fourth from the last bead that you picked up in Step 1 (bead 3 in the diagram), and then pull the thread taut.

9 Continue adding a new bead and passing back through a bead until you arrive at the beginning of the first row, passing back through the first bead that you picked up in Step 1 (bead 1 in the diagram).

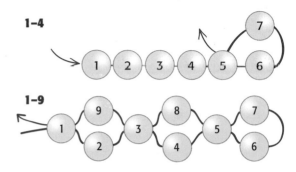

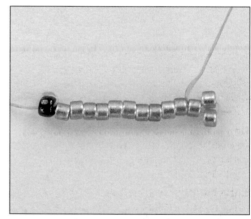

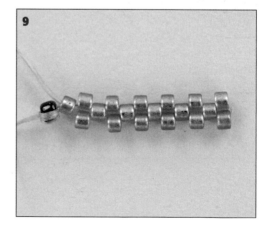

CONTINUED ON NEXT PAGE

⑩ Turn, and pick up a new bead (bead 10 in the diagram).

⑪ Pass back through the first bead in the second row (bead 9 in the diagram).

⑫ Continue this pattern to complete this and future rows, stitching each row in the opposite direction that you stitched the prior row.

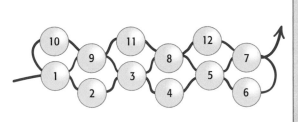

Even-count peyote stitch

ODD-COUNT FLAT PEYOTE

Odd-count flat peyote stitch has an odd number of columns. It requires that you weave back into the beadwork after completing every other row, in order to change the thread's direction.

❶ After preparing your thread, pick up an odd number of beads to equal the width that you'd like the beadwork to have.

❷ Stitch beads, using the same technique that you use for even-count flat peyote stitch, until you reach the end of the third row. The thread now exits the final bead in the third row (bead 11 in the diagram), which is a high bead that is not yet stitched into the beadwork.

❸ Pass back through the first bead that you picked up in Step 1 (bead 1 in the diagram).

❹ Moving upward diagonally, pass through the next two beads (beads 2 and 10 in the diagram), and pull the thread taut.

❺ Reversing direction, pass through the bead (bead 3 in the diagram) that is directly below the bead that the thread currently exits.

❻ Moving upward diagonally, pass through the next bead (bead 2 in the diagram).

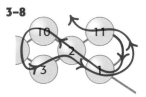

7 Moving downward diagonally, pass through the next bead (bead 1 in the diagram on the previous page), and then pull the thread taut.

8 Reverse direction and pass back through the last bead in the second row (bead 11 in the diagram on the previous page). You have now completed a turn.

9 Pull the thread taut again.

10 Pick up another bead, and continue stitching peyote stitch as usual.

11 Repeat Steps 3–9 to secure the last bead in every other row.

Odd-count peyote stitch

FAQ

When should I use the odd-count flat peyote stitch instead of the even-count stitch?

The even-count flat peyote stitch is less complicated and takes less time to complete than the odd-count stitch. However, the odd-count stitch allows you to center design features within your beadwork, and the even-count stitch does not. In the pattern on the right, the tapered end and the graphic design are centered along the middle column. If you attempted this pattern using even-count peyote, the taper and the design would be off-center by one column. (The taper is made with an outside peyote stitch decrease, which is covered on page 65.) Use the odd-count stitch whenever project directions instruct you to, or when you create a new design that contains elements that must be perfectly centered.

Center column

You can use *tubular peyote stitch* to create long beaded tubes, called *ropes*, or to cover objects seamlessly with beads. Just like flat peyote stitch, tubular peyote can be either even-count or odd-count. Before you begin, review "Holding Tubular Beadwork" on page 28.

Tubular Peyote Stitch Rows and Columns

In tubular peyote, beads are stacked and offset by half of a bead, just as they are in flat peyote. However, tubular peyote rows—called *rounds*—wrap around the tube, with the first and last beads in each row positioned against one another. With even-count tubular peyote, you must *step up* at the end of each row, in order to position the thread to begin the next row. When you step up, you simply pass the needle through two beads—one low and one high—before stitching the next bead, rather than passing through just one low bead (see "Even-Count Tubular Peyote Stitch" on the next page).

In these diagrams, each bead labeled with a "1" represents the first bead in each new row. Diagram a represents the even-count tubular peyote stitch, in which the first bead in each row is preceded by a step up.

Diagram b represents odd-count tubular peyote, which does not require a step up because the odd number of columns allows the rows to spiral seamlessly around the tube (see Odd-Count Tubular Peyote Stitch on page 59). This spiraled alignment creates rows that are slightly angled rather than straight.

As you can see, the first bead in each round of both even-count and odd-count tubular peyote moves forward by the space of one column.

a

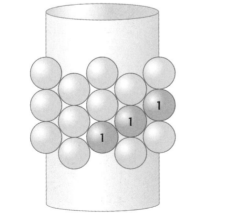

b

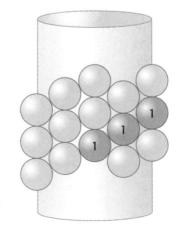

Even-Count Tubular Peyote Stitch

The first few rounds of tubular peyote may be challenging, but subsequent rounds are easier. Take care to hold those first rounds securely so that the beads do not flip and change position.

1 After preparing a new strand of thread, pick up an even number of beads sufficient to wrap all the way around your form, with a small space between the beads and the form. (The example uses ten size 11/0 Japanese seed beads on a ⅛-inch diameter copper tube from a hardware store.)

2 Pass through the first bead, in the same direction, and pull the thread taut.

3 Slide the ring onto the form.

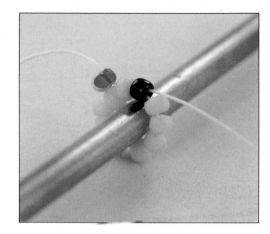

4 Use your fingers to slide the beads away from the bead stop far enough to create a space of bare thread that is about two or three beads wide. (This thread is taken up as the beads fall into alignment in the following steps.)

5 Press the thread tail against the form, just below the ring of beads. (Review "Holding Tubular Beadwork" on page 28 in Chapter 2).

6 Pick up a bead. This is a high bead.

7 Skip over the very next bead in the ring, and pass down through the following bead.

8 Pull the thread taut. The beads may look a little jumbled at this point, but thread tension should help to pull them into alignment after the first few rows.

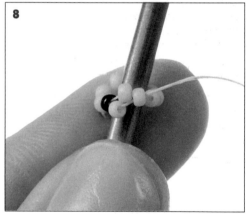

9 Continue adding a new bead, skipping a bead, and passing through the next bead in the ring, all the way around the ring one time, to complete three rounds of peyote stitch.

10 Pull the thread taut while using your fingers to align the beads so that they resemble the first three rows of flat peyote stitch, as shown here.

11 Use the spare fingers on your non-dominant hand to hold the first three rounds flat against the form.

CONTINUED ON NEXT PAGE

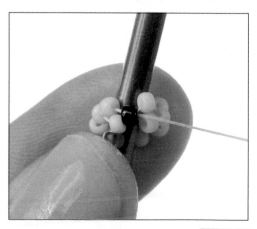

12 Step up by passing the needle through the next adjacent high bead.

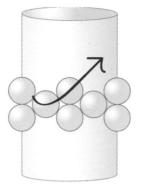

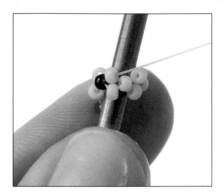

13 Continue stitching one round at a time, stepping up to begin each new round, to your desired length of tube. In the tube shown, a black bead was used as the first bead in each round.

TIP

Accommodating Inconsistent Thread Tension in the First Few Rounds

Once you have created about an inch of beaded tube, you may notice that the tension in the first few rounds is either tighter or looser than the tension in subsequent rounds. If this becomes a problem, make a habit of beginning tubular peyote with at least three temporary rounds, which are not part of your pattern or design. (In the example, the temporary rounds are worked in a contrasting color.) You can go back and remove the beads from these rounds later, and then end the thread by weaving into the rounds that have proper tension.

Odd-Count Tubular Peyote Stitch

1 Perform Step 1 of "Even-Count Tubular Peyote Stitch" on page 57, but this time pick up an odd number of beads. (The example uses eleven size 11/0 Japanese seed beads.)

2 Pass through the first bead, in the same direction, and pull the thread taut.

3 Perform Steps 3–11 of "Even-Count Tubular Peyote Stitch." (Remember that you do not need to step up.)

4 Continue stitching one bead at a time until you reach your desired length of tube. In the tube shown, a green bead is used as the first bead in each round.

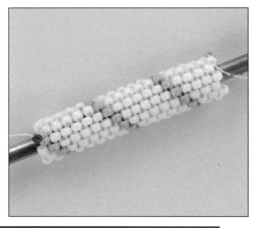

FAQ

When I design my own patterns, should I use the even-count tubular peyote stitch or the odd-count stitch?

Use the even-count stitch when you would like to create horizontal stripes, like those shown at right. It is easier to create them using the even-count stitch, because the rows are straight (with a distinct beginning and end); in contrast to the odd-count stitch, whose rows spiral continuously. For the same reason, it is also easier to create a grid pattern for the even-count stitch than it is for the odd-count stitch.

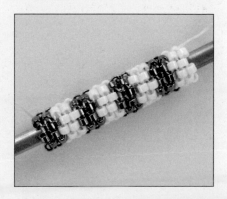

You can speed-up peyote stitch and change its appearance by skipping and stitching multiples of beads, rather than one bead at a time.

When you see this technique in project instructions, its name should specify the number of beads in each set, or *drop*, of beads that you skip and stitch. (Do not confuse this type of drop with drop beads, which are defined on page 7 in Chapter 1.) For example, in *two-drop peyote*, you work with two beads at a time; and in *three-drop peyote*, you work with three beads at a time.

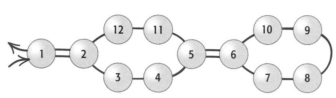

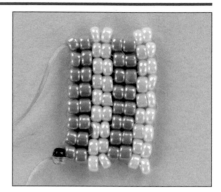

Two-drop flat peyote

You can use multiple-drop peyote to create either flat or tubular beadwork, using an even-count or an odd-count stitch. Keep in mind that whether a stitch is even-count or odd-count depends on the number of drops in a row—not on the total number of beads that you initially pick up.

Three-drop flat peyote

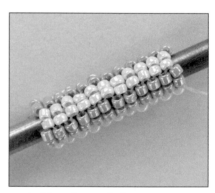

Two-drop tubular peyote

For instance, when you begin three-drop peyote by picking up 12 beads, you have an even-count stitch because there is an even number of drops (four drops containing three beads each). The same rule applies when you incorporate more than one size of drop in the same piece of beadwork. The example on the right contains two columns of two-drop peyote, two columns of three-drop peyote, and one column of regular peyote—for a total of five columns. Therefore, it is stitched using the odd-count peyote method.

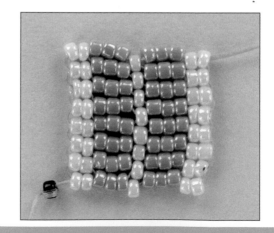

When you *zip-up* peyote stitch, you join the top and bottom ends of a length of beadwork by stitching them together. This technique is used to create peyote-stitch beaded beads, like those on the right, as well as the Tubular Peyote Napkin Rings on page 189.

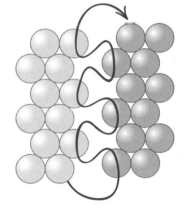

1 Begin by making sure that your beadwork has an even number of rows or rounds. If it does not, then either stitch one more row or round, or rip one row or round, to ensure that the ends of the beadwork will fit together properly.

2 Bring the two ends of beadwork together, positioning them so that each high bead or high drop (for multiple-drop peyote) on one end aligns with a matching low bead or low drop on the other end.

3 Using the existing thread tail from one end of the beadwork (or after weaving-in to add a new length of thread) bring the needle out through a low bead or low drop in the place where you plan to begin the join.

4 Pull the thread taut.

5 Reversing direction, pass through the corresponding high bead or high drop in the other end of the beadwork.

6 Pull the thread taut. The two ends of beadwork are now becoming joined, like the teeth of a zipper.

7 Pass the needle through the next adjacent high bead or high drop in the other end of the beadwork.

8 Continue this process to zip together both ends of beadwork. The needle now exits a high bead or high drop on one end.

9 Reverse direction again and pass through the corresponding low bead or low drop on the other end of the beadwork.

10 Pull the thread taut and weave-in to end the thread.

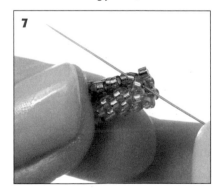

7

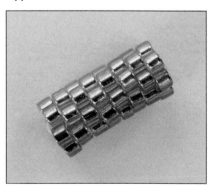

Zipped peyote stitch

Perform Peyote Stitch Increases and Decreases

Increases and decreases produce rows of varying lengths within a piece of beadwork. When you make an *increase*, you stitch more beads into a row than you stitched into the previous row. With a *decrease*, you stitch fewer beads than you did in the previous row. There are two primary types of peyote stitch increases and decreases: *outside* and *mid-row*.

Peyote Outside Increases and Decreases

Outside increases and decreases occur on the outside edges of flat bead-work. With an *outside increase*, you add one or more beads or drops to the beginning or end of a row; with an *outside decrease*, you subtract one or more beads or drops from the beginning or end of a row. (Keep in mind that adding or subtracting an odd number of columns to your bead-work may convert it from an even-count stitch to an odd-count stitch, or vice versa.)

Many outside increases and outside decreases require you to weave through the beadwork to reposition your needle before you can stitch the next row—much like odd-count flat peyote stitch. You can use any path that allows your needle to emerge from the correct bead and in the proper direction, while keeping the thread at the edges of the beadwork incon-spicuous. The path that you select depends on the exact configuration of the beads, the number of rows that are available to weave through, and your own personal preference. Here are some common approaches.

BASIC ONE-COLUMN OUTSIDE PEYOTE INCREASE

This method often works to increase peyote beadwork by one outside column. When you begin this increase, your needle may exit a high bead (a) or a low bead (b).

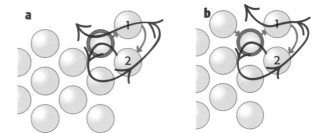

① At the end of the row that is *one row past* where you would like the new column to begin, pick up two beads (beads 1 and 2 in the diagram).

② Position the two new beads so that they are stacked on top of one another, with the holes running horizontally parallel. (Hold them between your finger and thumb.)

③ Pass back through the bead (outlined in the diagrams on the previous page) that your thread exited in Step 1 and pull the thread taut.

4. Reversing direction and moving downward, pass through the next vertically adjacent bead and back through the second bead that you picked up in Step 1 (bead 2).

5. Pull the thread taut.

6. Pass back through the first bead that you picked up in Step 1 (bead 1) and again pull the thread taut.

7. If you began with the thread exiting a high bead (a), pass back through that bead, and again pull the thread taut.

8. Resume peyote stitch as usual. Keep in mind that the stitch now becomes odd-count peyote, unless you perform a corresponding increase or decrease on the opposite edge of the beadwork.

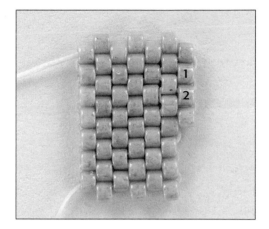

EVEN MULTIPLE-COLUMN OUTSIDE PEYOTE INCREASE

Use this technique to add an even number of columns to the edge of flat peyote beadwork, all at once. The example adds two columns; to add a larger even number of columns, begin by picking up a larger number of beads, and then follow the same general procedure described below. For this method to work, you generally need to start from a low bead (outlined in the diagram).

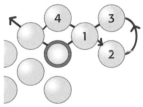

1. At the end of the row that is one row past where you would like the new columns to begin, pick up three beads (beads 1, 2, and 3 in the above diagram).

2. Arrange the beads as shown, with the third bead stacked on top of the second bead.

3. While holding those beads between your finger and thumb, pull the thread taut.

4. Pass back through the first bead that you picked up in Step 1 and again pull the thread taut.

5. Pick up another bead (bead 4).

6. Pass back through the bead that you started from and pull the thread taut.

7. Resume peyote stitch as usual.

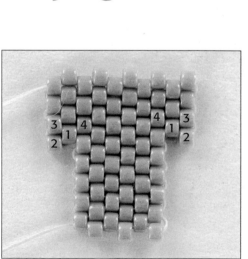

CONTINUED ON NEXT PAGE

ODD MULTIPLE-COLUMN OUTSIDE PEYOTE INCREASE

Use this technique to add an odd number of columns, greater than one, to the edge of flat peyote beadwork. The example adds three columns; to add a larger odd number of columns, begin by picking up a larger number of beads, and then follow the same general procedure described below. These directions apply to either a high-bead start (a) or a low-bead start (b).

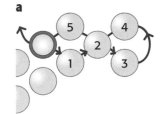

1 At the end of the row that is one row past where you would like the new columns to begin, pick up four beads (beads 1, 2, 3, and 4 in the diagrams).

2 Pass back through the second bead that you picked up in Step 1 (bead 2) and pull the thread taut.

3 Pick up another bead (bead 5).

4 Pass back through the bead that you started from (outlined in the diagrams) and pull the thread taut.

5 If the bead that you started from is a high bead (a), resume peyote stitch as usual; if it is a low bead (b), proceed to Step 6.

6 Moving downward, pass through the next vertically adjacent bead in the previous row and pull the thread taut.

7 Pass through the first and second beads that you picked up in Step 1 (beads 1 and 2) and pull the thread taut.

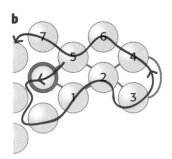

8 Pass through the third and fourth beads that you picked up in Step 1 (reversing direction) and pull the thread taut.

9 Pick up another bead (bead 6).

10 Pass through the fifth bead that you picked up in Step 1 and pull the thread taut.

11 Pick up another bead (bead 7) and pass back through the next adjacent bead in the previous row.

12 Resume peyote stitch as usual.

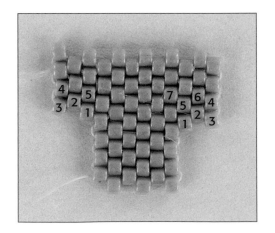

ONE-COLUMN OUTSIDE PEYOTE DECREASE

To create a decrease at the end of a row, you can often simply end the row early, turn, and begin the following row, as shown in this diagram (a).

However, to *begin* a row with a decrease, you usually need to weave into the beadwork to change the direction of the thread. This works with either a high-bead start (b) or a low-bead start (c). To use this technique with multiple-drop peyote, substitute a drop for each single bead in the directions.

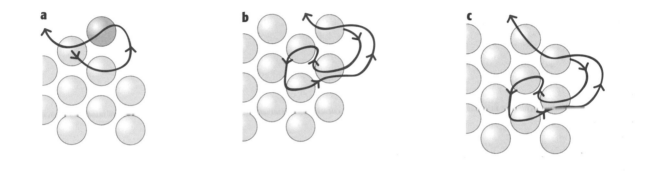

In this example (d), a one-column outside decrease is performed on either edge of each of the final (topmost) rows of even-count flat peyote. In this example (e), the same technique is used with odd-count flat peyote. Notice that the odd number of columns in odd-count flat peyote allows the beadwork to taper to a center point.

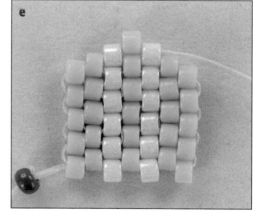

CONTINUED ON NEXT PAGE

MULTIPLE-COLUMN OUTSIDE PEYOTE DECREASE

You can perform an outside decrease of more than one column by beginning with the basic procedure for decreasing by one column, and then weaving through the beadwork to bring the needle out at the place where the new, shorter row should begin. This diagram shows one possible path. Your goal is to ensure that the needle emerges from the correct bead and in the proper direction.

If a project calls for a significant decrease, it is often easier to stitch the wider and shorter lengths separately, and then join them by zipping-up (see the section "Zip-Up Peyote Stitch" on page 61).

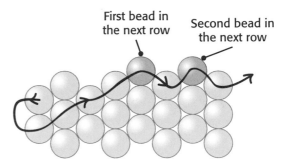

First bead in the next row

Second bead in the next row

FAQ

What Is Diagonal Peyote?

Diagonal peyote is flat peyote stitch performed with a special series of outside increases and decreases that make the beadwork appear to have diagonal rows. The most popular diagonal peyote technique, called *Russian leaf peyote*, also makes use of turning beads. You can see an example of this method in "Herringbone Rope and Peyote Leaf Necklace" on page 235.

Peyote Mid-Row Increases and Decreases

Mid-row (or "inside") increases and decreases occur within flat, tubular, or circular bead-work. (This is the only type of increase that you use for tubular and circular peyote, whose rows do not have edges.) With a *mid-row increase* you add one or more beads within a row or round, and with a *mid-row decrease* you subtract one or more beads within a row or round. A mid-row increase or decrease does not require that you weave through the beadwork to reposition your needle; however, it may convert your stitch from even-count to odd-count, or vice versa.

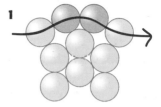

REGULAR PEYOTE MID-ROW RAPID INCREASE

This mid-row increase technique creates a *rapid increase*, which results in a sudden, dramatic increase in row length. (These directions are for regular, single-bead peyote; to make a mid-row increase in multiple-drop peyote, see page 69.)

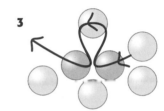

1 At the place in a row or round where you would like to begin an increase, pick up two beads instead of one.

2 Resume peyote stitch as usual to the end of the row and back again, or around the tube (for tubular peyote).

3 When you reach the two beads that you picked up in Step 1, pass back up through the first bead of the increase, pick up a new bead, and then pass back down through the second bead in the increase, as shown.

4 Pull the thread taut and resume peyote stitch as usual.

In the photo on this page, the two lighter-color beads are the beads added in Step 1.

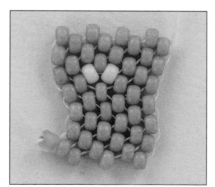

Flat peyote

Tubular peyote

CONTINUED ON NEXT PAGE

REGULAR PEYOTE MID-ROW GRADUAL INCREASE

This mid-row increase technique creates a *gradual increase*, which results in a slightly smoother, less abrupt widening than the rapid increase. It is worked over the course of four rows or rounds.

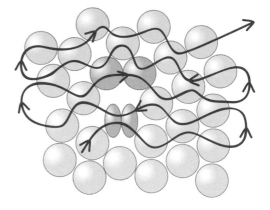

1 At the place in a row where you would like to begin an increase, stop and inspect your loose beads. Select either two that are noticeably thinner than average or one that is noticeably wider than average. (The diagram uses two thin orange beads.)

2 Pick up and stitch either the two thin beads or the one large bead in place of a single, average-size bead.

3 Resume peyote stitch as usual to the end of the row and back again, or around the tube (for tubular peyote).

4 When you reach the two thin beads or one wide bead, pass back through those two or that one, as if you are passing through a two-bead drop or a regular single bead.

5 Resume peyote stitch to the end of the row and back again.

6 When you reach the two thin beads or one wide bead in the previous row, pick up and stitch two average-size beads (the circular orange beads in the diagram), as if you were performing two-drop peyote.

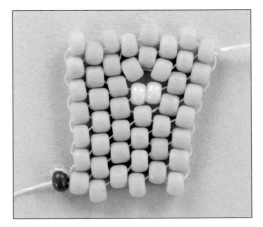

Flat peyote

7 Resume the regular peyote stitch to the end of the row and back.

8 When you reach the two average-size beads that you picked up in Step 6, pass up through the first bead, pick up another bead, and then pass down through the second bead, as you would for a mid-row rapid increase.

9 Resume peyote stitch as usual.

In the two photos on this page, lighter-color beads represent the two thin beads picked up in Step 1. In a real project, you typically use colors that blend-in, so that the point of the increase is less obvious.

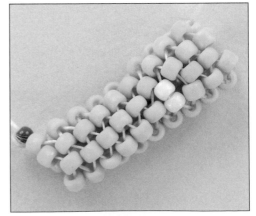

Tubular peyote

MULTIPLE-DROP PEYOTE MID-ROW INCREASE

With multiple-drop peyote, you typically make mid-row increases by increasing the number of beads in a drop. In this example, a series of increases occurs in the center column of blue beads. The first several bottom rows contain three-bead drops; the final top row contains a six-bead drop.

PEYOTE STITCH MID-ROW RAPID DECREASE

This mid-row technique creates a *rapid decrease*, which results in a sudden, dramatic decrease in row length. (These directions are for regular, single-bead peyote; to make a mid-row decrease in multiple-drop peyote, see page 70.)

① At the place in a row or round where you would like to begin the decrease, pass back through two beads from the previous row without adding a new bead in between them.

② Resume peyote stitch as usual to the end of the row and back, or around the tube (for tubular peyote).

③ When you reach the location where you skipped a bead (Step 1), string on one bead to fill the gap (orange in the diagram).

④ Resume peyote stitch as usual.

In these photos, the two lighter-color beads are the beads passed back through in Step 1.

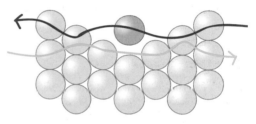

Flat peyote   *Tubular peyote*

CONTINUED ON NEXT PAGE

PEYOTE STITCH MID-ROW GRADUAL DECREASE

This mid-row decrease technique creates a *gradual decrease*, which results in a slightly smoother, less abrupt narrowing of the beadwork than the rapid decrease. It is worked over the course of four rows or rounds.

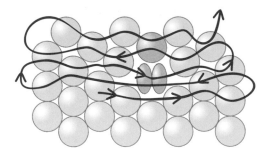

1 At the place in a row or round where you would like to begin the decrease, pass back through two high beads, without adding a bead in between them.

2 Resume peyote stitch as usual to the end of the row and back, or around the tube (for tubular peyote).

3 When you reach the place where you passed back through two beads (Step 1), stop and inspect your loose beads. Select either two that are noticeably thinner than average or one that is noticeably wider than average. (The diagram uses two thin orange beads.)

4 Pick up the two thin beads or one wide bead and pass the needle back through the next bead on the opposite side of the gap created by the two adjacent low beads.

5 Resume peyote stitch as usual.

6 When you reach the place where you added the two thin beads or one wide bead, pass back through them (or it), as if they were one average-size bead.

7 Resume peyote stitch.

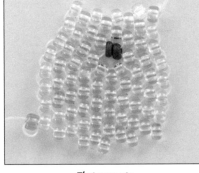

Flat peyote

Tubular peyote

8 When you reach the place where you added the two beads in Step 6, pick up and stitch one average-size bead (the circular orange bead) to fill the gap.

9 Resume peyote stitch.

In the two examples above, the darker-color beads represent the two thin beads added in Step 4.

MULTIPLE-DROP PEYOTE MID-ROW DECREASE

With multiple-drop peyote, you can make mid-row decreases by reducing the number of beads in a drop. In this example, a series of decreases occurs in the two columns of blue beads.

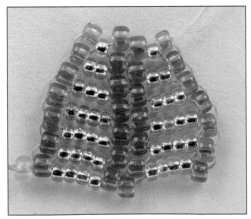

Flat peyote multiple-drop decreases

Make Circular Peyote

In *circular peyote* (also called *peyote in the round*), the rows are circles, near-circles, or ovals—called *rounds*—that develop outward from the center. As with tubular peyote, you can stitch the beadwork either clockwise or counterclockwise, whichever direction you find most comfortable.

BASIC THREE-BEAD-START CIRCULAR PEYOTE

This is the most basic circular peyote technique. Once you understand the process, you can experiment by starting with a larger number of beads in the initial ring, and by incorporating beads of different sizes.

1 After preparing your thread without a stop bead, pick up three beads to begin circular peyote. (The example uses three size 11/0 Japanese seed beads.)

2 Position the beads at least 6 inches from the loose end of the thread, and tie a square knot or a surgeon's knot to create a taut ring of three beads. This serves as the first round.

3 Pass through the first bead that you strung on and pull the thread taut.

4 Pick up two beads. (Notice that this is a mid-row increase.)

5 Pass through the next bead in the first round and pull the thread taut.

6 Repeat Steps 4 and 5 two more times to complete the second round.

7 Step up by passing through the two beads that you picked up in Step 4 and pull the thread taut.

CONTINUED ON NEXT PAGE

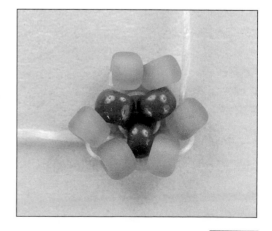

8. Pick up a bead to begin the third round.

9. Pass through the next bead in the second round and pull the thread taut.

10. Pick up another bead, pass through the next bead in the second round, and pull the thread taut.

11. Repeat Step 10 until you reach the end of the third round.

12. Step up by passing through the first bead of the third round and pull the thread taut.

13. Repeat the general procedure you used in Steps 8–12 to continue adding rounds of beads.

From this point on, the number of beads that you pick up at a time depends on how much space exists between beads in the previous round (which is related to the size of beads that you use). You need to adjust that number in order to keep the beadwork in your desired flat, ruffle, or dome shape. In the flat example shown, the fifth round (made up of green beads) is completed by picking up two beads at a time, and the final two rounds (made up of cream and purple beads) are completed by picking up one bead at a time.

TIP

Making Circular Peyote with a Hole at the Center

You can make circular peyote beadwork that has an open center by starting with a larger ring of beads. With this technique, you need to stitch the next round after the ring the same way you would stitch the fourth or fifth round of circular peyote. That is, instead of picking up a bead between each pair of beads in the ring, you pick up a bead and then skip a bead in the ring, and repeat that process for the entire round. For a project that uses this method, see "Tubular Netting and Peyote Bezel Necklace" on page 214.

In this example, one cream bead is stitched between every two pairs of green beads in the sixth round, rather than between every two beads. This curls the edges of the beadwork to create a dome (or, if you turn it upside-down, a bowl). In the seventh round, one purple bead is stitched after each cream bead in the previous row.

You are not limited to picking up the same number of beads for each stitch in a round as long as your increases and decreases remain uniformly spaced. For instance, you can stitch two beads at a time for one stitch, one bead for the next stitch, two beads for the next stitch, and so on, as shown in the final round of the example on the right.

TIP

Flat versus Ruffled Circular Peyote

As flat circular peyote beadwork expands, it becomes more prone to curling or ruffling. You can create intentional ruffles by adding more beads than necessary to fill the spaces between beads in a previous row, and by keeping tension relatively tight.

If ruffles occur unintentionally, try reducing the number of beads in the previous one or two rounds by ripping and re-stitching those rows. Keep in mind that you can also take advantage of the slightly different widths of beads in your bead dish. Select slightly shorter beads when you have less space to fill and slightly longer beads to fill a larger space.

Learn Dutch Spiral Stitch

Dutch spiral is a type of modified odd-count tubular peyote stitch. Instead of adding beads one at a time, you stitch drops of multiple beads. You can achieve more dramatic results by alternating between stitching single beads and multiple-bead drops.

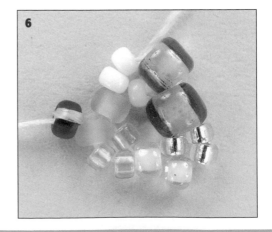

This stitch differs from multiple-drop peyote in that you do not pass through all of the beads that make up a drop when you stitch the next round. Instead, most of those beads are skipped over, creating the appearance of an open weave.

Dutch spiral traditionally begins and ends with *graduating* rounds. You perform increases for the first few (or more) rounds, and decreases for the final few (or more) rounds.

BASIC DUTCH SPIRAL ROPE

This approach to Dutch spiral stitch is a good way to learn the basic technique.

1. Pick up three sets of two beads each, with each set containing one larger size bead and one smaller size bead, in that order. The example uses this series of Japanese seed beads: one size 11/0, one size 14/0, one size 8/0, one size 14/0, one size 11/0, and one size 14/0. (The red bead is a stop bead.)

2. Pass through the first bead and pull the thread taut to create a ring. This serves as the first round. (Do not slip the ring onto a form.)

3. Pick up a set of three beads: two smaller beads and one larger bead, in that order. The smaller beads should match the next smaller bead in the ring, and the larger bead should match the next larger bead in the ring.

4. Pass through the next large bead in the ring. For now, you can hold the beadwork flat.

5. Pull the thread firmly taut.

6. Repeat Steps 3–5 two more times to complete the second round.

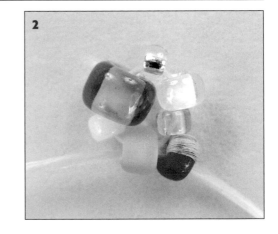

7 Pick up a set of four beads: three smaller beads and one larger bead, in that order. Once again, the smaller beads should match the next smaller bead in the previous round, and the larger bead should match the next larger bead in the previous round.

8 Pass through the next large high bead in the previous round and pull the thread taut. The beadwork is now taking on a bowl shape.

9 Repeat Steps 7 and 8 twice more to complete the third round.

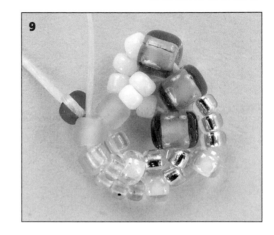

10 **Optional:** To create a wider rope, repeat Steps 7 and 8 three more times, this time adding sets of five beads: four smaller beads and one larger bead, in that order.

11 Continue adding three sets of the same number of beads until you reach your desired length, less the final two or three rounds. The beadwork takes on a tubular shape as you add rounds.

12 To stitch the final rounds, make decreases by eliminating one smaller bead per set for each round, finishing with a round that has a total of six beads.

In this example (a), the completed Dutch spiral has been reinforced by passing diagonally through all of the beads in one spiral column of single beads. This tightens the rope's tension, making the undulations more pronounced.

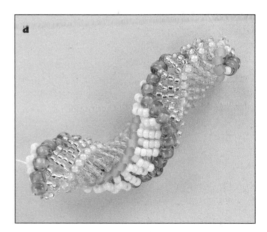

TIP

Dutch Spiral Rope Variations

You can alter the basic Dutch spiral stitch in many ways. For example, you can achieve a more undulating rope by alternating between single beads and multiple-bead drops of varying lengths. Because there are so many possibilities for the Dutch spiral, project instructions typically indicate how you should perform the stitch for a given project.

Peyote Stitch Graph Patterns

Peyote stitch graph patterns have cells that are offset like the bricks in a brick wall that is turned on its side. You read peyote graphs a little differently depending on whether they are for flat peyote, tubular peyote, or circular peyote.

FLAT PEYOTE GRAPH PATTERNS

You can read flat peyote patterns from the bottom up or the top down, whichever you prefer. The side from which you begin depends on the type of peyote stitch. Even-count flat peyote (a) begins with a high bead, and so you must begin with a corner that contains a high cell. Because odd-count flat peyote begins with a low bead (b), you must begin with a corner that contains a low cell.

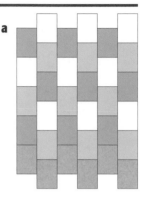

a

In the graph patterns on the right, the orange cells represent the beads that you initially pick up if you begin reading the pattern at the bottom. Each subsequent row is represented by a common cell color (green, blue or yellow).

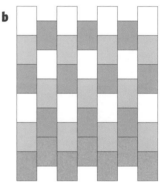

b

FAQ

I have an odd-count flat peyote pattern that has high cells at all four corners. Since odd-count peyote begins with a low bead, how do I begin working this pattern?

In this case, you can begin stitching the pattern as even-count peyote by temporarily leaving off the last bead in the first row. Then, at the end of the third row, make a one-column outside increase.

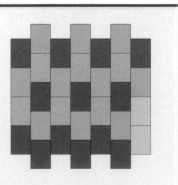

In the example on the right, you can begin by picking up the six brown beads in the lowest row, (reading the pattern left to right). Then turn and stitch the blue beads to complete a third row. Turn again and stitch the fourth row using orange beads. At the end of the fourth row, make the outside increase, which adds the two green beads. From this point forward, the stitch is odd-count peyote.

TUBULAR PEYOTE GRAPH PATTERNS

Tubular peyote graph patterns are flat representations of tubes. You do not read them back and forth as you do with flat peyote graphs. Instead, you follow each line moving in the same direction. Notice that the first bead in each round of tubular peyote moves over by the space of one bead. In these examples, the numbered, dark-blue cells represent the first bead in each round, if you begin reading the patterns at their lower-left corners. Most graph patterns include similar number labels to help you keep track of rounds. However, those numbers are only for reference; a numbered bead is not necessarily the first bead that you pick up to stitch a round.

Notice that with both even-count tubular peyote (a) and odd-count tubular peyote (b), the first *low* cell represents the first bead of the first round. This means that in even-count tubular peyote, which begins with a high bead, the first bead in the first round (reading left to right) is in the second column.

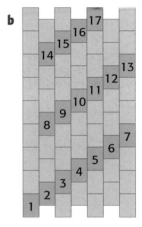

With odd-count tubular peyote, the first bead in the first column is also the first bead of that round; however, the graph becomes more complicated further along. In figure b, this occurs at round eight, where the first cell in the row of the graph represents the last bead in round seven, rather than the first bead in round eight. To avoid confusion, many beaders avoid creating graph patterns for odd-count tubular peyote designs. You may find it easier to create your design by experimenting with the stitch and then writing down the sequence of bead colors and sizes that you use.

CONTINUED ON NEXT PAGE

MULTIPLE-DROP PEYOTE GRAPH PATTERNS

Graph patterns for multiple-drop peyote have groups of columns whose cells are aligned horizontally, rather than being offset by a half cell. The number of cells that are grouped together horizontally indicates the size of the drop.

Many patterns combine regular peyote with multiple-drop peyote. In the graph pattern on the right, the orange columns call for regular peyote; that is, you pick up and stitch a single bead in that part of each row. The blue columns are two-drop peyote, where you pick up and stitch two beads at once.

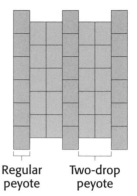

Regular peyote   Two-drop peyote

KEEPING YOUR PLACE IN A PEYOTE GRAPH PATTERN

In this example, a sheet of paper marks a beader's place in a peyote graph pattern. The edge of the paper aligns with the tops of the cells in the current row. You can ignore the half-covered cells; they are the cells for the next row, and you can align the paper along their tops when you move on to that row.

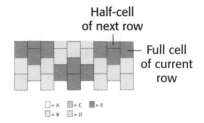

Half-cell of next row

Full cell of current row

☐ = A ☐ = C ■ = E
☐ = B ☐ = D

PEYOTE GRAPH INCREASES AND DECREASES

Outside increases and decreases are depicted in flat peyote stitch graph patterns the same way they appear in the actual beadwork: Either one or more new columns of cells begin, or a column decreases by one or more cells. Mid-row increases are indicated differently depending on the personal preference of the graph's author. If there are symbols drawn within some cells, look for a *graph key*, which should explain whether the symbols represent inside increases or decreases. If a graph looks like the one shown here, it usually means that each large, empty space between cells represents a decrease, and the addition of cells within those spaces is an increase. (Be aware that the spaces will not appear in the resulting beadwork; it will actually become narrower within those rows.)

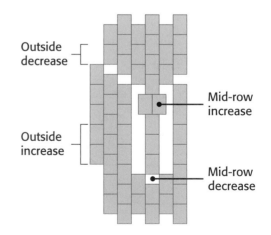

Outside decrease

Mid-row increase

Outside increase

Mid-row decrease

CIRCULAR PEYOTE PATTERNS

Circular peyote patterns are drawn to mirror the placement of beads in the design. Because these patterns are circular, you cannot easily use a sheet of paper to help you keep your place. Instead, try making a copy of the pattern that you can write on, and then, using a pen or pencil, mark off the cell for each bead that you pick up.

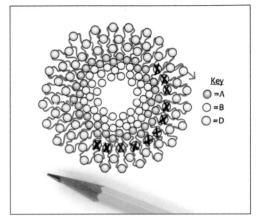

Key
○ = A
○ = B
○ = D

STITCHING PEYOTE PATTERNS USING BRICK STITCH

You can stitch many peyote graph pattern designs using brick stitch instead of peyote stitch. Simply turn the peyote graph pattern on its side and follow it as you would a brick stitch pattern. To learn about brick stitch and brick-stitch patterns, see Chapter 5.

TIP

Making the Most of Increases and Decreases

When you create your own designs from scratch, keep in mind that you can use outside and mid-row increases and decreases to achieve many interesting design effects. Some techniques call for spacing increases at set intervals, and others are more freeform in nature, allowing you to make increases and decreases where you see fit. In the peyote tube shown on the right, evenly-spaced rapid mid-row increases and decreases create the orange undulations.

chapter 4

Beaded Netting

Beaded netting is like peyote stitch in that you stitch beads after skipping other beads in previous rows or rounds. Unlike peyote, netting creates a supple, open weave that gives beadwork the appearance of a net or web. You can stitch flat beaded netting either horizontally or vertically, and you can use the horizontal version to make tubular and circular netting.

Create Flat Horizontal Netting

With *flat horizontal netting*, you stitch rows from one side to the other. You can vary the density of netting by altering the number of beads that you pick up for each stitch, and you can make increases and decreases either on the outside or mid-row. For an example of a flat horizontal netting project, see "Horizontal Netting Anklet" on page 211.

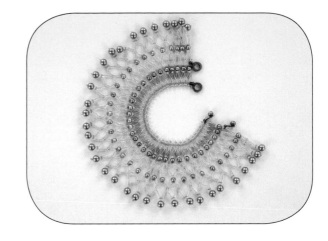

Flat Horizontal Netting Rows and Columns

Netting rows are made up of *loops*, which are short segments of odd-count, strung beads. The middle bead in each loop is called the *link bead*. This is the bead that you pass through to connect loops. In horizontal netting, the thread passes horizontally through link beads.

You can determine the number of rows and columns in netted beadwork by counting the link beads horizontally and vertically. Horizontal netting is typically even-count; that is, you stitch an even number of columns.

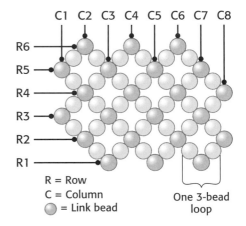

Horizontal netting stitches are named according to the number of beads in each loop. The diagram above shows *three-bead netting*, in which each loop contains three beads. The orange beads are the link beads.

Before you begin a horizontal netting project, you need to determine how many beads to pick up to establish your desired width and to accommodate complete loops of beads. An easy way to do this is to shade in cells on a blank netting graph pattern and then count them (see the section "Netting Graph Patterns" on page 94).

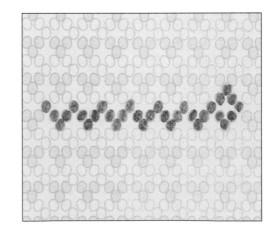

THREE-BEAD HORIZONTAL NETTING

This example creates flat beaded fabric with 10 columns.

1 After preparing your thread, pick up 15 beads. (This example uses size 11/0 Japanese seed beads; the teal beads represent link beads, and the red bead is a stop bead.)

2 Now pick up five more beads. These beads establish a turning chain (defined in Chapter 2), because they allow you to change direction and begin the next row.

3 Pass back through the third from the last bead that you picked up in Step 1 and pull the thread taut.

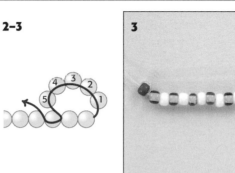

2–3

3

4 Pick up three more beads, skip three beads, and then pass back through a bead

5 Pull the thread taut.

6 Perform Steps 4 and 5 two more times to reach the end of the row.

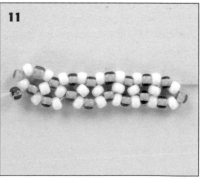

7 Pick up five beads. These make up the next turning chain.

8 Turn, and pass back through the next high link bead (the middle bead in the loop).

9 Pull the thread taut.

10 Pick up three beads, pass through the next high link bead, and pull the thread taut.

11 Repeat Step 10 until you reach the last high link bead in the previous row.

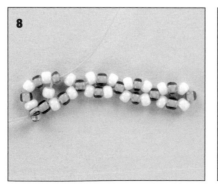

8

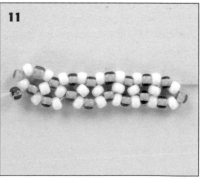

11

CONTINUED ON NEXT PAGE

⑫ Pick up five beads for the turning chain, and turn.

⑬ Repeat Steps 10–12 until you reach your desired length of beadwork.

3-bead horizontal netting

FIVE-BEAD HORIZONTAL NETTING

Five-bead horizontal netting is another popular netting stitch. You stitch it like three-bead netting, except that you pick up five beads for each loop instead of three, and for each turning chain, you pick up eight beads instead of five. This example begins with thirteen size 11/0 Japanese seed beads. The dark-green beads are the link beads.

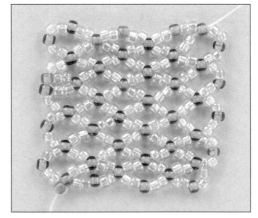

5-bead horizontal netting

TIP

Keep Horizontal Netting Flat

To avoid twisted rows of netting, hold the needle in line with the beadwork and as parallel as possible to the thread that is already running through a bead. Do your best to keep the threads from crossing inside of beads, and, as always, take care not to split thread.

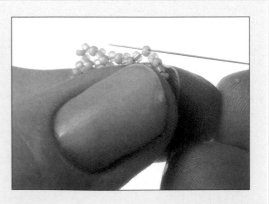

HORIZONTAL NETTING WITH TURNING-BEAD EDGES

This is an ornate version of horizontal netting in which a turning bead serves as an accent at the end of each row. It's a popular technique for dressing up netted bracelets and choker bands.

1. Pick up all of the beads for the first two rows of horizontal netting; (with a row defined as one row of link beads; see page 82). For five-bead netting with eight columns, these are the first nineteen beads.

2. Pick up a bead to serve as the turning bead (orange in the diagram). It can be the same size, smaller, or larger than the other beads in the netting.

3. Position the turning bead close to the last bead that you picked up in Step 1 and pass back through that last bead.

4. Hold the last bead and the turning bead between your finger and thumb and pull the thread taut.

5. Pick up all of the beads for the first loop of the third row of netting. For five-bead netting, this is five beads.

6. Continue the horizontal netting stitch as usual until you reach the end of the row.

7. To make the turn, pick up the first half of the loop beads plus the link bead, and then stitch another turning bead, as you did in Steps 2–4.

8. Continue this process to stitch each row to your desired length of netting.

In this example (a), the loops each contain five size 14/0 Japanese seed beads, and the turning beads are size 11/0 Japanese seed beads.

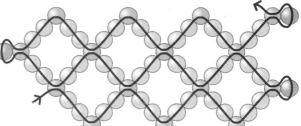

Horizontal netting with turning-bead edges

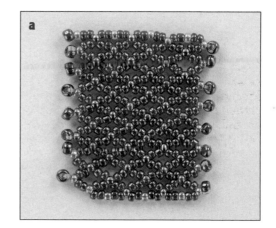

TIP

Use Multiple Turning Beads

You are not limited to using just one turning bead at the end of each netted row. You can use sets of three beads strung together, loops of multiple beads, or even long fringes. In this example, six turquoise beads create a loop with a gold turning-bead base at the end of each row. To learn more about fringe and other decorative details that you can add to the edges of beadwork, see Chapter 9.

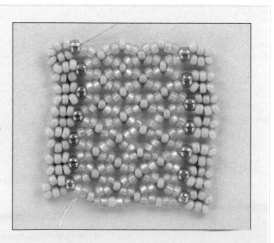

Increasing and Decreasing Flat Horizontal Netting

Just like with peyote stitch, you can increase or decrease the width of horizontal netting rows either on the outside edges or mid-row.

HORIZONTAL NETTING OUTSIDE INCREASE

Basic outside increases expand the beadwork by the width of two columns, or one "diamond" formation of beads. To make an outside increase, you need to pick up an additional set of beads that is large enough to form another full diamond. This lengthens two rows at once: Both the end of the current row and the beginning of the next row are extended.

In the three-bead netting diagram on the right, the orange beads are the five turning-chain beads that you normally pick up to end the row without an increase, and the green beads are the additional beads that you pick up to make the increase. Notice that you begin by picking up only the first two beads in the usual turning chain, the second of which is a link bead. You then pick up the additional seven beads for the increase, and pass back through the link bead, before picking up the next three beads. Those three form the next loop.

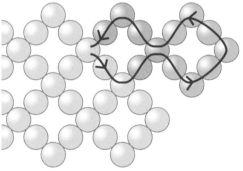

HORIZONTAL NETTING OUTSIDE DECREASE

For a two-column (single "diamond") outside decrease, you simply end a row two columns early, pick up all of the beads for the usual turning chain (orange in the diagram on the right), turn, and resume stitching.

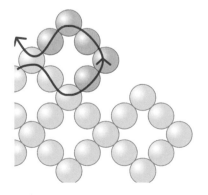

HORIZONTAL NETTING MID-ROW INCREASE

You can make a mid-row increase by adding more beads to a loop as shown on the right. Each increase must occur in multiples of two beads, to ensure that the loop maintains an odd number of beads with a link bead in the middle.

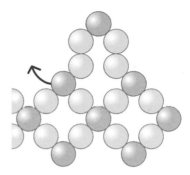

In the example shown on the right, increases convert the beadwork from three-bead horizontal netting into five-bead horizontal netting. (The darker-color beads represent the three-bead netting, and the lighter-color beads are the five-bead netting.) Notice that the turning chains also increase from five beads to eight beads.

You can make increases in all of the loops, beginning with a certain row, as shown in the example, or you can make increases in just one or two loops, depending on what your design calls for. This is also the type of increase that you use for tubular netting (see page 90 in this chapter).

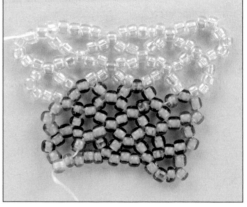

HORIZONTAL NETTING MID-ROW DECREASE

The mid-row decrease (a) is the opposite of the basic horizontal netting increase: Instead of adding beads to a loop, you reduce the number of beads. In this example (b), mid-row decreases convert the netting from five-bead to three-bead, beginning with the first row of lighter-color beads. This is also the type of decrease that you use for tubular netting (see page 90).

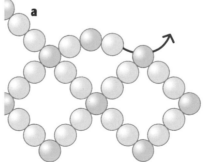

a

b

Create Vertical Netting

Vertical netting is a type of beaded lace. You stitch it one vertical column at a time, rather than one horizontal row at a time, and you alternate between working down one column and up the next.

This stitch typically flows from a base row, which may be a simple strand of beads or a band of beadwork made using a different stitch—like peyote or brick stitch. For a project that uses vertical netting, see "Netting and Right-Angle Weave Earrings" on page 192.

BASIC VERTICAL NETTING

Just like horizontal netting, vertical netting is made up of loops that connect together with link beads. In this example, the base row is a band of square stitch (see Chapter 6) using size 11/0 Japanese seed beads. The netting beads are size 11/0 Japanese seed beads.

1 After preparing your base row of strung beads or beadwork, pass or weave through the base row so that the thread exits at the place where you'd like to begin the vertical netting.

2 Pick up one bead (the first link bead) and then all of the beads for the first loop. The example uses nine beads per loop. (See page 83 to review loops.)

3 Pick up another link bead and slide all of the beads against the base row.

4 Repeat Steps 2 and 3 to your desired column length. The example creates three loops.

5 Pick up all of the beads for another loop. This is the bottom loop for the next column, and it serves as a turning chain.

6 Pass back through the fourth from the last link bead that you picked up.

7 Pull the thread taut while sliding all of the beads in the first column against the base row. There should be no spaces between beads, but the tension should not be so tight that it causes the beadwork to pucker. (You may find it helpful to position the beadwork flat on your work surface for the first two or three columns, after which it becomes easier to maintain proper thread tension.)

8 Pick up all of the beads for another loop.

9 Skip a link bead, and then pass through the next link bead in the first column.

10 Pull the thread taut.

11 Pick up all of the beads for another loop. In the example, this is the final loop for the second column. If your columns are longer, continue this process until you arrive back at the base row.

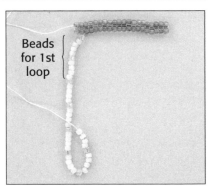

Beads for 1st loop

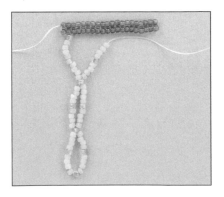

12 Pass back through the first bead that you picked up in Step 2 and pull the thread taut.

13 Pass back into the base row and, optionally, make a half-hitch knot over the thread there to secure the tension.

14 Bring the needle out where you would like to begin the next column.

15 Pick up a link bead and then enough beads for one half of a loop, less the next link bead. In the example, this is a total of five beads.

16 Pass back through the corresponding link bead from the previous column and pull the thread taut.

17 Pick up all of the beads for the next loop. In the example, this is a total of nine beads.

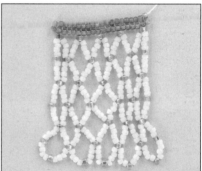

5 beads picked up in Step 15

9 beads picked up in Step 17

18 Pass back through the next corresponding link bead in the previous row and pull the thread taut.

19 Continue this process until you reach the end of the column.

20 Create the bottom loop, as you did in Step 5, to make the turn.

21 Keep stitching vertical netting, one column at a time, to your desired width of beadwork. To end the thread, you may either weave-in within the netting or within the base row, whichever is easier.

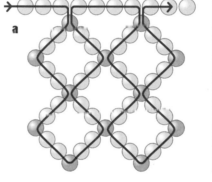

a

This diagram (a) demonstrates the path of the thread through five-row vertical netting from a base row of strung beads.

VERTICAL NETTING VARIATIONS, INCREASES, AND DECREASES

You do not need to use the same number of beads in each vertical loop as long as the link beads match up in each row. You can also add detail to the bottom loops of vertical netting by stitching one or more turning beads, using the same technique that you use to end rows with turning beads in horizontal netting (see page 83).

In addition to altering the numbers of beads in vertical loops, you can vary the lengths of columns. To make a set of columns longer than the previous set, simply pick up enough extra beads to create an extra loop. To make a set of columns shorter, stop and turn at the point of the decrease.

Make Tubular Netting

Tubular netting is horizontal netting performed in seamless rounds, much like tubular peyote, and it is easiest to stitch using a form. Because tubular netting is very soft, netted ropes are sometimes slipped over cord or ribbon for extra support. This is also a popular stitch for covering decorative objects. For a project that uses tubular netting, see "Tubular Netting and Peyote Bezel Necklace" on page 214.

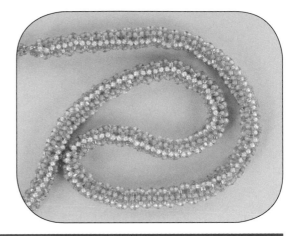

BASIC TUBULAR NETTING

1 After preparing your thread, pick up enough beads to form a strand long enough to wrap all the way around your form, with an *even* number of equally spaced link beads. Which beads become link beads depends on the size of the netting stitch; for instance, with three-bead netting, every other bead is a link bead, and with five-bead netting, every third bead is a link bead. (The example is for three-bead netting and uses sixteen size 11/0 Japanese seed beads to encircle a ¼-inch wooden dowel used as a form.)

2 Pass through all of the beads again and pull the thread taut to form a ring. (If you used a bead stop, you may remove it now.)

3 **Optional:** Make a square knot or surgeon's knot to secure the thread tension in the ring.

4 Pass into the ring and bring the needle out after the first link bead that you picked up.

5 Slip the ring onto the form and press the thread tail firmly against the form.

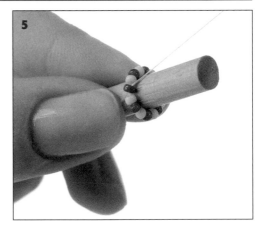

5

6 Pick up all of the beads to make one loop of netting. The example is for three-bead netting.

7 Skip the same number of beads on the ring, and then pass through the next bead (a link bead). Use your thumb to stack this new loop on top of the initial ring, so that it doesn't flip down below the ring.

8 Pull the thread taut.

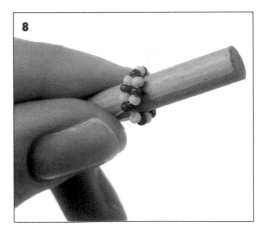

8

9 Repeat Steps 4–6 until you reach the first set of beads that you picked up the first time that you performed Step 4. The thread now exits a low link bead.

10 Step up by passing through the first half of the next loop and bring the needle out after the link bead.

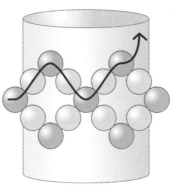

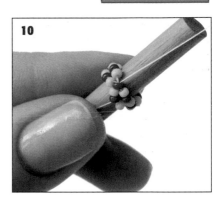

11 Pick up another set of loop beads and then pass through the next high link bead.

12 Continue this process to add loops, keeping the thread pulled taut, until you complete the current round.

13 Step up again (as you did in Step 10) to begin the next round.

14 Continue stitching each round and then stepping up to begin the next round until you reach your desired length.

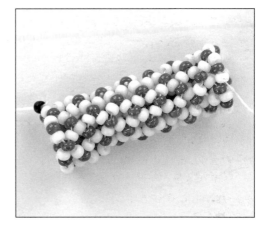

TUBULAR NETTING INCREASES AND DECREASES

You can make tubular netting rounds expand and contract using mid-row increases and mid-row decreases (see page 87). In the example on the right, the rounds graduate in size, ranging from three-bead netting for the first and last rounds to nine-bead netting for the middle round.

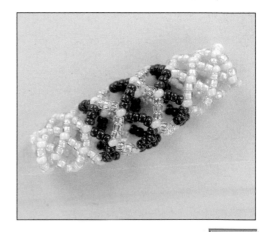

Make Circular Netting

With *circular netting*, increases in each round create horizontally netted circles that expand outward from a central ring of beads. Because of these increases, the link beads in the central rings are closer together than they are in any of the subsequent rounds.

 After preparing your thread, pick up an even number of beads to create your desired size of center ring. This number must allow the link beads to be evenly spaced. The example uses eight size 11/0 Japanese seed beads, with the orange beads representing the link beads that are spaced one bead apart.

② **Optional:** Use a square knot or surgeon's knot to tie the beads into a ring, leaving a thread tail at least 6–8 inches long (so that you can weave it in later).

③ Pass into the ring and bring the needle out through a link bead.

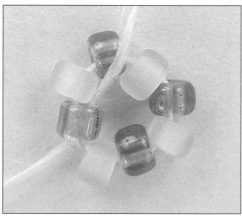

④ To begin the second round, create an increase by picking up a loop of beads that is longer than the distance between two link beads in the ring. Keep in mind that this must be an odd number of beads, with a center bead that becomes a link bead in the next round. (The example uses a loop of three beads, which is longer than the one-bead distance between link beads in the ring.) When you plan your own design, you may need to experiment by completing the entire round to find out whether the length you choose is correct to allow the beadwork to lie flat; if it doesn't, remove that round and try a different size of loops.

⑤ Pass through the very next link bead in the ring (do not skip over one link bead as you would for regular flat or tubular horizontal netting) and pull the thread taut.

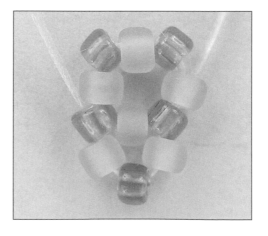

6 Repeat this process using the same length of loop to stitch all of the loops in the round.

7 At the end of the round, step up by passing into the first loop of the round and bring the needle out after the link bead.

8 Pick up another loop of beads that is longer than the distance between two link beads in the previous round (remember that this must always be an odd number). The example uses a five-bead loop.

9 Repeat this process using the same length of loop to stitch all of the loops in the round.

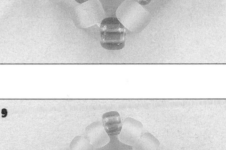

10 At the end of the round, step up to position the thread for the next round.

11 Continue stitching to create one round at a time, each larger than the previous round as needed to keep the beadwork flat. Alternatively, create a dome or bowl shape by repeating rows of the same size. (When you keep many rounds the same size, you create tubular netting.) You can also create ruffles by making rounds slightly longer than they need to be.

Netting Graph Patterns

In most netting-stitch graph patterns, each cell is an oval that roughly mimics the shape of a true seed bead. The positions of the ovals indicate which direction the thread should run through each link bead, and accordingly whether the pattern is for horizontal or vertical netting.

FLAT HORIZONTAL NETTING PATTERNS

With horizontal netting, the thread runs horizontally through most link beads. Because seed beads are shaped like donuts—wider than they are tall—the link-bead cells in a horizontal-netting graph pattern often look like donuts standing on their sides. (The outermost side beads are an exception, because you pass through them vertically unless you add turning beads.)

You can usually follow a horizontal-netting graph pattern from either bottom to top or top to bottom. However, you need to begin on the side that is short by one column. This is because the first row of horizontal netting is one column shorter than subsequent rows.

If you begin reading this three-bead pattern (a) or this five-bead netting pattern (b) from the bottom up, then you need to read it from left to right. The initial beads that you pick up are shown in green, and the beads in the first turning chain are purple.

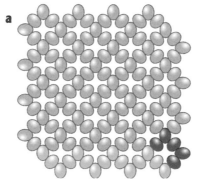

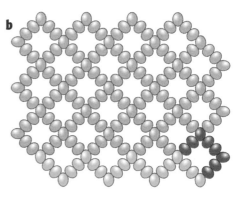

VERTICAL NETTING PATTERNS

With vertical netting, the thread runs vertically through the link beads, and so the cells representing link beads look like donuts lying flat. If you make vertical netting with loops that are all the same size, then you can use a blank horizontal-netting graph turned on its side to design your pattern. You can usually begin reading a vertical-netting graph pattern on either the right or the left. Then, alternate between following the pattern first downward and then upward, the same way you perform the stitch. If you read this example (c) from left to right, then the green cells are the initial beads that you pick up to establish the length of the columns, and the purple cells make up the loops that you add as you work back up toward the base row. The base row is shown as a simple strand of blue beads.

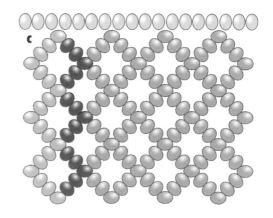

d

For designs with varying sizes of loops, graph patterns are typically customized for a particular project (d). To design your own, you can sketch out the design on blank paper and then color it in as usual.

TUBULAR NETTING PATTERNS

Tubular netting graph patterns look like flat horizontal netting patterns, except that all of their rows are typically of equal length, and the final column on the graph is not made up of link beads. Begin the pattern at either end (top or bottom), on the side that contains a column of link beads.

If you begin reading this pattern (e) from the bottom, then you need to start at the bottom-left corner. The green cells are the beads that make up the initial ring of beads, which becomes the first two rounds. The purple cells make up the loops that create the third round, and the orange cells make up the fourth round. Because you step up to begin each round, the first link bead shifts by the space of one column. In the example, the first link bead in each round is labeled with the number of the round.

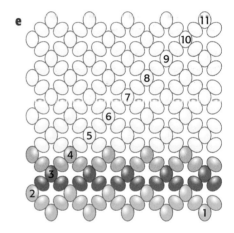
e

CIRCULAR NETTING PATTERNS

In circular netting patterns, the cells are arranged to exactly match the configuration of the beads. Typically, you can begin anywhere in the central ring, as long as you bring the needle out through a link bead.

NETTING PATTERN INCREASES AND DECREASES

Netting increases and decreases, whether outside or mid-row, are drawn into a pattern to mimic the way the beads are actually arranged in the beadwork. The places where increases or decreases occur tend to look much like they do in the increase and decreases diagrams earlier in this chapter; however, they may not indicate the path or direction of the thread.

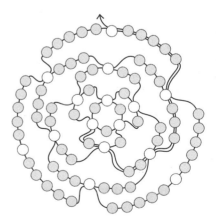

5

Ladder Stitch and Brick Stitch

With *ladder stitch*, beads are stacked next to one another and aligned like rungs in a ladder. You can use ladder stitch by itself to create a band of stitched beads, or as a foundational row for *brick stitch*. With brick stitch, beads are offset by one-half, just as they are in peyote stitch—but they are offset horizontally, rather than vertically. For this reason, brick stitch looks much like peyote stitch turned on its side. When you try it for the first time, begin by creating a base row of ladder stitch, and then transition into the basic *flat brick stitch*. You can also use *tubular brick stitch* to weave a rope or to bead around an object, and *circular brick stitch* to create a flat, domed, or ruffled circle.

Weave a Row of Ladder Stitch

You typically use ladder stitch to create the first row of brick stitch beadwork. You can also use this stitch by itself or in combination with other stitches.

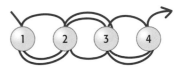

Basic Ladder Stitch

1. After preparing your thread without a stop bead, pick up two beads and position them 6–8 inches from the end of the thread. (The example uses size 11/0 Japanese seed beads.)

2. Pass through the first bead but do not pull the thread taut; instead, pull it into a small loop, with the beads positioned side by side and their holes parallel.

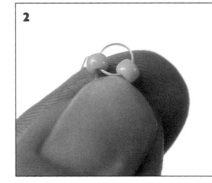

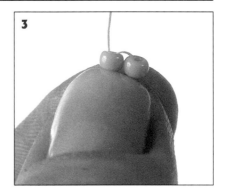

3. Holding the beads in that position with your fingers, gently pull the thread taut. The beads are now stacked.

4. Pass through the second bead and pull the thread taut. Do your best to keep the beads in their stacked position.

5. Pick up another bead, pass through the previous bead, and pull the thread taut.

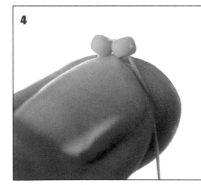

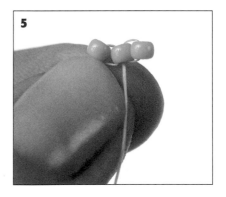

6 Now pass through the bead that you picked up in Step 5 and pull the thread taut. Continue to use your fingers to hold the beads in a stack, with the holes parallel.

7 Repeat Steps 5 and 6 to your desired length, which is the width of the beadwork if you plan to transition into brick stitch.

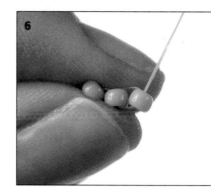

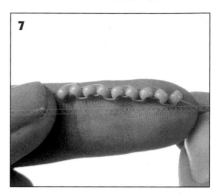

8 **Optional:** *Stabilize* the ladder stitch row by weaving back through each bead—top to bottom, and then bottom to top—until you arrive back at the beginning of the row. This helps to lock the beads into their proper, ladder rung positions.

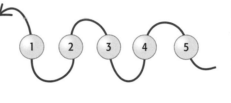

TIP

Multiple-Bead Ladder Stitch

In the above example, one bead is stitched into the ladder at a time. You can make the ladder row taller—and more textural and colorful—by stitching in more than one bead at a time. In this example, units of three beads are substituted for each single bead in the steps above. You begin by picking up six beads instead of two: one seed bead, one bugle bead, two seed beads, one bugle bead, and one final seed bead, in that order. You then pass through the first seed bead, the first bugle bead, and the second seed bead, treating them as if they were a single bead. Continue ladder stitch as usual, stitching each set of three beads as one unit. Notice that this allows you to use bugle beads in a ladder, while still buffering their ends with seed beads so that the sharp edges do not damage your thread. It also allows you to make an entire bracelet or choker band using the ladder stitch.

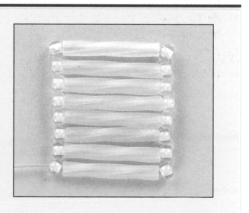

Brick stitch (sometimes called *Comanche stitch*) creates dense beaded fabric in which you stitch beads by connecting them to bridges of thread. You can begin stitching flat brick stitch after you create an initial row of ladder stitch. For a project that uses flat brick stitch to create a necklace bail, see "Tubular Netting and Peyote Bezel Necklace" on page 214.

FLAT BRICK STITCH ROWS AND COLUMNS

Before you perform brick stitch for the first time, take the time to review how its rows and columns align. As shown here, each horizontal row is a straight, sideways stack of beads. To count rows, you simply count the beads along one side of the beadwork.

Brick-stitch columns, on the other hand, are offset by the space of one-half bead (much like rows in flat peyote stitch). You can count them diagonally, either left to right (as shown) or right to left.

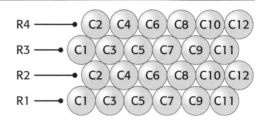

R4 — C2 C4 C6 C8 C10 C12
R3 — C1 C3 C5 C7 C9 C11
R2 — C2 C4 C6 C8 C10 C12
R1 — C1 C3 C5 C7 C9 C11

C = Column
R = Row

BASIC FLAT BRICK STITCH

In this example, the foundational ladder row has been stabilized (see Step 8 on the previous page).

❶ After creating a ladder row, pick up two new beads. These are the first and second beads for the second row of beadwork.

❷ Pass the needle beneath the bridge of thread that runs between the second and third beads in the ladder row and gently pull the thread taut.

❸ Pass back up through the second bead that you picked up in Step 1. Do your best to keep the bead from rising up as you pass it through; try using your fingers to temporarily hold down the thread below the bead until you are ready to complete the stitch.

❹ Pass back down through the first bead that you picked up in Step 1 and pull the thread taut.

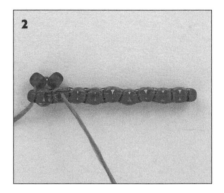

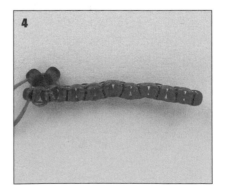

5 Pass up through the second bead that you picked up in Step 1 one more time and pull the thread taut again.

6 Pick up another bead.

7 Pass the needle beneath the bridge of thread that runs between the next two beads in the ladder row and gently pull the thread taut.

8 Pass back through the bead that you picked up in Step 6 and pull the thread taut again.

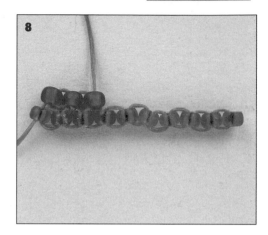

9 Repeat Steps 6–8 to the end of the row.

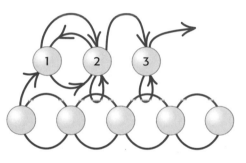

10 Turn, and then pick up two beads to begin the next row.

11 Stitch in these two beads the same way you stitched in the first two beads of the previous row (Steps 3–5).

12 Continue this process to complete each row—remembering to begin by picking up two beads—to your desired length of beadwork. This example (a) demonstrates how the rows automatically decrease in length away from the ladder row. You can compensate for these natural decreases by making outside increases (see the section "Perform Brick Stitch Increases and Decreases" on page 106).

CONTINUED ON NEXT PAGE

MULTIPLE-DROP BRICK STITCH

You can stitch a multiple-drop version of brick stitch by treating units of multiple beads (called *drops*, like they are with multiple-drop peyote) as if they were single beads. For *two-drop brick stitch*, you use sets of two beads in place of single beads; in *three-drop brick stitch* you use sets of three beads in place of single beads.

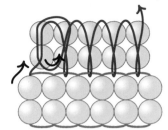

1. Begin by making a ladder-stitch row. You can make this row match the multiple-drop rows by stitching it with sets of multiple beads (see the tip "Multiple-Bead Ladder Stitch" on page 99).

2. To begin the second row, pick up twice the number of beads that you plan for each drop—for two-drop brick stitch, pick up four beads; for three-drop brick stitch, pick up six beads.

3. Perform Steps 2–12 of "Basic Flat Brick Stitch," substituting drops for single beads. Remember to begin each new row with twice the number of beads in each drop.

FAQ

Why pick up two beads, instead of one bead, to start each new row?

If you begin a brick stitch row by stitching one bead, as you do for the rest of the beads in each row, then the thread wraps around the outside of the first bead. This can be unsightly, and it's inconsistent with the rest of the beadwork, where thread only runs through beads and not down their sides. By picking up two beads to start each row and weaving through them correctly, you eliminate the need for an outside thread. Additionally, by weaving back through the first bead that you pick up and then back again, you stabilize the first bead in the row for a more uniform appearance.

In the multiple-drop brick stitch example on the previous page, the first row is ladder stitched with two beads in each stitch, and the subsequent rows contain two-bead drops. Keep in mind that you are not limited to using the same-size drop throughout the beadwork. For instance, a common approach is to separate each multiple-drop row with a row of regular, single-bead brick stitch. The example on the right alternates between two-drop and three-drop brick stitch, separated by rows of regular brick stitch.

ZIPPING-UP BRICK STITCH

You can join two edges of brick stitch using the same technique that you use to zip-up peyote stitch (see page 61). Notice that with brick stitch, you join the sides of beadwork, rather than the ends. In order to make a successful join, you need to plan your beadwork so that each protruding bead on one side matches a recessed bead on the other. This diagram shows the path you might take to zip-up beadwork that includes a row of two-drop brick stitch.

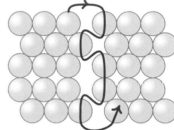

When you join the sides of the same piece of flat beadwork to create a tube, you can ensure that the sides join properly by making a one-column outside increase at the end of each row (see the section "Perform Brick Stitch Increases and Decreases" on page 106). Zipped brick stitch tubes have the same appearance as tubular brick stitch (see the next page).

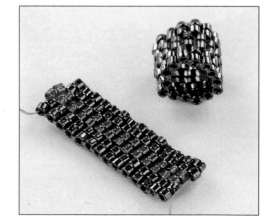

Create Tubular Brick Stitch

Tubular brick stitch beadwork has straight ends and horizontal rounds. It's a popular stitch for beading around decorative objects and for making simple finger rings. Unlike flat brick stitch, tubular brick stitch rounds do not automatically decrease. For an example of a project that uses tubular brick stitch to cover an object, see "Tubular Brick Stitch Slider Necklace" on page 196.

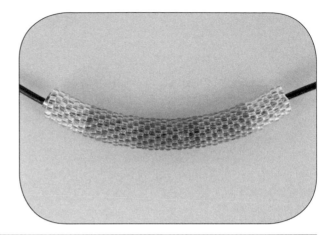

TUBULAR BRICK STITCH

As with tubular peyote and tubular netting, it helps to use a form to support your beadwork, especially for the first several rows.

 Weave a ladder-stitch row that is long enough to wrap around your form. (The example uses 15 size 11/0 cylinder beads and a ¼-inch wooden dowel as a form.)

2 Pass up through the first bead in the ladder, then down through the last bead, and then up through the first bead again, to form a ring. (Optional: Do this twice to stabilize the stitch.)

TIP

Holding Tubular Brick Stitch Beadwork

You may find it more challenging to hold tubular brick stitch on a form than it is to hold other stitches. That is because you need to reverse the direction of the thread with each stitch. You may find it most comfortable to change the angle at which you hold the form when you make these reversals, which allows your dominant hand and wrist to work in a more neutral position with the needle.

3 Slip the ring onto the form.

4 Pick up two beads to begin the second round.

5 Pass the needle beneath the bridge of thread between the second and third beads in the ladder round, moving from the inside of the tube toward the outside of the tube. (You can use the form to help angle your needle as you do this.)

6 Pass back up through the second bead that you picked up in Step 4 and pull the thread taut.

7 Pick up a third bead and stitch it in by passing beneath the next bridge of thread in the ladder round and then back through the same bead.

8 Perform brick stitch as usual all the way around until you arrive back at the beginning of the round.

9 Connect the last and first beads in the round by passing down through the first bead and then up through the last bead.

10 If you are stitching the second round of beadwork (the first round of brick stitch above the ladder row), repeat Step 9. (For subsequent rounds, you only need to pass through the first and last beads in each round once).

11 Pick up two new beads to begin the next round.

12 Continue this process to stitch one round at a time to your desired length of beadwork. To make horizontal stripes, as shown, simply change bead colors when you begin a new round.

FAQ

What if the thread exits the ladder row in the wrong direction?

For both flat brick stitch and tubular brick stitch, the thread needs to exit the ladder row pointing toward the next row or round of beadwork. Usually, this means that the needle-end of the thread and the thread tail emerge on opposite sides. (You can think of the tail as pointing downward and the needle-end as pointing upward.) This is normally the case when you stitch and then stabilize a ladder row (a) (see page 99).

However, in some cases, both thread ends may exit on the same side. For instance, this happens when the ladder row contains an even number of beads and you do not stabilize the row (b). In that case, you can simply flip the beadwork so that the thread effectively changes direction but remains on the same end of the row. Just be sure to make the thread tail long enough that you can easily hold it out of the way until you're ready to weave it in.

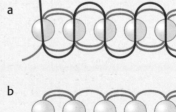

a

b

Perform Brick Stitch Increases and Decreases

Brick stitch increases and decreases can occur on the outsides of flat beadwork, or within rows of flat or tubular beadwork. You can make all of these increases and decreases with multiple-drop brick stitch by substituting drops for single beads in the directions.

Brick Stitch Outside Increases

This section covers one-column outside increases, which are the most common increases used with flat brick stitch. (You can learn multiple-column brick-stitch increases in books that cover more-advanced beadwork.) If one portion of a pattern contains rows that are longer than others by more than one column, it's often easiest to begin stitching the widest part of the pattern first, and then make decreases when you reach the narrower portion (see page 108)—rather than trying to make increases to stitch a wider area of beadwork.

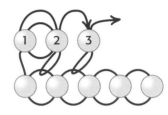

Keep in mind that because flat brick stitch automatically decreases by one column per row, one-column increases at either the beginning or end of a row make it the *same* length as the previous row. In order to make a row longer than the previous row, you need an increase at both the beginning and the end of the row.

OUTSIDE BRICK STITCH INCREASE: BEGINNING OF ROW

Use this technique to add one column at the beginning of a new row.

1 At the beginning of the new row, pick up two beads as usual.

2 Instead of passing the needle beneath the bridge of thread between the second and third beads in the previous row, pass it beneath the bridge of thread between the *first* and *second* beads in that row.

3 Resume brick stitch as usual.

In this example, a one-column outside increase is made at the beginning of each new row. This creates an even, rather than tapered, band of beadwork.

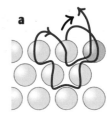

OUTSIDE BRICK STITCH INCREASE: END OF ROW

Use this increase to add one column at the end of a row (a).

1 Instead of turning at the end of the row, pick up one bead (orange in the diagram).

2 Moving downward, pass through the next diagonally adjacent bead and pull the thread taut.

3 Reversing direction, pass up through the next two horizontally adjacent beads, moving back toward the beginning of the row.

4 Pull the thread taut.

5 Reverse direction again, passing down into the next horizontally adjacent bead toward the end of the row, and pull the thread taut.

6 Reverse direction one more time and pass up through the bead that you picked up in Step 1.

7 Pull the thread taut and resume brick stitch as usual.

In this example (b), the fourth row both begins and ends with an outside increase, which results in the beadwork expanding evenly, by one column, on both sides. The decreases are those which occur automatically with brick stitch.

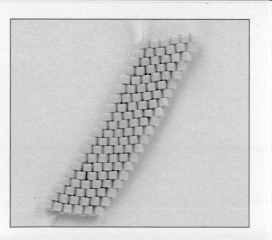

What is Diagonal Brick Stitch?

Just like with peyote stitch (see the FAQ on page 66), you can make flat brick stitch rows appear to run diagonally. *Diagonal brick stitch* is simpler than diagonal peyote, however, because its automatic outside decreases mean that you only need to make increases; those increases occur along one side of the bead-work, and the other side is allowed to decrease naturally.

CONTINUED ON NEXT PAGE

Brick Stitch Outside Decreases

Because flat brick stitch automatically decreases by one column per row, you use outside decreases to make *additional* decreases. Accordingly, a *one-column outside decrease*—if performed without a corresponding increase at the other end of the row—results in a cumulative decrease of two columns, and a *multiple-column outside decrease* results in a cumulative decrease of three or more columns.

EVEN MULTIPLE-COLUMN OUTSIDE BRICK STITCH DECREASE: BEGINNING OF ROW

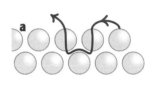

To decrease the length of a new row by an even number of columns, you can simply weave back through the previous row (a) and bring the needle out at the place where you would like to begin the next row.

ONE-COLUMN OR ODD MULTIPLE-COLUMN OUTSIDE BRICK STITCH DECREASE: BEGINNING OF ROW

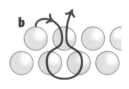

In order to decrease by one column at the beginning of a row you need to weave through the beadwork farther in order to change the direction of the thread (b).

1 After completing the current row, turn, and then weave back, as shown, until you reach the bead from which you would like to begin stitching the next, shorter row. (The diagram shows a one-column decrease.)

2 Pass down into the next horizontally adjacent bead toward the end of the row and pull the thread taut.

3 Reversing direction, pass up through the next horizontally adjacent bead toward the beginning of the row, and then pass up through the bead that you started from.

4 Begin the next row as usual.

OUTSIDE BRICK STITCH DECREASE: END OF ROW

To make the current row shorter by one or more columns, simply stop stitching at the place where you would like to begin the decrease, and begin the next row as usual. This diagram (c) shows a decrease of one column at the end of the row.

In this example (d), a two-column decrease occurs at both the beginning and the end of the fourth row.

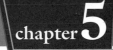

Brick Stitch Mid-Row Increases and Decreases

Mid-row increases and decreases occur between columns. They are the only increases and decreases that you use with tubular brick stitch, which has no outside edges.

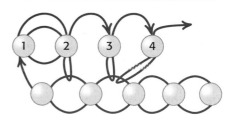

BRICK STITCH MID-ROW INCREASE

Use this increase to lengthen a flat row from the inside, or to lengthen a round of tubular brick stitch.

1 When you reach the point where you would like to perform the increase, pick up a bead (bead 4 in the diagram).

2 Pass the needle beneath the *same* bridge of thread that you passed under for the previous bead.

3 Pass back up through the bead that you picked up in Step 1 and pull the thread taut.

4 Resume brick stitch as usual. When you reach the point of the increase in the next row or round, treat it as you would any other bead in that row or round.

In this example (a), each row begins with a one-column outside increase, and a one-column mid-row increase occurs in the sixth row (the first row of lighter-color beads). Here (b), two mid-row increases occur in different places within the fourth round (the first round of lighter-color beads), and two more mid-row increases occur in the sixth round. Matching mid-row decreases (see the next section) occur on the other end of the tube, creating a taper.

BRICK STITCH MID-ROW DECREASE

You can shorten a row or round simply by skipping a bridge of thread in the previous row or round. Keep in mind that in flat brick stitch, this results in a cumulative decrease of two columns, unless you also make an increase in the same row.

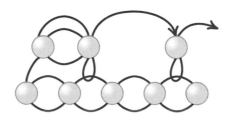

In this flat brick stitch example (c), the first five rows each begin with a one-column outside increase, and the sixth row (the first row of lighter-color beads) has no out-side increases and one mid-row decrease. Each of the final three rows ends with a one-column increase. You can see that the beadwork is slightly puckered, and there is a small gap between beads where the mid-row decrease occurs. This makes the mid-row decrease better suited to tubular brick stitch (b).

Create Circular Brick Stitch

Like other circular stitches, circular brick stitch begins with a central ring, and then expands outward with increasingly longer rows, called *rounds*. This section describes the most basic circular brick stitch technique, which begins with a ladder row pulled into a loop.

CIRCULAR BRICK STITCH BEGINNING WITH A LADDER ROW

Circular brick stitch can form a disc of solid beadwork, or a circle with a hole at the center. For a solid circle, you begin with a short ladder stitch row, and for a hole you begin with a longer one. This example begins with a short ladder row of only three beads. Feel free to begin with a longer one to create the center-hole size of your choice.

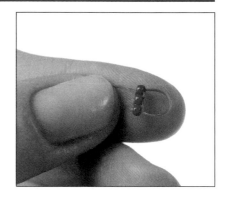

1 Stitch and reinforce a ladder row that is at least three beads long. (The example uses three size 11/0 Japanese seed beads.)

2 From the first bead, pass through the last bead, as shown, but do not pull the thread taut.

3 Holding the ladder row flat, use your fingers to bring the first bead toward the last bead, so that the two are touching.

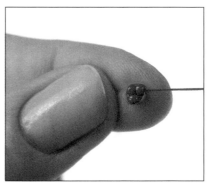

4 Now slowly pull the thread taut, using your fingers to keep the beads from flipping; you need a ring of beads with the bridges of thread facing *outward* so that you can brick-stitch the next round.

5 Pass through both the first and last beads again. The beads now form a ring, with a bridge of thread between each set of two beads, facing outward. If you use more than three beads for the ladder row, there may be a hole at the center of the ring.

6 Pick up two beads to begin the next round.

7 Pass the needle beneath the next bridge of thread.

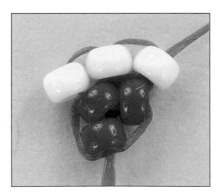

8 Pass back through the second bead that you picked up in Step 6 and pull the thread taut.

9 From this point on, you decide on the placement of beads based on what is needed to fill gaps in the round, and to keep the beadwork in your desired form (flat, domed, or ruffled). In the example, the third bead in the round is stitched by passing beneath the same bridge of thread onto which the first two beads were stitched.

10 Continue stitching beads onto bridges of thread from the first round until you reach the beginning of the second round.

11 Connect the last and first beads in the second round by passing down through the first bead and then back up through the last bead.

12 Pull the thread taut.

13 Continue this process to stitch each round, using your best judgment to estimate how many beads to include in each round, and where to stitch each one. As with other circular stitches, you can create a dome or bowl shape by decreasing the numbers of beads in rounds, and you can create ruffles by increasing them.

TIP

Alternative Circular Brick Stitch Starting Methods

There are other methods for starting circular brick stitch that you can try. One involves stitching the first round of beads onto a loop of bare thread. With another, you begin with a simple ring of beads and complete the next round by brick-stitching beads onto the thread between beads in the ring. Yet another approach is to stitch a larger-size bead at the center of the beadwork. For an example of a project that features a large central bead, see "Circular Brick Stitch Fringe Earrings" on page 228.

Brick Stitch Graph Patterns

The cells in brick stitch graph patterns are offset like the bricks in a wall. The top and bottom rows are flat, and the sides are jagged with protruding and recessed beads.

FLAT BRICK STITCH GRAPH PATTERNS

Flat brick stitch graph patterns look like peyote stitch patterns turned on their sides. For this reason, you can use the same blank graph pattern for both stitches—just be sure to change to the direction of the pattern to match the layout of the beads for each stitch.

You can read a flat brick stitch pattern from bottom to top or top to bottom, and you can begin at any corner. Keep in mind that a flat brick stitch pattern with no increases tapers into a triangle. This means that when a brick stitch pattern depicts rows of uniform width, you need to perform a one-column outside increase at the beginning or end of each row. Whether the increase occurs at the beginning or end of the row depends on which corner you begin reading the pattern.

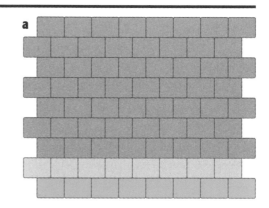

In this example (a), if you begin reading in the lower-left corner and then stabilize the row (so that your needle exits the first bead that you picked up, rather than the last), then you need to make an increase at the beginning of each subsequent row. However, if you begin reading from the lower-right corner and reinforce the first row, then you perform the increase at the end of each row.

For patterns that taper, it's often easiest to begin with the longest row so that you can take advantage of the automatic decreases, and because extra decreases are easier to make than increases.

TUBULAR BRICK STITCH GRAPH PATTERNS

You read a tubular brick stitch pattern moving in the same direction for each round; either right to left or left to right. Similar to tubular peyote patterns, the first bead in each round shifts by the space of one-half cell. In this example (b), each of the numbered beads represents the first bead in each round, if you begin reading the pattern from the bottom-left corner and stabilize the initial ladder row.

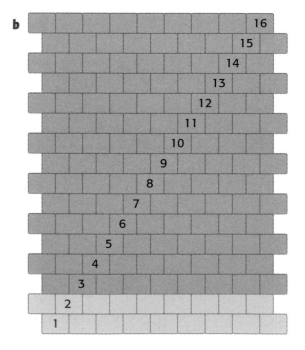

MULTIPLE-DROP BRICK STITCH GRAPH PATTERNS

Multiple-drop brick stitch graph patterns for flat or tubular brick stitch have cells in aligned stacks that show how many beads are included in each drop. In the example on the right, the initial ladder row (shown in green) is a regular, single-bead stitch, and the second row (shown in blue) is two-drop brick stitch. Subsequent rows alternate between single and two-drop brick stitch.

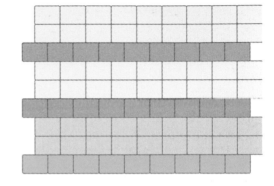

CIRCULAR BRICK STITCH PATTERNS

Circular brick stitch patterns are drawn to indicate exactly how the beads are arranged for a given project. Some include lines that show the actual path of the thread, so that you can determine which bridges of thread each bead is stitched onto. Others (like the project on page 228) use special symbols to designate sets of beads that are stitched onto the same bridge of thread.

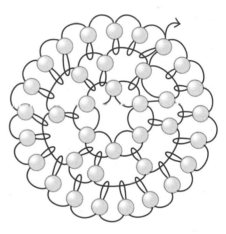

TIP

Brick Stitch Pattern Increases and Decreases

In flat brick stitch patterns, outside increases and decreases are simply indicated by cells that expand beyond, or fall short of, a natural brick stitch row. Since flat brick stitch rows automatically decrease by one column without an increase, you know that rows that contain the same number of cells require an outside increase (see "Flat Brick Stitch Graph Patterns" on the previous page). Mid-row increases and decreases can be indicated by symbols, or by the spacing of cells (as with some peyote stitch graph patterns; see page 76). Patterns that contain them are typically accompanied by written project instructions that explain them.

Square Stitch
and Spiral Rope

Unlike peyote stitch and brick stitch, *square stitch* rows and columns
align horizontally and vertically in a true grid formation. This allows you
to create flat beadwork with even sides, and to design patterns that
contain single-row and single-column lines or stripes. *Spiral rope*, which
creates a solid rope of beadwork, uses a technique similar to square
stitch. Thread may be more visible with these stitches than with others,
so be sure to select a complementary or neutral thread color.

Create Flat Square Stitch

With *flat square stitch*, you stack and stitch beads one on top of the other, moving back and forth to stitch each row. Because you need to change the direction of the thread at least twice for every stitch, you may find that you hold square stitch beadwork a little differently than you hold other beadwork. As always, experiment to discover which position you find most comfortable. For a project that uses flat square stitch, see "Flat Square Stitch Finger Ring" on page 198.

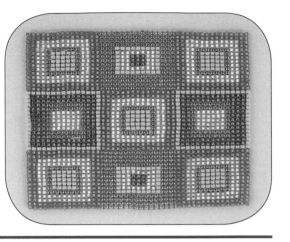

It's a good idea to practice stitching in both directions with flat square stitch, rather than turning the beadwork around to begin each new row. This makes it easier to learn tubular square stitch (see page 118), where you stitch each round in the opposite direction of the previous round.

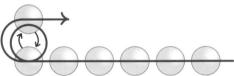

1 After preparing a length of thread, pick up all of the beads for the first row and position them against the bead stop. (The example below uses nine size 11/0 Japanese seed beads.)

2 Pick up one more bead, and turn. This is the first bead of the second row.

3 Pass through the last bead in the first row, and then through the first bead in the second row again, and pull the thread taut. As you do this, keep the last bead in the first row from moving by squeezing it between your finger and thumb. Make sure that the first bead in the second row stacks on top of the last bead in the first row, with the holes of both beads running parallel.

④ Pick up another bead.

⑤ Pass through the second to last bead in the first row, and then pass through the bead that you picked up in Step 4.

⑥ Pull the thread taut.

⑦ Continue this process to add one bead at a time until you reach the end of the second row.

⑧ At the end of the row, turn, and then stitch the first bead of the third row using the same technique you used to stitch the first bead of the second row (Step 3).

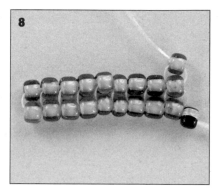

⑨ Continue adding beads and stitching rows back and forth to your desired length of beadwork.

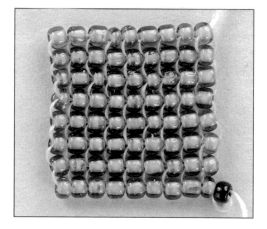

TIP

Reinforcing Square Stitch Rows

If your square stitch beadwork feels loose, you can add bulk to each row, and strengthen it, by passing through it again. After completing every other row, pass through all of the beads in the previous row and then through all of the beads in the current row again.

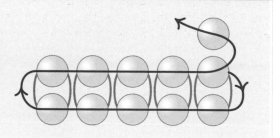

Like other tubular stitches, *tubular square stitch* creates a tube or "rope" of beadwork, and you can also use it to bead seamlessly around decorative objects. Unlike other tubular stitches, however, you switch direction to begin each new round.

1 After preparing your thread without a bead stop, pick up all of the beads for the first round. (The example uses 18 size 11/0 cylinder beads and a ⁵⁄₁₆-inch diameter pencil as a form.)

2 Position the beads at least 6–8 inches from the end of the thread.

3 Pass through all of the beads again, and then through the first bead again.

4 Pull the thread gently taut. (Do not make a knot, because the ring will expand slightly in the following steps.)

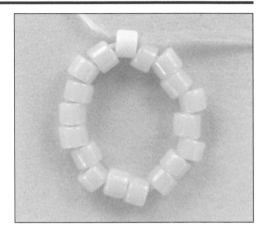

5 Slip the ring onto the form. It should fit relatively snugly for this stitch.

6 Pick up one bead. This is the first bead in the second round.

7 Use basic square stitch (see the section "Create Flat Square Stitch") to stitch in the bead directly on top of the first bead in the first round, as shown.

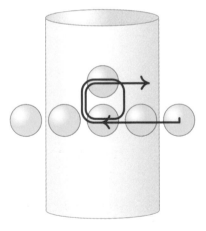

8 Pull the thread taut. Notice that you just performed a turn; you stitch the second round in the opposite direction that you strung the first round.

9 Repeat this procedure to add beads, one at a time, until you arrive back at the beginning of the second round.

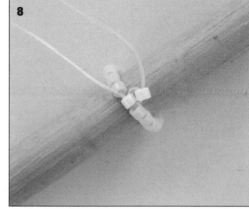

10 Close the ends of the round by passing through the first bead again and pull the thread taut.

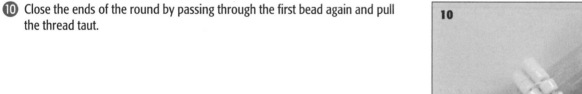

11 Pick up the first bead of the third round and square-stitch it directly on top of the first bead in the second round. Here, you automatically reverse direction again.

12 Continue stitching beads and completing rounds, one by one, until you reach your desired length of beadwork.

13 **Optional:** Pass back through all of the beads in the final round again and pull the thread taut. This increases the tension of the last round, which is especially helpful when you bead around a decorative object instead of using a temporary form.

In the example on the right, each lighter-color bead represents the first bead in a round. Notice that these beads stack vertically, rather than shifting.

Multiple-bead square stitch is similar to the multiple-drop versions of peyote stitch and brick stitch; you stitch sets of multiple beads, treating each set like a single bead. As with drop stitches, the name of the stitch designates how many beads make up each set.

1 Pick up all of the beads for the first row or round, making sure that their total number is divisible by the number of beads in each stitch. (The example is for two-bead square stitch and uses 12 size 11/0 Japanese seed beads for the first row.)

2 To begin the second row, pick up the first set of beads and stitch them to the matching set of beads at the end of the first row.

3 Continue square stitch, picking up and passing through sets of beads.

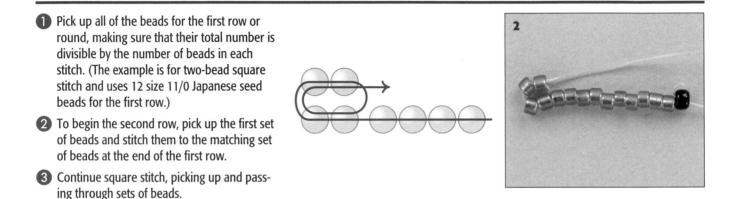

You are not limited to using bead sets that each contain the same number of beads, as shown here. For instance, you might begin with a column of two-bead sets, followed by a column of three-bead sets—or you might alternate between columns of multiple-bead sets and single-bead square stitch. Just ensure that the number of beads that you pick up in Step 1 can accommodate the number and sizes of sets that you plan to use.

You can change the length of a flat square stitch row using an outside increase or decrease. Use mid-row increases and decreases to alter the width of flat square stitch beadwork or to lengthen tubular square stitch rounds.

Square Stitch Outside Increases and Decreases

With square stitch outside increases, you increase the number of columns in two rows at once, rather than one. This means that you make an outside increase at the end of a row at the same time that you stitch the first bead of the next row. Square stitch outside decreases, on the other hand, shorten one row at a time.

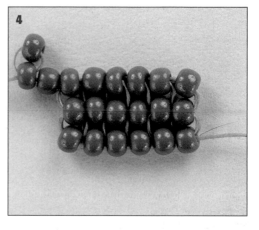

SQUARE STITCH OUTSIDE INCREASE: FIRST SIDE

If you need to make an increase on one side of the beadwork, use this "first side" method. To make an increase on the other end of the same row, use the "second side" method on the next page.

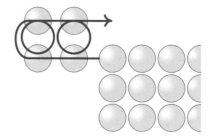

1 After completing the row, pick up one bead for each column that you would like to add. The example shows a two-column increase.

2 Position and hold these beads against the last bead in the row.

3 Pick up another bead. This is the first bead in the next row.

4 Stitch this bead directly on top of the last bead that you picked up in Step 1. Do your best to keep the thread pulled firmly taut. (Spaces are left between beads in the diagram only to show the path of the thread.)

5 Continue stitching the row as usual. Take the time to stop and pull the thread taut as needed.

CONTINUED ON NEXT PAGE

SQUARE STITCH OUTSIDE INCREASE: SECOND SIDE

Use this technique to make a matching increase on the other side of a row that has a first-side outside increase.

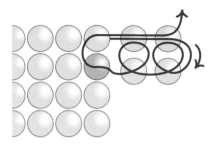

1. When you reach the end of the row, pick up one bead for each column that you would like to add. The example shows a two-column increase.

2. Position and hold these beads against the last bead in the row.

3. Pick up another bead. This becomes the new first bead of the *previous* row, which you are now increasing along with the current row.

4. Stitch that bead directly beneath the last bead that you picked up in Step 1.

5. If your increase is larger than one column, stitch in a bead for each of the remaining beads in the increase until you arrive back at the original edge of the beadwork.

6. Pass through the next horizontally adjacent bead (orange in the above diagram), and pull the thread taut.

7. Reverse direction and pass through the rest of the beads in the last row, bringing the needle out of the last bead.

8. Pull the thread taut and resume square stitch as usual.

In the example on the right, a two-column increase occurs on both sides of the beadwork beginning with the third row.

SQUARE STITCH OUTSIDE DECREASE: BEGINNING OF ROW

Before you can begin a new row with a decrease, you need to weave through the beadwork to change the direction of the thread.

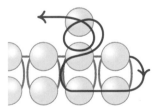

1. At the end of the current row, pass down and through the second to last row and bring the needle out after the bead that is just below where you plan to start the next row. The example shows a decrease of one column.

2. Pull the thread taut, then change direction and pass through the next bead in the last row.

3. Pick up a bead. This is the first bead in the new, shorter row.

4. Stitch this bead directly on top of the bead from which your thread emerges.

5. Resume square stitch as usual.

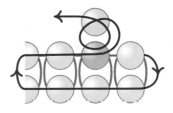

The example on the previous page was performed without the optional row reinforcement (see the tip on page 117). When you reinforce rows, you take a slightly different path to change the direction of the thread before making the decrease. In the diagram on the right, the first row is passed through for reinforcement before the decrease is performed.

SQUARE STITCH OUTSIDE DECREASE: END OF ROW

To make a decrease at the end of a row, simply stop adding beads at the point of the decrease and begin the next row. In the example on the right, a two-column outside decrease occurs at the beginning and end of the fourth row.

CONTINUED ON NEXT PAGE

FAQ

When I pass through a row to reinforce it, can I simply bring the needle out at the point where I want the next row to begin?

When the thread exits the bead that is adjacent to where you would like to begin a decreased row, you may be tempted to stop and begin the row, as shown in this diagram. However, this can pull the first bead in the shorter row out of alignment, and it exposes more thread than necessary along the edge of the beadwork. It's a good idea to take the time to change the direction of the thread instead.

Avoid this bridge of thread.

DIAGONAL SQUARE STITCH INCREASES AND DECREASES

Diagonal square stitch is flat square stitch performed with increases on one side and decreases on the other. There are many approaches to this stitch, which you can learn by following project patterns. Here is a basic technique that creates an even band of diagonal square stitch.

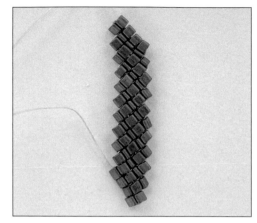

1 Pick up all of the beads for the first row of square stitch. Make this row slightly wider than your desired width of the completed band. (The example uses four size 11/0 triangle beads, and each row is reinforced.)

2 Stitch the second row, making a "first side" one-column outside increase at the end of the row (see page 121).

3 Stitch the third row, stopping short by one column to create a one-column decrease at the end of the row (see page 123).

4 Stitch the fourth row with a one-column outside decrease at the beginning of the row (see page 122), and a "second side" one-column increase at the end of the row (see page 122).

5 Stitch the fifth row with a "first side" one-column increase at the beginning of the row, and end it with a one-column decrease.

6 Stitch the sixth row with a one-column decrease at the beginning of the row, and a one-column "second side" increase at the end of the row.

7 Continue this process of increasing on one side and decreasing on the other to create a stair-step effect along both sides of the beadwork. Make sure that each of these "steps" contains only one bead. (You do this by alternating between "first side" and "second side" increases, rather than only using "first side" increases.)

8 Complete the band with a row that is the same length as the first row of the band (which is one column shorter than the other rows).

TIP

Avoid Outside Bridges of Thread During Turns

When you reinforce rows that contain outside increases or decreases, always choose a path that avoids exposing a bridge of thread on the side of the beadwork. For instance, if you plan to make an outside increase at the end of a row, first pass back through the previous row (the red line in the diagram). When you make an end-of-row decrease, reinforce by passing into the previous row beginning with the bead that is vertically adjacent to the last bead in the row (the blue line in the diagram).

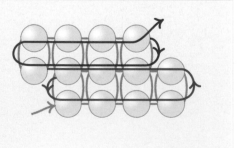

Square Stitch Mid-Row Increases and Decreases

Square stitch mid-row increases and decreases alter the lengths of rows from within the beadwork.

SQUARE STITCH MID-ROW INCREASE

To increase the length of one row or round by one column, pick up two beads—instead of one—at the point of the increase (see the red line in diagram a). Then, in the next row or round (see the blue line in diagram a), stitch into those beads individually. To create a more dramatic increase, you can pick up three extra beads and stitch into each one individually in the next row or round.

In example b, a series of one-column mid-row increases gives the beadwork a fan-shape.

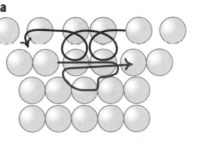

SQUARE STITCH MID-ROW DECREASE

To eliminate one column from a row of flat square stitch, or to make a decrease in tubular square stitch, simply skip one or more beads in the previous row. Diagram c shows a one-bead decrease; for a more dramatic decrease, you can skip more than one bead in the row or round.

In example d, a series of one-column mid-row decreases gives the beadwork a reverse fan shape.

In example e, increases and matching decreases occur in the tan and brown rounds of a length of tubular square stitch.

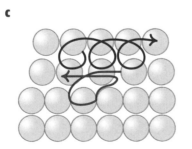

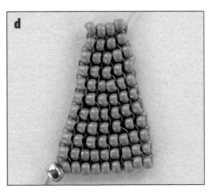

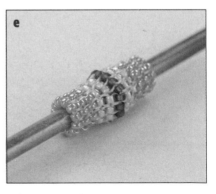

Perform Circular Square Stitch

As with other circular stitches, you begin *circular square stitch* with a central ring of beads, and then expand each row by using mid-row increases. In order to produce a circular shape with this stitch, you need to leave an opening at the center. As with tubular square stitch, you switch the direction of your stitches with each new round.

① Pick up an even number of beads to create the central ring, which is also the first round. The number of beads that you pick up establishes the size of the central opening. (The example uses eight size 11/0 Japanese seed beads.)

② Pass through all of the beads again, bringing them into a reinforced ring.

③ **Optional:** Pull the thread taut and make a square knot or surgeon's knot to maintain the tension.

④ Pass through the first bead that you picked up in Step 1 and pull the thread taut again.

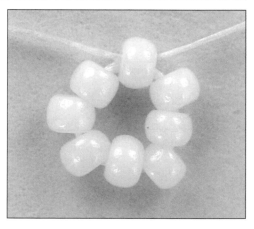

⑤ To begin the next round, pick up enough beads to make a mid-row increase. The example makes a one-bead increase in the second round for every bead in the first round. That is, you simply stitch two beads onto every single bead in the first round. When you make your own design (rather than follow a pattern), you may need to experiment to determine how large an increase to make; that is, how many extra beads to pick up per stitch. You can either repeat the same-size increase for the entire round, or alternate between larger and smaller increases, spacing them as uniformly as possible. The goal is to fill as much space in the beadwork as you can while preserving its circular shape and creating your desired form: flat, domed, or ruffled.

⑥ At the end of the second round, pass through the first bead in the round again to pull the last and first beads together.

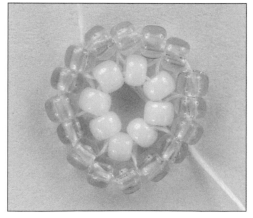

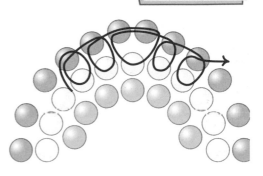

7 **Optional:** Reinforce the entire round by passing through all of its beads once more.

8 Stitch the third round, making the increases needed to fill the entire round with beads. As with other circular stitches, adding fewer beads than necessary creates domed or bowl-shaped beadwork, and adding more beads than necessary creates ruffles. In the example (which is flat), the third row is made by performing two stitches without an increase and one stitch with a one-bead increase, in that order, and repeating that sequence to complete the round.

9 **Optional:** Pass through the entire third round again to reinforce it.

10 Continue this process to stitch each round until you reach your desired size of beadwork. In the example, the fourth round is stitched primarily by alternating between single stitches and stitches containing two beads each. The fifth round is stitched in generally the same pattern as the third round (Step 8).

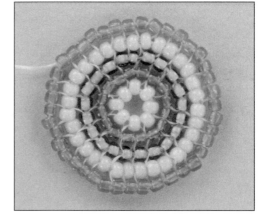

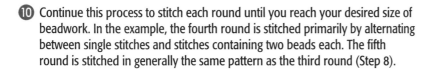

FAQ

How can I mark my place when I pass through an entire round to reinforce it?

Unless your circular beadwork is extremely large, you can usually leave a small loop of thread between the first and second beads in the round to mark the place where the round begins and ends. Then, after you pass through the entire round to reinforce it, bring the needle out and gently pull the thread taut to remove the loop.

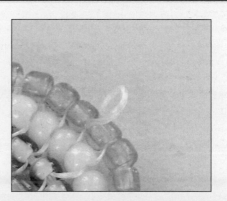

In square stitch graph patterns, the rows and columns align to form a grid. (These are the same patterns used for beading on a loom.)

FLAT SQUARE STITCH GRAPH PATTERNS

You may begin reading a flat square stitch graph pattern from either corner at either end of the pattern. Read each row in the opposite direction of the previous row, either right to left or left to right. In this example, if you begin at either end of the bottom row, then the green cells are the beads that you initially pick up, and the blue cells represent the beads that you stitch to complete the second row.

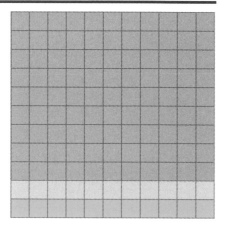

TUBULAR SQUARE STITCH GRAPH PATTERNS

Unlike peyote and brick stitch tubular patterns, in which you follow each round moving in the same direction, you need to switch direction at the end of each round of a tubular square stitch pattern. Begin at either the top or bottom of the pattern, at either corner, and work your way toward the opposite side. When you finish the first round, move up to the next horizontal row in the graph and follow it in the opposite direction.

In this example, if you start at the lower-left corner, then you pick up all of the green beads first, beginning with the bead labeled "1" (the first bead in the first round). After you pull those beads into a ring, you pass through that first bead again, which allows you to then pick up and stitch the first bead in the second round (labeled "2"). Next, switch to the *other side* of the pattern, and stitch the bead that is marked with "*." Continue stitching the second round, right to left, until you complete that round with the thread exiting bead 2. Pick up the first bead for the third round (labeled "3"), and follow this row of the pattern left to right. Continue this process for each round, remembering to jump to the other side of the pattern after stitching the first bead in every other round.

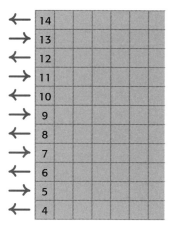

MULTIPLE-BEAD SQUARE STITCH GRAPH PATTERNS

Multiple-bead square stitch graph patterns contain columns that are more than one bead wide. In order to show both the beads and the columns in the pattern, these graphs may use bolded lines to define bead sets. The example is for three-bead square stitch, where you stitch sets of three beads at a time. Multiple-bead graph patterns can be used for either flat or tubular square stitch.

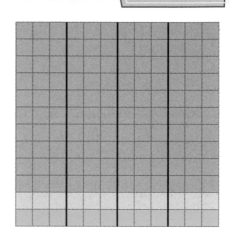

CIRCULAR SQUARE STITCH PATTERNS

Circular square stitch patterns are drawn to represent the actual placement of the beads. Often, they include lines that indicate the path of the thread, and they are typically accompanied by written instructions that you should follow along with them.

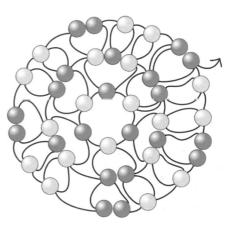

TIP

Square Stitch Pattern Increases and Decreases

In flat square stitch patterns, outside increases and decreases are simply indicated by cells that expand beyond, or fall short of, a natural square stitch row. Mid-row increases and decreases can be indicated by symbols, or by the spacing of cells (as with some peyote stitch patterns; see the section "Peyote Stitch Graph Patterns" in Chapter 3). These patterns are typically accompanied by written project instructions.

Spiral rope is similar to square stitch in that you loop through beads twice, moving in the same direction, in order to stitch new beads. However, instead of making beaded fabric, you stitch sets of multiple *loop beads* onto a central strand of *core beads* to create a long, spiraling rope. For a project that uses spiral rope, see "Spiral Rope and Herringbone Pendant Necklace" on page 220.

BASIC SPIRAL ROPE

You can make a spiral rope with various combinations of core beads and loop beads. This example is a basic version that begins with four core beads and three loop beads.

1. Prepare a length of thread that is as long as you feel comfortable working with (because it can be more difficult to begin a new thread with this stitch than with others).

2. Thread the needle, and pick up four beads to serve as core beads, and three beads to serve as loop beads. In most designs, the core beads and the loop beads are different colors. (The example uses size 11/0 seed beads in black for the core and silver for the loops; the red bead is a stop bead.)

3. Pass back through all four core beads and pull the thread taut.

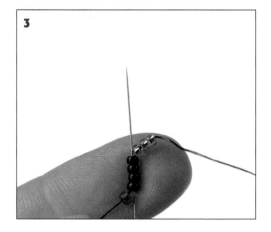

4. Position the loop beads so that they flip toward your non-dominant hand. If you are right-handed, position them to the left of the core beads; if you are left-handed, position them to the right of the core beads.

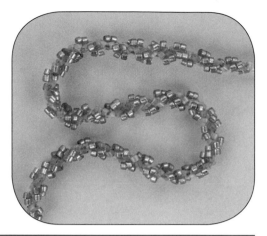

5 Pick up one core bead and three loop beads.

6 Pass back through the last three of the core beads that you picked up in Step 2, and through the single core bead that you picked up in Step 5.

7 Stack the new loop on top of the previous loop, and hold the loops under your thumb in your non-dominant hand.

8 Pull the thread taut and repeat Step 5.

9 Pass back through the last three core beads plus the single core bead that you picked up in Step 8.

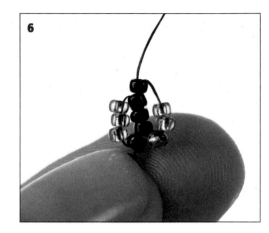

10 Continue this process, picking up one core bead and three loop beads, and then passing through the last three core beads, until you reach your desired length of spiral rope. After several rounds, the loop beads begin to spiral around the core beads. Be sure to always hold the most recently made loops under your thumb to keep your place.

TIP

Selecting Needle, Thread, and Beads for Spiral Rope

With spiral rope, you need to pass through most core beads several times. This limits the sizes of beads, needles, and thread that you can use. If the bead holes are very small, or if your needle or thread is too thick, the needle can become stuck as you attempt to pass through core beads. To keep this from happening, take the time to experiment with scrap thread before you begin a design from scratch. Test to see which needle-and-thread combinations work with the beads that you plan to use. If you cannot find a combination that works, you may need to reduce the number of core beads that you initially pick up, or switch to larger core beads.

chapter

Right-Angle Weave

Right-angle weave (which is sometimes referred to by the acronym "RAW") creates a gridlike net of beads that align in interlocking, square or rectangular groups of four beads or bead sets each. The thread takes a figure-eight path through the beadwork as you incrementally build each row or round.

Create Flat Right-Angle Weave

The traditional form of right-angle weave is stitched using two needles, with one at each end of the thread. (You may see it referred to as *two-needle right-angle weave*.) The more common method used by American beaders today requires just one needle. This section covers the flat version of this *single-needle right-angle weave* stitch. For some projects that use flat right-angle weave, see "Netting and Right-Angle Weave Earrings" on page 192 and "Embellished Right-Angle Weave Bracelet" on page 224.

FLAT RIGHT-ANGLE WEAVE ROWS AND COLUMNS

With flat right-angle weave, the holes in row beads run at right angles to the holes in column beads. You achieve this by stitching beads in sets of four, called *units*, and connecting them by passing through the beadwork in a figure-eight pattern.

When you begin right-angle weave, you stitch the first two rows of beads at once, moving from one side of the beadwork to the other. After the first two rows, you stitch one row of beads at a time.

Because you stitch flat right-angle weave in units, many project instructions define right-angle weave "rows" and "columns" as rows and columns of units, rather than rows and columns of individual beads. As shown in the diagram on the right, each *unit row* and *unit column* contains two rows and two columns of beads.

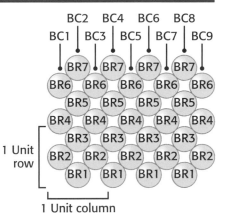

BR = Bead row
BC = Bead column

TIP

Selecting Beads and Thread for Right-Angle Weave

Ideally, right-angle-weave row beads stack horizontally, and column beads stack vertically. However, when you use smaller beads (size 11/0 seed beads and smaller) or beads that have large holes, they may look crooked or appear to align diagonally.

To achieve more orderly rows and columns, try using larger beads (such as the size 6/0 seed beads used on the next page), and increase the bulk of your thread by using a larger size thread, doubling the thread, or passing through each unit twice for reinforcement.

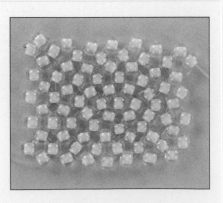

BASIC SINGLE-NEEDLE RIGHT ANGLE-WEAVE

1 After preparing your thread without a stop bead, pick up four beads. (The example uses size 6/0 Japanese seed beads.)

2 Pass through all four beads again, pulling them into a ring.

3 Make a square knot or surgeon's knot to secure the ring's thread tension.

4 Pass through the first three beads again.

5 Pull the thread taut.

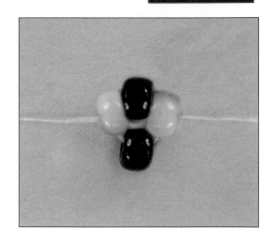

6 Pick up three beads.

7 Pass through the third bead that you picked up in Step 1 and pull the thread taut.

8 Pass through the first two beads that you picked up in Step 6 and pull the thread taut. You now have two units of four beads, which share a connecting bead at their center.

9 Pick up three beads to form the next unit.

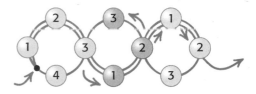

10 Pass through the second bead that you picked up in Step 6 and pull the thread taut.

11 Pass through the first and second beads that you picked up in Step 9 and pull the thread taut. This completes the third unit.

CONTINUED ON NEXT PAGE

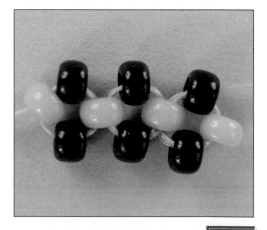

12 Continue this process, adding three beads at a time, until you reach your desired width of beadwork. If the thread points *upward* at the end of the unit row, pass through one more bead (a); if the thread points *downward* at the end of the unit row, pass through the next three beads in the unit (b). Pull the thread taut.

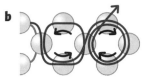

13 Pick up three beads and pass through the last high bead in the previous unit row (which is the bead that your thread last exited). This creates the first unit of the next unit row.

14 Pull the thread taut.

15 If the thread points toward the beginning of the previous unit row in Step 13, pass through the first bead that you picked up in Step 13 (c); if the thread points toward the end of the first unit row, pass through all three beads again, and then through the second to last high bead in the first unit row (d).

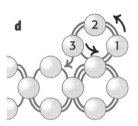

FAQ

Why might the direction of the thread vary?

The direction that your thread points at a given place in the beadwork depends on the number of units in the first unit row. As long as you complete the first unit with the thread pointing down (as shown in the example on page 135), an odd number of units results in the thread pointing upward at the end of the first unit row, and an even number of units results in the thread pointing downward. This direction in turn determines whether the thread exits toward the beginning or the end of the unit row after Step 13.

If you prefer one direction over the other, you can flip your beadwork after completing the first unit row, as necessary, to effectively change the direction of the thread. However, this can be confusing when you follow a graph pattern, and—more importantly—it does not keep the thread from pointing in the opposite direction at the ends of later unit rows. For this reason, you need to learn both techniques.

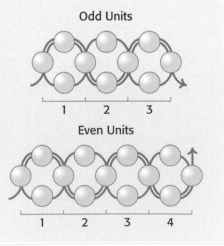

Odd Units

Even Units

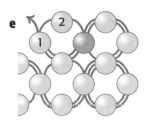

16 Pull the thread taut and pick up two beads.

17 If the thread pointed upward (away from the beadwork), pass through all of the beads in the unit again, and then through the next high bead in the previous unit row (e); if the thread pointed downward (toward the beadwork) after Step 15, pass through the third bead that you picked up in Step 14 (orange in the diagram) and through the next high bead in the previous unit row (f).

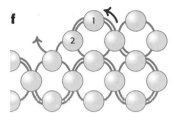

18 Pull the thread taut.

19 Continue this process, adding two beads at a time to complete each unit within each unit row, and beginning each new unit row by picking up three beads.

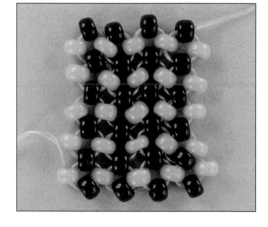

TIP

Navigating Through Right-Angle Weave Beadwork

When you weave through right-angle weave beadwork—whether to begin or end a thread, to reinforce a unit with an extra pass, or to change thread direction—always follow the path of the existing thread. Thread should run diagonally between beads, and not straight across from one bead hole to the next.

Create Tubular Right-Angle Weave

You can use *tubular right-angle weave* to create a hollow tube of beadwork or to bead around a decorative object. As with most other tubular stitches, it helps to use a form to support your beadwork, especially for the first several rounds. Like tubular peyote stitch and tubular brick stitch, you stitch each round of tubular right-angle weave in the same direction.

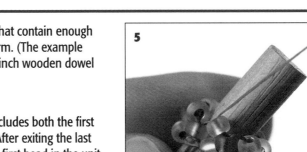

1. Begin by stitching two unit rows of flat right-angle weave that contain enough complete units to *almost* wrap all the way around your form. (The example uses seven units of size 8/0 Japanese seed beads and a ¼-inch wooden dowel as a form.)

2. Hold the beadwork against the form, as shown.

3. To close the ring, you need to complete a final unit that includes both the first and last beads in the unit row that you created in Step 1. After exiting the last bead in the unit row, pick up a bead and pass through the first bead in the unit row, then pick up another bead and pass through the last bead in the unit row again.

4. Pull the thread taut.

5. Weave through the unit again for reinforcement and bring the needle out through the high bead (the second bead that you picked up in Step 3). You now have a closed ring of right-angle weave, which comprises the first two rounds of beadwork, and the needle is in the proper position to begin the next round.

6. To begin the next round, pick up three beads using the same technique you use to begin a new unit row in flat right-angle weave.

7. Stitch right-angle weave until you arrive back at the beginning of the round.

8 To complete the round, pick up just one bead (orange in the diagram) and then pass through the first bead in the round, the lower bead from the previous round, and the last bead in the current round. (This completes the last unit in the round.) The path you take depends on whether your thread was pointing upward (a) or downward (b).

a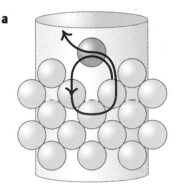

b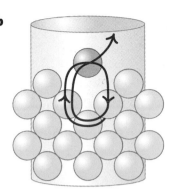

9 Pick up three beads to begin the next round.

10 Continue this process to stitch one unit row at a time until you reach your desired length of beadwork.

MULTIPLE-BEAD RIGHT-ANGLE WEAVE

In multiple-bead right-angle weave, you substitute some or all of the single beads in the basic stitch with groups of beads. In the example on the right, the left and right sides of the units contain one bead each, and the tops and bottoms of the units contain three beads each. Keep in mind that with this technique, you can make increases and decreases by adding to and reducing the number of beads on the top of a unit, rather than using the traditional increasing and decreasing methods described on the next page.

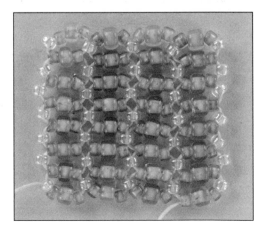

Make Right-Angle Weave Increases and Decreases

As with most stitches, you can alter the lengths of right-angle weave rows by making either outside or mid-row increases and decreases. Because you stitch right-angle weave in units, increases and decreases lengthen and shorten unit rows by units, rather than by columns of individual beads.

Right-Angle Weave Outside Increases and Decreases

Use these techniques to add or subtract unit columns at the edges of flat beadwork.

RIGHT-ANGLE WEAVE OUTSIDE INCREASE: BEGINNING OF ROW

1 At the end of the current unit row, pick up three beads (beads 1, 2, and 3 in the diagrams) and stitch them as you normally would to begin the next unit row without an increase.

2 Weave through this unit until the thread exits toward the beginning of the next unit row, pointing either upward (a) or downward (b).

3 Pick up three beads (beads 4, 5, and 6 in the diagrams) and stitch them to create a new unit at the edge of the beadwork. The new unit row now contains its first two units of beads.

4 **Optional:** To increase by more than one unit, continue adding units, stitching outward, until you reach your desired width of increase.

5 Weave back through the unit row, taking care to follow the path of the existing thread (see the tip on page 137), and resume right-angle weave as usual.

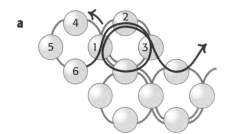 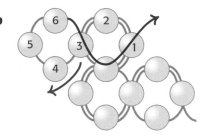

RIGHT-ANGLE WEAVE OUTSIDE INCREASE: END OF ROW

1. Navigate through the beadwork, as necessary, so that the thread exits the last bead in the unit row (orange in the diagrams), pointing either upward (c) or downward (d).

2. Pick up three new beads and stitch them to create a new unit at the edge of the beadwork (beads 1, 2, and 3 in the diagrams).

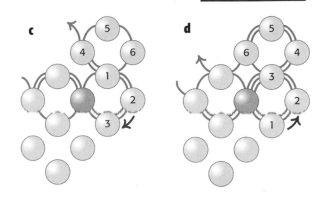

3. **Optional:** To increase by more than one unit, continue stitching outward until you reach your desired width.

4. Pick up three beads to turn and begin the next unit row (beads 4, 5, and 6 in the diagrams).

5. Resume right-angle weave as usual.

In this example (a), a one-unit increase is made at the beginning and end of the third unit row.

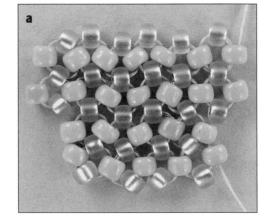

RIGHT-ANGLE WEAVE OUTSIDE DECREASE

To make a decrease at the beginning of a unit row, weave back through the beadwork after completing the previous unit row and bring the needle out through the high bead upon which you would like to start the next, shorter unit row. Begin the new unit row by stitching three beads as usual.

To make a decrease at the end of a unit row, simply stop short of the usual end of the unit row by one or more units and begin the next unit row. In this example (b), a one-unit decrease occurs at the beginning and end of the third unit row.

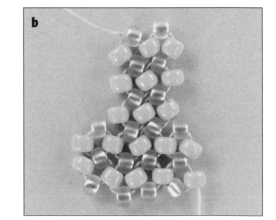

CONTINUED ON NEXT PAGE

Right-Angle Weave Mid-Row Increases and Decreases

RIGHT-ANGLE WEAVE MID-ROW INCREASE

To make a mid-row increase in flat or tubular right-angle weave, pick up one extra bead at the point of the increase. For regular right-angle weave, this is a total of three beads (orange in the diagram) instead of two (for multiple-bead right-angle weave, the number depends on the pattern). On the next unit row or round, treat that unit as having an additional high bead and stitch a separate unit of beads onto that high bead.

In this example of flat right-angle weave (a) and this example of tubular right-angle weave (c), the lighter-color beads mark the place where an extra bead is stitched into a unit to begin the increase. For a more dramatic increase, you can make the increase in more than one place within a unit row or round, or you can add more beads to the increased unit.

RIGHT-ANGLE WEAVE MID-ROW DECREASE

To make a mid-row decrease in flat or tubular right-angle weave, stitch through two high beads (orange in the diagram) from the previous unit row when you stitch a unit at the point of the decrease.

In this example of flat right-angle weave (b) and this example of tubular right-angle weave (d), the lighter-color beads are the two beads passed through together to begin the decrease. For a more dramatic decrease, you can either make decreases in other places in the unit row or round, or you can pass through more than two consecutive high beads from the previous unit row or round.

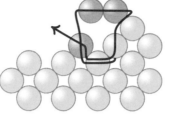

Mid-row increase

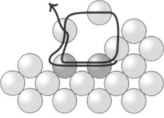

Mid-row decrease

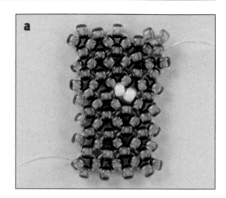

a

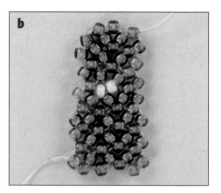

b

c

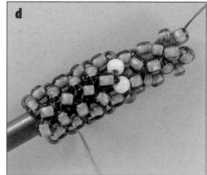

d

Right-angle weave is challenging to stitch into perfect circles, but you can experiment with it to make unique and interesting shapes. It begins with a single unit of four beads. You make increases all the way around that first unit and around each subsequent round.

Basic Circular Right-Angle Weave Technique

1 Begin by stitching the first unit of four beads as you would to begin any other right-angle weave stitch. (The example uses size 8/0 Japanese seed beads.)

2 Stitch the first unit of the second round, using the same technique that you use to begin the second round of tubular right-angle weave, but this time make a mid-row increase. (In the example, one extra bead is picked up.)

3 Stitch two more units, one on top of each bead in the initial ring, making an increase in each unit. (The example increases by one bead in each unit of this round.)

4 To complete the round, stitch one bead plus the number of beads in your increases. (In the example, this is a total of two beads.)

5 Continue stitching rounds, making increases as necessary to fill the entire round with beads. As with other circular stitches, adding fewer beads than necessary creates domed or bowl-shaped beadwork, and adding more beads than necessary creates ruffles.

Right-Angle Weave Graph Patterns

In right-angle weave graph patterns, the cells may be squares, rectangles, or ovals separated by spaces, to mimic the alignment of beads in the stitch. In these examples, the cells are squares.

FLAT RIGHT-ANGLE WEAVE GRAPH PATTERNS

You can begin reading a flat right-angle weave pattern at either corner at either end, and then work back and forth across each unit row, stitching one unit at a time. Outside increases and decreases are depicted the same way they actually appear in the beadwork. Patterns that contain mid-row increases and decreases are usually customized to depict the way they appear in the beadwork, as well.

If you begin reading this pattern from the bottom, then the green cells define the first unit row that you stitch, and the blue cells are the units that you complete for the next unit row.

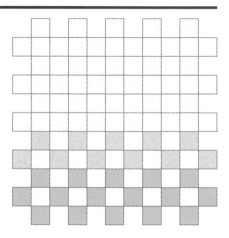

Multiple-bead graph patterns are often customized for use with specific projects. The cells are shown in stacks to indicate the number of beads on each side of each unit. If you begin reading this pattern at the bottom, then the green cells define the first unit row that you pick up. Notice that the bottom, top, and sides of the units each contain two beads. The units in the next row, shown in blue, are taller; their sides each contain four beads. In subsequent unit rows, the sides contain only one bead each, and—because there are no increases or decreases—the tops and bottoms still contain two beads each.

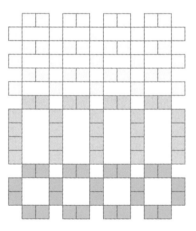

TUBULAR RIGHT-ANGLE WEAVE GRAPH PATTERNS

With a tubular right-angle weave graph pattern, you can begin at either end on the side that starts with a bead through which the thread runs vertically.

In this example, the first bead in each round of beads is labeled with its number, assuming that you begin at the bottom. You can see that the first unit establishes the first three bead rounds. At the end of that first round, you step up and stitch the unit that begins the fourth and fifth rounds of beads. Each time you complete a round by stepping up, the first beads in the new rounds shift by the space of one column.

CIRCULAR RIGHT-ANGLE WEAVE PATTERNS

Circular right-angle weave patterns are typically customized for use with particular projects. They are drawn to reflect the actual placement of the beads in each unit and in each round.

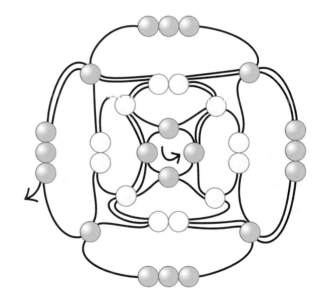

8

Herringbone Stitch

With *herringbone stitch*, also called *Ndebele stitch*, beads lie at slight angles to one another within each row or round. This stitch is thought to have originated with the master beadworkers of the Ndebele tribe of South Africa and recently has become a popular stitch among American beaders. There are many possible variations of herringbone stitch. This chapter covers the basic techniques that most commonly appear in beadwork project books and magazines.

Weave Flat Herringbone Stitch

Basic herringbone stitch consists of straight rows and columns. You can begin from a base row of a different stitch, or with an initial strand of beads that becomes the first two rows of beadwork.

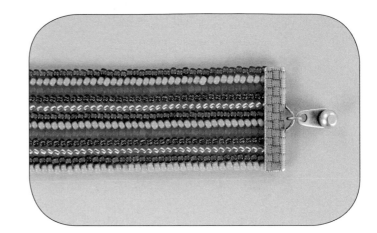

FLAT HERRINGBONE ROWS AND COLUMNS

Each full herringbone stitch contains two beads whose bottom ends are angled away from one another. These sets of beads stack vertically to create herringbone columns, called *spines*, which each contain two single columns of beads. Herringbone stitch rows are made up of single beads that lie at alternating angles to one another. Depending on how you begin the herringbone stitch, your beadwork may start with either a *full spine* (made up of full stitches) or a *half spine* made up of half stitches).

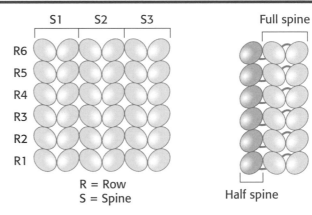

FLAT HERRINGBONE STITCH FROM A BASE ROW

The easiest way to begin herringbone stitch is with an even-count base row of a more orderly stitch, such as the ladder row used here. With this method, all of the columns are full spines.

1 Stitch and reinforce a row of ladder stitch (see page 117) with an even number of beads. This row establishes the width of the beadwork. (The example uses eight size 11/0 Japanese seed beads.)

2 Pick up two beads. This is the first set of two beads for the second row.

3 Pass down into the second from last bead in the first row and pull the thread taut.

4 Pass up through the third from the last bead and pull the thread taut.

5 Pick up two more beads. This is the second set of two beads for the second row.

6 Pass down into the fourth from last bead in the first row and pull the thread taut.

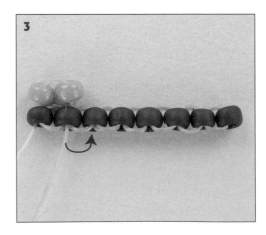

7 Continue this process, stitching two beads at a time, to the end of the row. The thread now exits the first bead in the first row, and points downward.

8 Bring the thread up over the outer side of the first bead in the first row (for an alternative turn, see the tip on page 160) and pass back through the last bead in the second row.

9 Pull the thread taut.

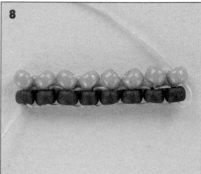

10 Pick up two beads to begin the third row.

11 Pass down through the second bead in the second row, and then up through the third bead in the second row, and pull the thread taut. (With a little practice, you should be able to pass through both of these beads at the same time.)

12 Pick up and stitch the next set of two beads.

13 Continue this process, stitching sets of two beads, to the end of the row.

14 At the end of the row, bring the thread up over the outer side of the last bead, as you did at the end of the first row (Step 8).

15 Continue stitching sets of two beads, one row a time, until you reach your desired length of beadwork less one final row, remembering to bring the thread up over the outer side of the last bead in each row to make a turn (a).

16 To reinforce the last row and to match it with the base row, stitch through it again using ladder stitch.

A completed swatch of herringbone from a base row is shown here (b).

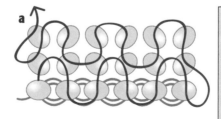

CONTINUED ON NEXT PAGE

FLAT HERRINGBONE WITHOUT-A-BASE ROW

The first three rows of flat herringbone are more difficult to stitch when you do not begin with a base row. However, *herringbone without-a-base row* results in more supple beadwork, and it allows all of the beads to align at their intended "herringbone" angles. With this method, the edges of the beadwork are half spines.

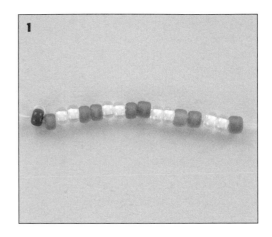

1 Begin by picking up a total number of beads that is divisible by four and that creates a strand about twice your desired width of beadwork. These beads create the first two rows. (The example uses 16 size 11/0 Japanese seed beads; the light blue beads are for the first row and the green beads are for the second row. The red bead is a stop bead.)

2 If you're using a bead stop that doesn't slide, like a Mini Bead Stopper, position the beads a few bead-widths away from the bead stop.

3 Pick up the first bead for the third row. (In the example, this is a cream-colored bead.)

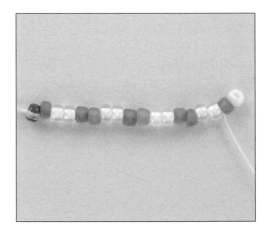

4 Pass back through the last bead in the initial strand of beads that you picked up in Step 1.

5 Pull the thread taut while positioning the bead that you picked up in Step 3 against the last bead that you picked up in Step 1.

6 Skip the next two beads in the initial strand (light blue beads in the example) and pass back through the next bead (green in the example).

7 Pull the thread taut. The beads now begin to align in a zigzag formation that, when pulled together at the top, becomes the first three rows of the first two columns of beadwork.

8 Pick up two more beads—the second and third beads of the third row—and pass back through the very next bead in the initial strand.

9 Pull the thread taut again.

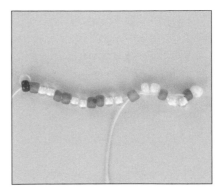

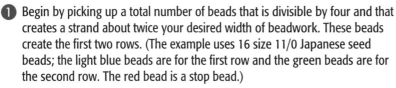

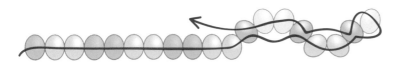

⑩ Skip the next two beads (blue) in the initial strand and pass back through the following bead (green).

⑪ Pick up two more beads (cream) for the third row and pass back through the very next bead (green) in the initial strand. (If these beads twist so that the thread crosses below them, use your fingers to straighten them.)

⑫ Continue this process, skipping two beads and stitching two beads between single beads, until you reach the end of the second row, with the thread exiting the last bead. (Don't worry if the beadwork appears somewhat jumbled at this stage.)

⑬ Pick up two beads—the last bead of the third row and the first bead of the fourth row.

16

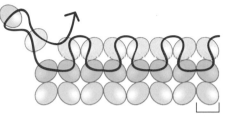

Half spine

⑭ Slide these beads together against the beadwork and pass back through the first bead that you picked up in Step 13.

⑮ Holding the beads in position, pull the thread taut.

⑯ Pass through the next bead (cream) in the third row.

⑰ Pick up the next two beads (blue) for the fourth row.

⑱ Pass through the very next two beads (cream) in the third row and pull the thread taut. At this point, the first three rows should begin to align properly.

⑲ Continue picking up two beads and passing through the very next two beads to the end of the row.

⑳ At the end of the row, pick up two beads—the last bead in the fourth row and first bead in the fifth row—and slide them against the beadwork as you did in Steps 13 and 14.

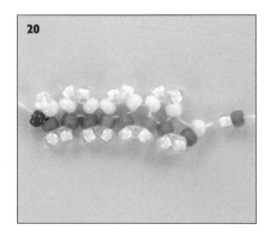

20

㉑ Pass back through the first bead that you picked up in Step 20 and pull the thread taut.

㉒ Continue this process, stitching two beads at a time and picking up two beads to make each turn, until you reach your desired length of beadwork.

A completed swatch of herringbone without-a-base row is shown here (a).

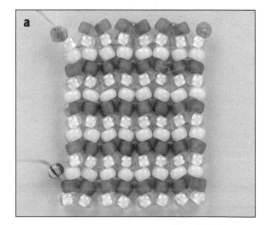

a

Create Tubular Herringbone

Tubular herringbone typically begins with a ladder-stitch base row. The basic technique creates a tube with straight columns, but you can create spiraled—or "twisted"—columns by slightly varying the stitch.

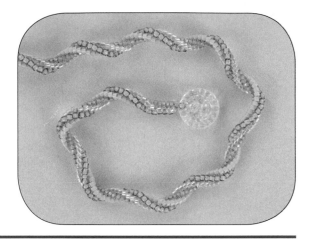

TUBULAR HERRINGBONE WITH STRAIGHT COLUMNS

1. Stitch and reinforce a row of ladder stitch with an even number of beads that is long enough to wrap all the way around your form. (The example uses eight size 11/0 Japanese seed beads and a ⅛-inch cooper tube as a form.)

2. Bring the first and last beads of the ladder row together and ladder-stitch them twice through to create a ring.

3. Slip the ring onto the form.

4. Pick up the first two beads of the second round.

5. Pass down into the ladder row and up again, as you would for flat herringbone stitch from a base row (see page 148).

6. Continue stitching two beads at a time until you arrive back at the beginning of the round.

7. At the end of the second round, pass up through both the first bead in the first round and the first bead in the second round and pull the thread taut.

8. Use herringbone stitch (base-row method) to stitch the third round until you arrive back at the beginning of the round.

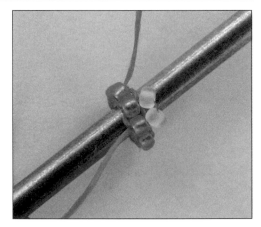

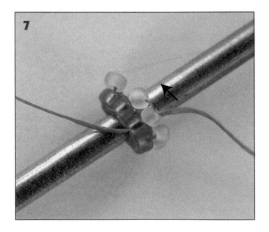

9 Step up by passing through both the first bead in the second round and the first bead in the third round (orange in the diagram) and pull the thread taut. (If you would like to give the columns a gently-twisted appearance, you can skip the step up and simply pass up through the first bead in the third round, which is the upper-most orange bead in the diagram.)

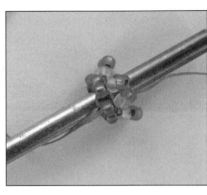

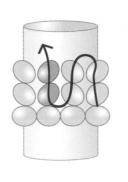

10 Continue this process to stitch each round.

11 To stitch the last round so that it matches the first, reinforce it with ladder stitch, just as you would for flat herringbone stitch from a base row (see page 149).

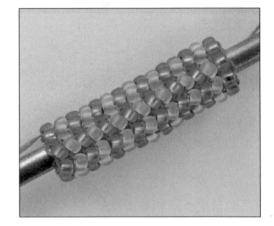

TUBULAR HERRINGBONE WITH TWISTED COLUMNS

You can stitch columns that appear to twist around the tube by bringing the needle up through two or more rounds after stitching each set of two beads.

1 Begin by stitching the first three rounds of tubular herringbone with straight columns (see previous page). Complete the third round by stepping up as usual.

2 Pick up the first two beads of the fourth round (orange in the diagram) and pass down through the very next bead in the third round as usual.

3 Instead of passing up through the next third-round bead in the next spine, pass up through the bead in the *second* round as shown.

Third round —
Second round —

CONTINUED ON NEXT PAGE

4 Continue picking up two beads, and then passing down through the third round and up through the second round, until you arrive back at the beginning of the fourth round.

5 To step up, pass though the first beads in the second, third, and fourth rounds (orange in the diagram) and pull the thread taut.

6 Continue this process for each round, stitching beads and passing up through the previous two rounds, until you reach your desired length of twisted columns.

7 To stitch the last three rounds so that they match the first three, stitch the final two or three rounds with straight columns (see page 152) and reinforce the final round with ladder stitch.

You can reverse the direction of the twist in tubular herringbone by passing down into previous rows in the *same* spine that supports the two beads that you just stitched, and then passing up through only the last round in the next spine.

TIP

Make More Dramatic Tubular Herringbone Twists

You can make more dramatic twists by passing through deeper rounds in the tube after you stitch each set of two beads. In the example on the right, the thread passes up through three rounds instead of two. Begin by stitching the first three rounds with straight columns and the fourth round with regular twisted columns. For the fifth round, pass up through the next bead in the *second* round (rather than the third) after stitching each set of two beads. At the end of each round, step up by passing through four beads instead of three. Continue this more dramatic twist until you reach your desired length. End the tube with one round of regular twisted columns and a final round of straight columns reinforced with ladder stitch.

TUBULAR HERRINGBONE BEADED-RING START

Instead of beginning tubular herringbone with a stitched base row (such as the ladder row used in previous examples), you can begin with a simple ring of beads. This creates an initial round with a slightly smaller circumference than later rounds. For this reason, you usually do not use a form with this method.

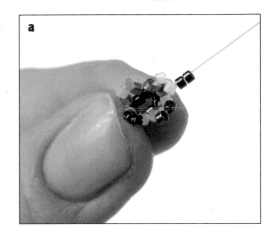

a

1 Begin by picking up an even number of beads to establish the number of spines in the tube. Pass through all of the beads again and pull them into a ring.

2 **Optional:** Make a square knot or surgeon's knot to secure the thread tension.

3 Pass through the first bead again and gently pull the thread taut.

4 Stitch the next round by picking up two beads and passing through two beads in the ring until you arrive back at the beginning of the round. At this stage, you can hold the beadwork as you would hold circular beadwork.

5 Step up and continue tubular herringbone stitch as usual. For the first several rounds (until a tube forms), hold the thread tail between your thumb and finger, with the beadwork perched on your fingertips (a).

6 Pass through all of the beads in the final round once or twice to reinforce the round and pull the beads together to better match the initial ring.

Here (b) is a completed length of eight-column, tubular herringbone started with an eight-bead ring. To create more-graduated ends, as shown here (c), you can begin with a ring that contains *half* of the total number of bead columns for the tube. Instead of passing through two beads at a time in Step 4, pass through only one bead in the ring. To stitch the last round of the tube, decrease by stitching only one bead per pass (rather than two beads), and then reinforce the round to cinch-up the thread tension at the end.

b

c

Perform Herringbone Increases and Decreases

You can make outside increases and decreases in flat herringbone beadwork, and mid-row increases and decreases in flat and tubular herringbone beadwork.

Herringbone Outside Increases

This section covers outside increases for beadwork that has full spines at the edges, which is the case with herringbone from a base row. (You can find instructions for outside increases from half spines, which are less common, in books on advanced bead weaving.)

Herringbone outside increases generally lengthen two rows at once: the current row at its end and the previous row at its beginning. To make an increase on one side of the beadwork, use a "first-side" method (below), and to make a matching increase on the opposite side, use a "second-side" method (on the next page).

HALF-SPINE OUTSIDE INCREASE: FIRST SIDE

You can use this method to add a half spine to the edge of a full spine. (The example uses size 11/0 Japanese cylinder beads.)

1. After stitching the last two-bead set in the row, allow the thread to exit the bottom of the last bead in the previous row. (That is, do not bring the thread up and pass through the last bead in the current row as usual.)

2. Pick up three beads (orange on the diagram).

3. While holding these beads against the side of the beadwork, pass back through the second bead that you picked up and pull the thread taut.

4. Now pass up through the last bead in the row that you just completed and continue the herringbone stitch as usual.

Note that because your beadwork now includes a half spine, you must use the herringbone without-a-base-row technique on this side going forward (see page 150): Pick up two beads at the end of the row and use the second one as a turning bead.

HALF-SPINE OUTSIDE INCREASE: SECOND SIDE

You can use this method to add a half spine to the edge of the full spine on the opposite edge of the beadwork. (This example uses size 11/0 Japanese cylinder beads.)

1 When you reach the end of the row where you would like to make a half-spine increase to match the one you made on the first side, pass down through the last bead in the third from last row and pick up the three beads (orange in the diagram) for the increase.

2 While holding these beads against the side of the beadwork, pass back through the second bead that you picked up and pull the thread taut.

3 Pass up through the next edge-bead and back up through the third bead that you picked up in Step 1.

4 Begin the next row by picking up one bead to use as a turning bead.

5 Pass back through the next two beads and pull the thread taut.

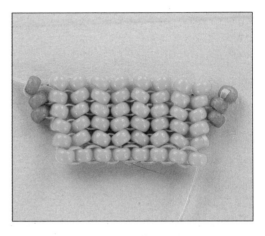

6 Continue the herringbone stitch as usual, making turns using the herringbone without-a-base-row method.

On the right, an outside increase of a half spine is made on both sides of the same two rows, beginning with the fourth row. The orange beads represent each set of three beads that you pick up to make the increases.

CONTINUED ON NEXT PAGE

FULL-SPINE OUTSIDE INCREASE: FIRST SIDE

Use this technique to increase by one full spine at the end of a row.

1 After stitching the last two-bead set in the row, allow the thread to exit the bottom of the last bead in the previous row.

2 Pick up four beads for the increase (orange in the diagram).

3 Using the fourth bead as a turning bead, pass back through the third bead, keeping the thread taut.

4 Pick up the first set of two beads for the next row and continue the herring-bone stitch as usual.

FULL-SPINE OUTSIDE INCREASE: SECOND SIDE

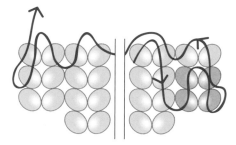

It is more challenging to create a matching full-spine increase on the second side of the beadwork than on the first, without weaving a path that is inconsistent with the path of existing thread. Here is one approach, which involves weaving all the way back to the opposite end of the row, and beginning the next row from that side (as shown on the right). Notice that you begin by picking up four beads (orange in the diagram), as usual, and then the next set of two beads (which serve as the last two beads in the current row). You then return to the other side and use the first bead in the previous row as a turning bead.

In the example on the right, a full-spine increase is made on both sides of the beadwork, beginning with the fifth row.

Herringbone Outside Decreases

This section covers outside decreases for beadwork that has full spines at the edges, which is the case with herringbone from a base row. (You can find instructions for outside decreases from half spines, which are less common, in books on advanced bead weaving.) Herringbone outside decreases shorten one row at a time. Just like with outside increases, you can decrease on the outside by a half spine or a full spine.

The examples in this section use size 11/0 cylinder beads. In this herring-bone swatch (as shown on the right), a half-spine decrease over a full spine occurs at both the beginning and the end of the fifth row.

HALF-SPINE DECREASE: BEGINNING OF ROW

Use this method to make an outside decrease of a half spine at the begin-ning of a new row when the previous row ended with a full spine (as shown on the right).

1 At the end of the previous row, pass back through the second from last bead in the row and pull the thread taut.

2 Pick up one bead (orange in the diagram). This is the first bead in the new, shorter row.

3 Moving toward the beadwork, pass through the second from last bead in the previous row again.

4 Pass up through the third from last bead in the previous row and continue the herringbone stitch as usual.

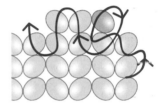

HALF-SPINE DECREASE: END OF ROW

To make an outside decrease at the end of a row that ends with a full spine (as shown on the right), simply pick up two beads (orange in the diagram; as you would to begin a new row when you stitch herringbone without-a-base row), and use the second bead as a turning bead to begin the new, shorter row.

CONTINUED ON NEXT PAGE

FULL-SPINE DECREASE: BEGINNING OF ROW

For an outside decrease of a full spine at the beginning of a row, weave back through the row as shown on the right, and stitch the first two beads for the new row (orange in the diagram) above the second from last full spine in the previous row.

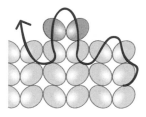

FULL-SPINE DECREASE: END OF ROW

To decrease by a full spine at the end of a row (a), you need to pass down into the third from last row as shown and then weave back toward the point of the decrease, following the path of existing thread. Pass straight up and out of the beadwork to stitch the first two beads in the next row (orange in the diagram).

In this example (b), a full-spine decrease occurs at both the beginning and the end of the fifth row.

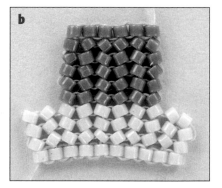

TIP

Use an Alternative Turn to Better Hide the Thread with Herringbone from a Base Row

When you stitch flat herringbone from a base row, you can use an alternative turn at the end of each row to avoid wrapping thread along the outsides of beads. Instead of bringing the thread over the side of the first bead in the previous row, weave back into the beadwork and exit the last bead in the current row. The disadvantage of this method is that it pulls the first two and last two beads in each row slightly out of alignment, which alters the traditional "herringbone" look of the beadwork.

Herringbone Mid-Row Increases and Decreases

You can make herringbone mid-row increases either between spines or within spines. You can also add strung beads between spines to make an increase with a more decorative effect. Mid-row decreases are more limited than mid-row increases, but they are simple to perform. All of these mid-row techniques work with flat herringbone, and they are the only increases and decreases that you make with tubular herringbone.

2

HERRINGBONE INCREASE BETWEEN SPINES

① To begin the increase, pick up an extra bead (orange in the first diagram) immediately after passing down through the previous row or round to stitch one set of two beads.

② Pass up through the next bead as usual and stitch the next set of two beads.

③ Continue the herringbone stitch, and when you arrive back at the place where you began the increase, pick up and stitch two beads (orange in the second diagram) directly above the extra bead that you picked up in Step 1.

④ Resume the herringbone stitch, and when you arrive back at the place where you picked up the two beads in Step 3, pass up through the first, pick up a new set of two beads, and then pass down through the second. An increase of one spine is now complete.

3–4

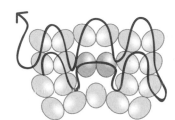

⑤ Continue the herringbone stitch as usual.

In this example (a), the yellow beads represent two between-spine increases that begin in the fifth row. In this example (b), the blue beads mark the location of a between-spine increase in tubular herringbone.

CONTINUED ON NEXT PAGE

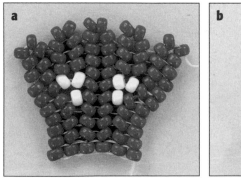

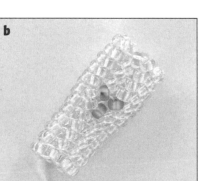

HERRINGBONE INCREASE WITHIN A SPINE

1 To begin the increase, pick up four beads instead of two when you perform a stitch. In the example on the right, the red beads are the two extra beads picked up, and the rest of the row is complete.

2 Continue stitching until you arrive back at the stitch that contains the four beads.

3 Pass up through the first of the four beads, pick up a new set of two beads, and then pass down through both the second and third of the four beads, and pull the thread taut.

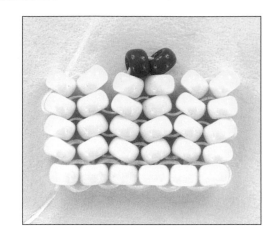

4 Pick up another set of two beads and pass down through the fourth bead from Step 1. What was previously a single spine is now split into two spines (orange in the diagram).

5 Continue the herringbone stitch, and when you arrive back at the point of the increase, stitch through the set from Step 3 and the set from Step 4 as two individual spines. (Be sure to skip over the second and third beads from Step 1 when you do this; those beads are only passed through a total of twice.)

6 Continue the herringbone stitch as usual.

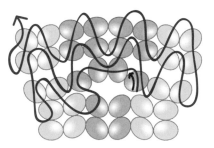

In this example (a), an increase occurs within the second spine, beginning with the fifth row. The two red beads in the fifth row are the two extra beads picked up in Step 1. The four red beads in the sixth row are the two sets of two beads stitched in Steps 3 and 4. In this example (b), the blue beads mark the location of a similar increase in tubular herringbone.

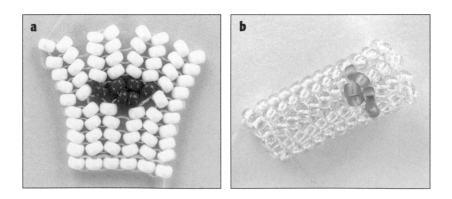

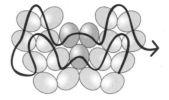

HERRINGBONE INCLUSIONS AS INCREASES

Another way to create mid-row increases in the herringbone stitch is to pick up extra beads between spines. The extra beads remain simply strung; you typically do not pass through them more than once. These increases are often called *inclusions*. When you use beads with contrasting colors, sizes, or shapes, your inclusions can serve as interesting design elements in either flat or tubular herringbone. In this diagram on the right, the orange beads are the inclusions.

In the flat herringbone example on the right, the darker beads are inclusions: In the third row, a single dark bead is added between the second and third spines. In the fourth row, two dark beads are added between those spines. The inclusions continue to increase in length by one bead per row for two more rows, and then they shorten by one bead in each of the next three rows. This puckers the beadwork and causes some of the inclusion beads to overlap.

HERRINGBONE MID-ROW DECREASES

To make a mid-row decrease, you can pick up just one bead in a spine rather than two. Then, when you reach that bead while stitching the next row, pass through it between spines. In the next row, skip the bead completely as you stitch sets of two beads. This decreases the width of the beadwork by one full spine. In this flat herringbone example (a), the decrease occurs in the fifth row. In this tubular herringbone example (b), it occurs in the seventh round.

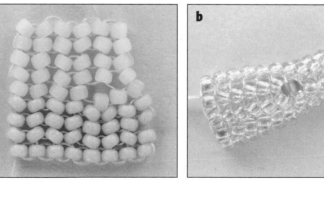

The herringbone stitch is not well suited for stitching perfect circles, but you can create other interesting shapes—some of which resemble snowflakes—by applying a basic circular stitch technique.

Begin with an initial ring that contains an even number of beads (as you would for "Tubular Herringbone Beaded-Ring Start," see page 155), and then stitch the second round by passing through each of those beads individually, as shown in the diagram. Use evenly spaced, mid-row increases in each subsequent round to enlarge the beadwork. In the diagram, the orange beads represent between-spine increases (inclusions). As with tubular herringbone, you need to step up to complete each round.

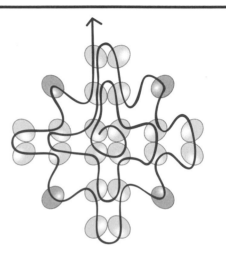

In the example on the right, the initial ring (which serves as the first round) contains four beads. Between-column increases begin in the third round, where you pick up one extra bead between spines. In the fourth round, three extra beads are picked up between spines, and in the fifth round, two sets of two beads are stitched into each three-bead increase. In the final round, just one bead is stitched onto each spine.

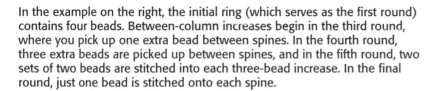

TIP

Keep Pairs of Beads from Twisting with Herringbone Stitch
With circular herringbone, as well as flat and tubular herringbone, take care to keep pairs of beads from twisting (and reversing their alignment) before you pass through them to stitch the next round or row. If a pair of beads does twist, use your fingers to straighten the beads and hold them in their proper position while you make the stitch.

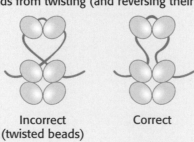

Incorrect
(twisted beads)

Correct

Herringbone stitch graph patterns contain cells that are angled to match the angles of beads in full spines and half spines. Cells are often rectangles or ovals, and you follow one row of a pattern at a time.

SPINES IN FLAT HERRINGBONE PATTERNS

When a pattern comes with instructions, always follow their recommendation regarding where to start. When there are no instructions, you need to consider which method you plan to use to begin the beadwork. Recall that for herringbone from a base row (beginning with an even-count base row, as described on page 148), your beadwork contains all full spines (assuming that you do not make any half-spine increases or decreases). Accordingly, you can only use the base-row method with a pattern that begins with full spines.

Whether a given row in a pattern contains half spines depends on which end you begin reading the graph. For instance, if you read this pattern (a) beginning at the bottom, you will only stitch full spines. However, if you begin reading it from the top, then the angles of the cells are reversed, and the rows begin and end with half spines. This is the alignment of beads that you use to stitch herringbone *without*-a-base row. Here (b), the same graph is flipped top to bottom and the colors changed to more clearly show the half spines.

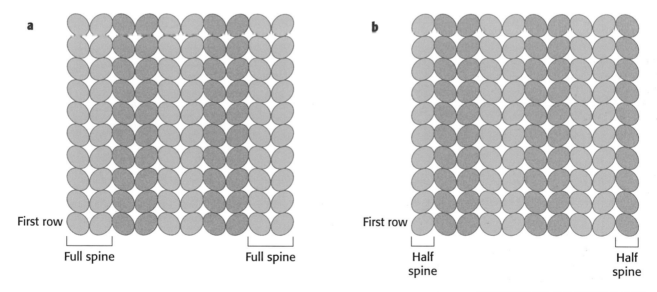

a

First row

Full spine   Full spine

b

First row

Half spine   Half spine

CONTINUED ON NEXT PAGE

HOW TO READ THE FIRST TWO ROWS OF A HERRINGBONE-WITHOUT-A-BASE ROW PATTERN

Remember that you begin the flat herringbone stitch without a base row by picking up all of the beads for the first *two* rows (see page 150). The order in which you pick them up is not the same order in which they appear in the first two rows of a graph pattern. For this reason, you may find it helpful to chart the initial strand of beads on paper before you begin.

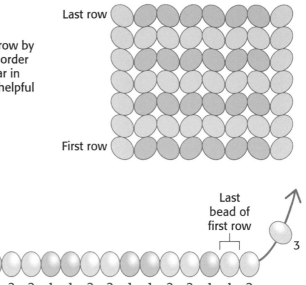

Last row

First row

The order of beads that you pick up always follows the sequence shown on the right, which corresponds to the graph shown above: Pick up the first bead of the second row, the first and second beads of the first row, the second and third beads of the second row, and so on, ending the initial strand with the last bead in the second row. The next bead that you pick up after the initial strand is the first bead in the third row (labeled "3" in the diagram). From this point forward you can read the pattern row by row, picking up beads in the order shown in the graph. Switch direction at the beginning of each new row.

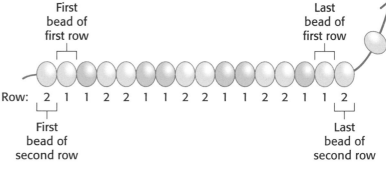

First bead of first row

Last bead of first row

Row: 2 1 1 2 2 1 1 2 2 1 1 2 2 1 1 2

First bead of second row

Last bead of second row

3

FAQ

What should I do if project instructions suggest that I follow the pattern differently?

That depends on the pattern and on your personal preference. However, as a general rule, you should attempt to follow any written instructions that accompany a pattern. This is especially important when the pattern has characteristics that you are unfamiliar with. For instance, although herringbone from a base row is usually an even-count stitch, some patterns may use an odd-count stitch. In that case, you need to alter your technique to accommodate the extra column—and the project instructions should tell you how.

TUBULAR HERRINGBONE GRAPH PATTERNS

Tubular herringbone graph patterns are like flat herringbone patterns that begin from a base row, except that you read each row in the same direction. If you read the pattern on the right beginning at the bottom, then the blue cells are the beads that make up the base row. If you begin at the lower-left corner and ladder-stitch the beads moving left to right, and then reverse direction to reinforce the ladder before securing it into a ring, your thread ultimately exits the first bead in the base row (labeled "1"). You then pick up each pair of two green beads for the second round, reading left to right. At the end of the second round, you step up and begin stitching each pair of yellow beads for the third round, again reading left to right. Notice that the first bead in each row (numbered in the diagram) aligns vertically with the first bead in the previous row.

If a pattern is intended to have twisted columns (see page 153), the accompanying project instructions typically indicate the degree of twist you should create. The twist does not affect the graph pattern because you always stitch sets of two beads at a time.

CIRCULAR HERRINGBONE, INCREASES, AND DECREASES IN PATTERNS

As with other circular patterns, circular herringbone patterns are normally drawn to mimic the actual arrangement of beads in the design. You begin with the central ring, reading the pattern in either direction, and then stitch one round at a time in the same direction, as you would for tubular herringbone. A typical circular herringbone pattern looks like the circular herringbone diagram on page 164.

Outside and mid-row increases and decreases in regular flat and tubular herringbone are also usually drawn into graph patterns to show the actual placement of the beads, as they are in the diagrams in the section "Perform Herringbone Increases and Decreases." In all of these patterns, the thread path is also often shown.

chapter

9

Details and Jewelry Finishing Techniques

Once you are familiar with some of the basic bead-weaving stitches, you can start experimenting with decorative details like picots, fringe, and drops. This chapter provides an introduction to these basic techniques, which are popular embellishments in bead-weaving projects. It also covers some essential techniques for converting beadwork bands and tubes into wearable pieces of jewelry.

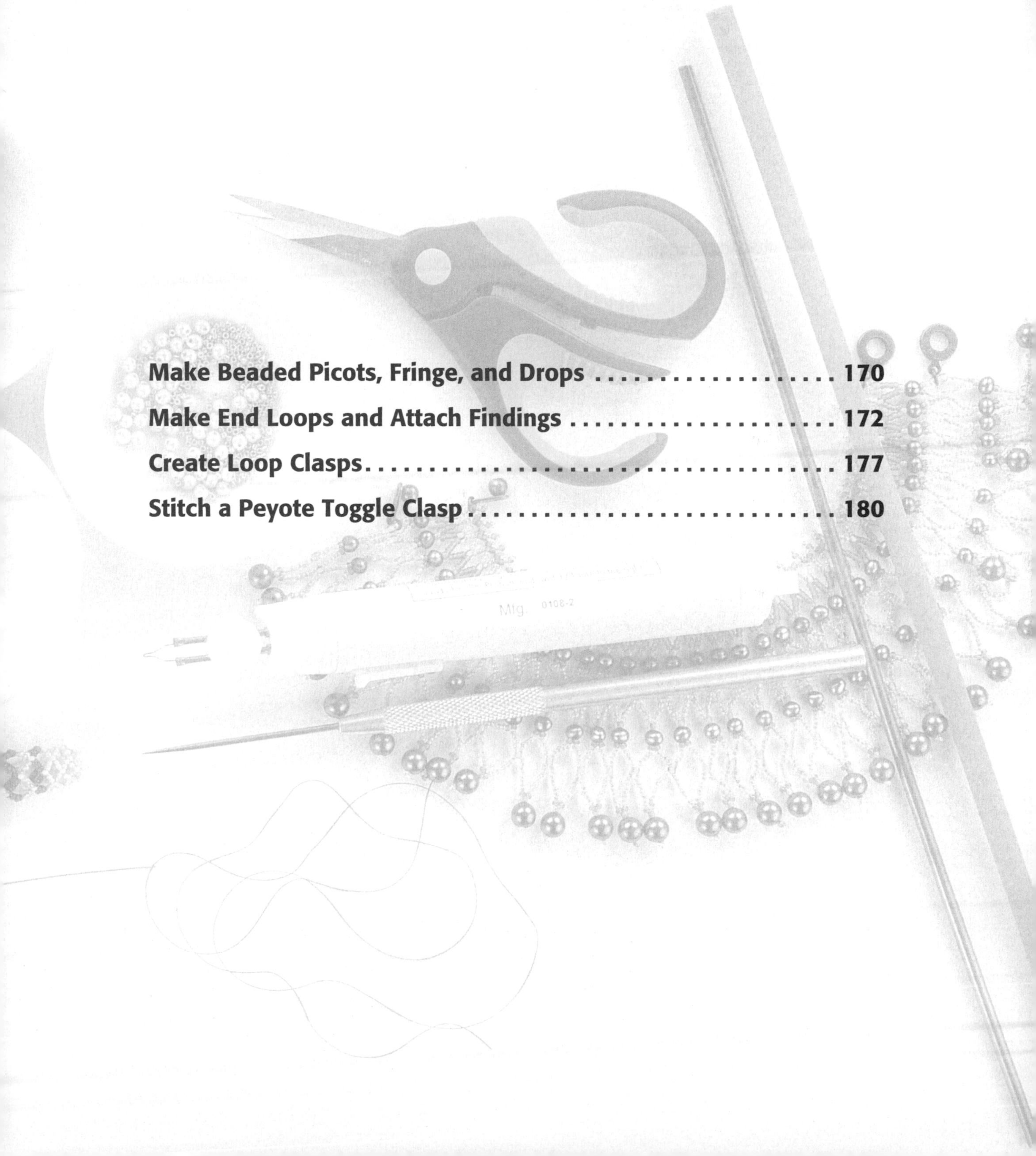

You can add beaded picots, fringe, and drops to the edges or ends of bead-work to give it extra personality and style.

Beaded Picots

Basic *picots* are small loops of beads that you add to the edges of beadwork. Depending on the type of stitch and the requirements of a given project, you can sometimes make picots while you stitch the main portion of the beadwork. For instance, with flat peyote stitch, you can make a picot simply by picking up extra beads at the end of a row. Other times, it's easier to go back and add picots after you finish stitching the main beadwork. An example is herringbone stitch, where you can pass through an outside bead-column, bring the needle out to add a picot, and then pass back into the beadwork.

When you bring the needle out at the edge of beadwork to make a picot, follow the path of existing thread as much as possible, just as you do when weaving-in. The diagrams below show examples of how you can make picots with some of the basic stitches: peyote stitch (a), horizontal netting with turning-bead edges (b), brick stitch (c), square stitch (d), right-angle weave (e), and herringbone (f). To practice making simple picots with peyote stitch, try "Flat Peyote Stitch Bracelet with Picots" on page 186.

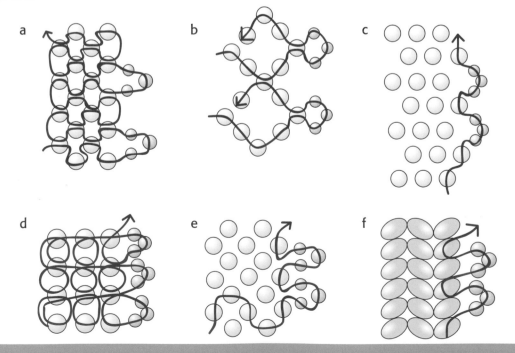

Beaded Fringe and Drops

Fringe is usually added after the main portion of beadwork is stitched. Basic fringe is either *straight* or *looped*. With some projects, it helps to tape the beadwork to your work surface when you make fringe, as shown in the photo below. Keep in mind that your fringe pieces do not need to be the same size. For an example project that includes graduating fringe, see "Circular Brick Stitch Fringe Earrings" on page 228.

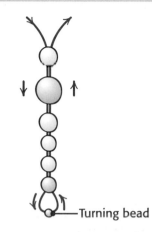

STRAIGHT FRINGE

A straight fringe piece is a strand of beads with one or more turning beads at the end.

1. To begin straight fringe, weave through the beadwork and bring the needle out at the edge, just as you would do for a picot.

2. Pick up all of the beads for the fringe piece, ending with one or more turning beads.

3. Turn and pass through all of the beads in the fringe piece again. To keep the thread taut but not too tight, hold the turning bead, or the thread behind the turning bead, with the fingers of your non-dominant hand. Allow the turning bead to slowly slide toward the beadwork as you pass back through the fringe beads.

4. Pass back into the beadwork, as you would to complete a picot.

5. Weave through the beadwork to bring the needle out again next to the first piece of fringe.

6. Repeat this process until you reach your desired length of fringe.

—Turning bead

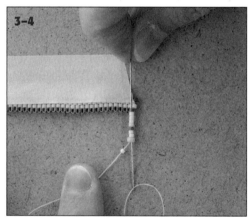

LOOPED FRINGE AND DROPS

Looped fringe is made up of extra-long picots. You can make open loops (a) or linked loops (b) by using link beads as you do for netting (see Chapter 4). Beaded drops (c) are essentially picots and fringe combined; they are loops with very short lengths of fringe at their center points.

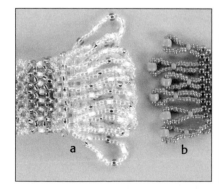

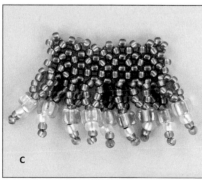

Make End Loops and Attach Findings

When you make a beaded necklace, bracelet, or anklet, you usually need to attach or construct a clasp to make the jewelry wearable. You can attach pre-made findings, like lobster clasps, using beaded loops called *end loops*. With some flat beadwork designs, you can use clamp ends (see page 175) instead.

Use End Loops to Attach Findings

With flat beadwork, you usually center a single loop as much as possible along the edge of the beadwork, and you should evenly space loops when you make more than one. With tubular beadwork, you can flatten the end of the tube so that the sides touch, and then stitch a loop across the opening, passing from one side to the other.

SIMPLE LOOPS

Simple loops lie directly against the edge of the beadwork.

This example uses a new thread to attach the loops. Alternatively, you can use a thread tail that is at least 12–14 inches long.

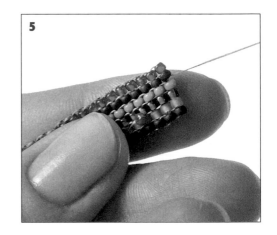

5

1. Complete all of the stitching required for the main portion of your design, end the thread, and weave-in the thread tail. (The example is a square stitch band using size 11 beads.)

2. Decide where you would like to place an end loop on the beadwork. (With narrow, flat beadwork that requires only one loop, the loop is typically centered.)

3. Prepare a new length of thread that is about 1½ feet long.

4. Weave-in with the new thread, beginning several rows from the edge of the design where you would like to create the end loop.

5. Bring the thread out in the exact place where you would like the first side of the end loop to begin.

6. String on enough beads to create the loop. (Seven size 11 beads are used in the example.)

7. String on the jump ring or jewelry finding and position it over the beads.

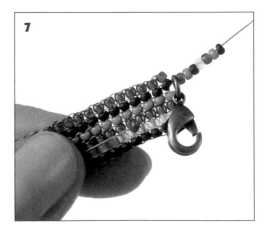

7

8 Pass the needle back into the beadwork at the place where you would like the loop to end. In the example, the loop begins and ends exactly two beads away from either edge.

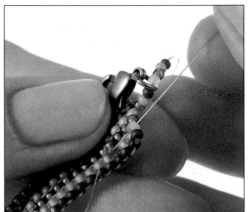

9 Weave back through the beadwork toward the place where you began the loop, and bring the needle back out through the same bead that you initially exited to begin the loop.

10 Pass the needle through all of the beads in the loop again, going through one or two beads at a time.

11 Pull the thread taut as needed to ensure consistent tension.

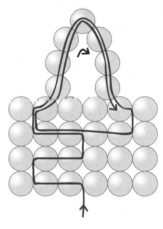

12 Weave-in to end the thread.

CONTINUED ON NEXT PAGE

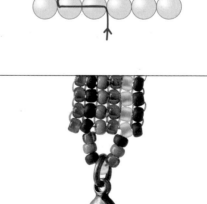

LOOPS WITH BASE BEADS

When you make a *loop with a base bead,* you stitch a bead at the base of the loop through which the thread passes in one direction to begin the loop, and then in the opposite direction to complete the loop. (This is similar to a link bead in netting.)

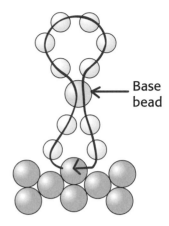

Base
bead

1 Bring the thread out of the beadwork in the place where you would like the beaded loop to begin.

2 Pick up at least two beads, the last of which is the base bead. (In the diagram, three beads are picked up.)

3 Pick up enough beads to create the loop.

4 String on the jump ring or finding and position it over the beads.

5 Pass back through the base bead and pull the thread taut.

6 Pick up another bead to match the first bead that you picked up in Step 2.

7 Pass into the beadwork, weave through to reverse direction, and then pass through the entire loop again.

8 Pull the thread taut and weave-in to end the thread within the beadwork.

Alternatively, you can pick up just one bead—the base bead—in Step 2, as shown in the photo on the right

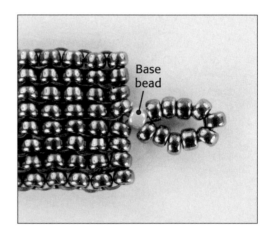

Base
bead

TIP

Opening and Closing Jump Rings

You can use jump rings (see page 18) to connect clasp parts to jewelry. *Open jump rings* are jump rings that are cut, allowing you to open and close them using two pairs of chain nose pliers. To open one, hold it in front of you using two pairs of pliers, with the opening of the jump ring facing upward. Gently bend one side of the ring toward you and the other side away from you. To close a jump ring, bend the ends back in the opposite direction and wiggle them together until the ring is completely closed; there should be no visible opening at the seam.

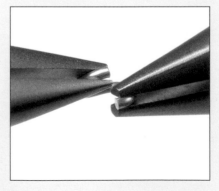

Attach Clamp Ends

You can use findings called clamp ends to connect clasps to flat beadwork stitched with 11/0 or smaller cylinder beads or seed beads. Here are two alternative methods for securing them to your beadwork.

ATTACH A CLAMP END BY SQUEEZING

When you attach a clamp end using this method, you need to be very careful not to crush and break beads in your beadwork as you squeeze the clamp end using pliers.

1️⃣ Select a pair of clamp ends that are the same width as, or slightly wider than, the end of your beadwork.

2️⃣ If the beadwork is stitched with true seed beads rather than cylinder beads, apply a narrow strip of fabric first-aid tape to the end, as shown. Make sure the tape is narrow enough that it will disappear within the clamp end (trim it with scissors, if necessary). If the tape does not stick well, use E6000 glue to secure it to the beadwork.

3️⃣ Apply a thin layer of E6000 glue to the top surface of the tape.

4️⃣ Insert the end of the beadwork into a clamp end and use chain nose or flat nose pliers to *gently* squeeze the clamp against the beads.

5️⃣ Repeat this process to attach the other clamp end to the other end of the beadwork.

6️⃣ Allow the glue to set and attach a clasp using jump rings.

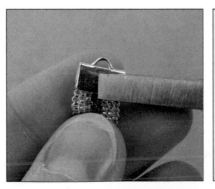

ATTACH A CLAMP END BY SLIDING

This alternative method avoids the risk of breaking beads. It is similar to that recommended by Designer's Findings, a reputable supplier of clamp ends. (For a list of suppliers and their contact information, see the online Appendix at www.wiley.com/go/tyvbeadwork).

① After selecting a pair of clamp ends, slide one onto the end of your beadwork, moving side to side (a). If the space inside the clamp end is too narrow to fit over the beadwork, remove the clamp end and use two pairs of chain nose pliers to gently widen it (b).

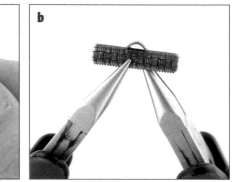

② Hold the clamp end a few inches over your work surface and allow the beadwork to hang down below it.

③ If the beadwork falls out of the clamp end, remove the clamp end and use chain nose pliers to slightly squeeze down and narrow the clamp end. Make at least two or three squeezes along the length of the clamp end, holding the pliers perpendicular to the clamp end.

④ Repeat Step 2, and if the beadwork falls free again, repeat Step 3.

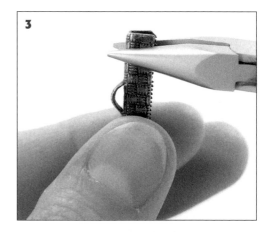

⑤ When the clamp end is narrow enough to hold the beadwork without the beadwork falling out, slide the clamp end off and apply a small amount of E6000 glue to the end of the beadwork.

⑥ Slide the clamp end onto the beadwork one final time and use a paper towel to wipe away any excess glue.

⑦ Repeat this process at the other end of the beadwork.

⑧ Allow the glue to set before attaching jump rings and a clasp.

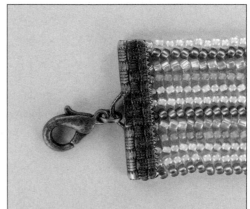

Bead-and-loop clasps and button-and-loop clasps are popular finishing techniques for bead-woven jewelry. They are simpler to make than beaded toggles (see page 180), and you can design them to match or complement a design.

Basic Loop Clasps

BEAD-AND-LOOP CLASP

1 Select a clasp bead that is large enough to hold securely within a loop, but that is not so large or heavy that it detracts from your design or strains your beadwork. At one end of the beadwork, create a simple end loop or a loop with a base bead (see pages 172–174) that is just large enough to slip over the clasp bead.

2 At the other end of the beadwork, using either a new thread or an existing thread tail, pick up two or three beads to form a *clasp shank*, or stalk, that will connect the clasp bead to the beadwork. Make sure that the bead that will be closest to the clasp bead is larger than the clasp bead's hole (so that it doesn't slip inside the clasp bead).

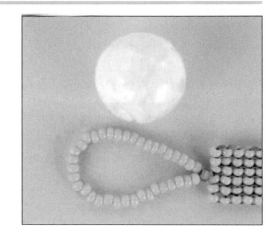

3 Pick up the clasp bead and one smaller bead to use as a turning bead and slide them against the clasp shank.

4 Pass back through the clasp bead and through all of the beads in the clasp shank, and pull the thread taut.

5 Weave into the beadwork to change direction and then pass though the clasp shank beads, clasp bead, and turning bead again.

6 Pass back through the clasp beads and the shank beads one more time.

7 Pull the thread taut and weave-in to end the thread.

8 To secure the clasp, pass the clasp bead through the loop.

Clasp bead

Clasp shank

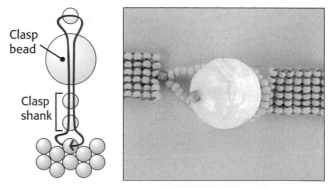

CONTINUED ON NEXT PAGE

BUTTON-AND-LOOP CLASP

With button-and-loop clasps, you use a button in place of a clasp bead.

1 Perform Steps 1–3 of "Bead-and-Loop Clasp," substituting a button for a clasp bead. The button should have either two holes at the center or a *button shank*, which is a built-in loop attached to its underside.

2 If the button has a button shank (a), pick up enough beads to reach the shank hole, then string on the button and pick up the same number of beads that you picked up before stringing on the button.

3 If the button has holes instead of a button shank (b), pick up several beads, pass through one button hole, pick up one or two more beads (which will show on top of the button), then pass down through the other button hole and pick up the same number of beads that you picked up at the beginning of this step.

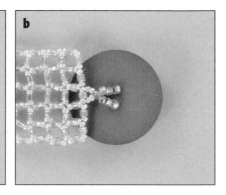

Clasp shank

Button shank

4 Pick up the same number of beads that you picked up in Step 1 for the clasp shank, and pull the thread taut.

5 Weave into the beadwork to reverse direction and then pass through all of the beads in the button clasp again for reinforcement.

6 Weave-in to end the thread within the beadwork.

7 To secure the clasp, pass the button through the loop.

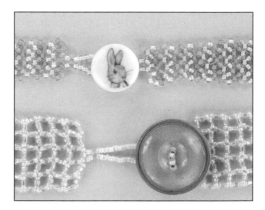

TIP

Placing Button Clasps on Top of Beadwork

When you use a button as a clasp with flat beadwork, another option is to position the button on the surface of the beadwork near the end, rather than at the edge. You can do this by weaving through the beadwork, bringing the needle out, stitching on the button the same way you would at the end of the beadwork, and then weaving back into the beadwork. With this style of clasp, be sure to make the loop at the other end of the beadwork long enough to pass all the way over the button without causing the ends of the beadwork to overlap.

Adjustable Loop Clasps

You can make a necklace, bracelet, or anklet adjustable in size by stitching a chain of more than one loop in place of a single loop. This technique is much like making a piece of looped fringe with link beads (see page 171) at the edge of your beadwork. The example creates a chain containing two loops, but you can also make more.

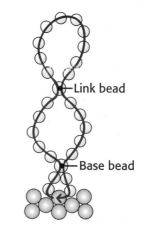

Link bead

Base bead

1. Complete Steps 1 and 2 of "Loops with Base Beads" on page 174.

2. Pick up an even number of beads that, when looped, fit over the bead or button in your clasp, then *remove* half of those beads.

3. Pick up a bead to serve as a link bead.

4. Pick up the same number of beads that you originally picked up in Step 2 (before you removed half of them).

5. Turn, and pass back through the link bead that you picked up in Step 3.

6. Pull the thread taut as if you were making a piece of fringe (page 171).

7. Pick up the same number of beads that remained on the thread *after* you removed half of the beads in Step 2.

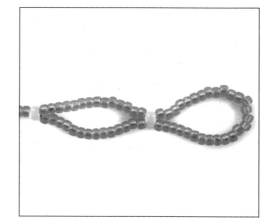

8. Pass back through the base bead and pull the thread taut.

9. Pick up the same number of beads that you originally picked up before stringing the base bead.

10. Weave-in to end the thread.

You can now secure the clasp by passing the clasp bead or button through either of the two loops.

Stitch a Peyote Toggle Clasp

You can use peyote stitch to create a beaded toggle clasp that matches your pattern. Begin by making a toggle bar on one end of the beadwork. Then, create a large end loop on the other end to slip over the toggle bar.

Basic Peyote Toggle Clasp

ADD A TOGGLE TO FLAT BEADWORK

This example adds a toggle clasp to a band of flat peyote stitch. To add one to a different flat stitch, use the same general technique, but ignore the references to high and low beads. Instead, do your best to center the toggle and bring the needle out at the end of the beadwork following the path of existing thread.

1. Bring the needle out at the place in the last row where you would like to begin the *toggle shank*, which is the narrow band that connects the toggle to the beadwork. The needle should exit a high bead and emerge toward the center-most column.

2. Pick up the first bead for the shank (bead 1 in the diagram).

3. Pass through the next high bead and then pick up the second bead for the shank (bead 2 in the diagram).

4. Pass back through the bead that you picked up in Step 2 and pull the thread taut.

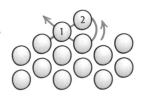

5. Using the first two beads of the toggle shank as a base, stitch two columns of peyote stitch outward for a total of six to eight rows.

6. Stop, but do not weave-in the thread.

7. Prepare a new, approximately 1½-foot length of size 0 or size B thread, with a size 12 or 13 needle threaded.

8. Stitch a swatch of flat peyote that is just long enough to form a narrow tube when the ends come together, and wide enough to hold securely within an end loop. The example uses eight rows and ten columns of size 11/0 cylinder beads.

9. **Optional:** Make small picots at the edges as you stitch for a more ornate toggle.

   Note: *To make the toggle bar stiffer, you can enclose a bugle bead inside the beadwork when you zip it up.*

10. Zip-up the ends of the swatch and weave-in both thread tails. This is the *toggle bar*.

11. Align the shank so that it is centered on the toggle bar.

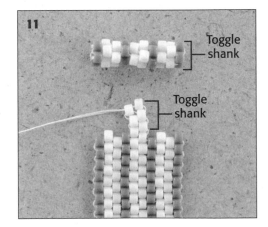

Toggle shank

Toggle shank

⑫ Thread the needle on the tail exiting the shank.

⑬ Pass through two adjacent beads at the center of the toggle bar that properly zip together with the beads in the final row of the shank; a high toggle bead should align with a low shank bead, and a low toggle bead should align with a high shank bead.

⑭ Pass through one more bead in the toggle bar and then weave back and forth all the way down the shank, as shown in the diagram.

⑮ Weave back into the beadwork and weave-in to end the thread.

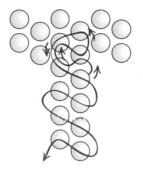

ADD A TOGGLE TO TUBULAR BEADWORK

❶ Flatten the end of the tube so that the sides come together.

❷ Pick up the first two beads for the toggle shank (blue in the diagram).

❸ Reversing direction, pass into the bead directly opposite the bead from which the thread currently exits, on the other side of the tube end (see the red line in the diagram). (If there is an odd number of beads in the final round, pass into the bead that is closest to being directly opposite; in this case, the loop cannot be perfectly centered.)

❹ Pull the thread tight and then pass back through the first two shank beads (see the black line in the diagram).

❺ Pass through the same bead on the opposite side of the tube end that the thread originally exited, moving in the *same* direction.

❻ Pull the thread taut and then pass through the first two shank beads again.

❼ Pick up the first bead for the second row of the shank and peyote-stitch it in place.

❽ Continue stitching two-column peyote for a total of six to eight rows.

❾ Stop, but do not weave-in the thread.

❿ Stitch and attach the toggle, following Steps 7–14 of "Add a Toggle to Flat Beadwork."

⓫ Weave-in to the end the thread within the tubular beadwork.

Flattened end of tube

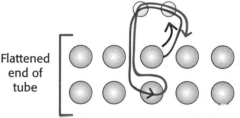

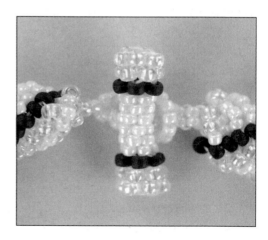

10

Beginner Projects

This chapter contains examples of the types of beginner-level projects that you can find in popular beading magazines. Before you begin, be sure to review Chapter 2 for guidance on following project instructions, preparing thread, beginning and ending thread, holding beadwork, and stitching beads. Remember that you can substitute different bead colors in these projects, and you can embellish most designs by adding your own drops, picots, or fringe. For the jewelry projects, you can substitute the suggested closures with different findings, or you can design your own loop or toggle clasps using the methods covered in Chapter 9. Keep in mind that most bead-weaving projects take time to complete, and many require more than one sitting. Be patient, and enjoy the process of learning as you work. For help finding the materials used in the projects, see "Internet Resources" in the online Appendix (www.wiley.com/go/tyvbeadwork).

Patterned Flat Peyote Bracelets

Use the two patterns on the next page to practice following basic peyote graph patterns. Remember that you can use a sheet of paper or a straight edge to keep your place. Repeat each motif shown until you reach your desired bracelet length, less about ½ inch for the clasp, and weave-in your thread tails without using knots. Attach a clamp end and lobster clasp to complete each design.

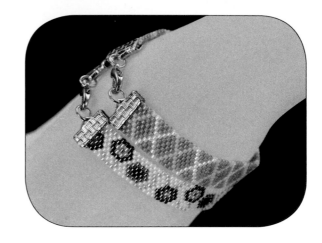

Techniques and Materials

TECHNIQUES

In addition to the general techniques covered in Chapter 2, this project uses techniques from the following chapters and sections.

Chapter 3:

- "Weave Flat Peyote Stitch"
- "Peyote Stitch Graph Patterns"

Chapter 9:

- "Make End Loops and Attach Findings"

SUPPLIES AND FINDINGS

The items below are in addition to those listed under "Essential Tools and Supplies" in Chapter 1 (see page 16).

- Size 12 beading needle
- Size D Nymo beading thread in cream
- 4½-inch gold-tone clamp ends (one pair for each bracelet)
- 2 gold-tone 11mm lobster clasps (one for each bracelet)
- 4 gold-tone 6mm OD (outside diameter) jump rings (one pair for each bracelet)
- Pliers for attaching jump rings and clamp ends
- E6000 (or similar) glue for gluing the clamp ends
- A paper towel (for wiping away excess glue)
- **Optional:** Fabric first-aid tape, if you decide to use that technique to affix the clamp ends (see page 175).

BEADS FOR THE EVEN-COUNT BRACELET

The cylinder beads used in both patterns are Miyuki Delicas. Weights are rounded up to the nearest 0.5 gram and are estimates based on an average-length bracelet.

- 2 grams size 11/0 opaque alabaster luster cylinder beads (**A**)
- 1 gram size 11/0 sparkling peridot-lined crystal cylinder beads (**B**)
- 0.5 grams size 11/0 silver-lined orange cylinder beads (**C**)
- 1 gram size 11/0 metallic olive green cylinder beads (**D**)

BEADS FOR THE ODD-COUNT BRACELET

- 1 gram opaque bisque white ceylon cylinder beads (**A**)
- 1.5 gram opaque periwinkle cylinder beads (**B**)
- 1 gram matte opaque light mauve cylinder beads (**C**)
- 1 gram opaque chartreuse cylinder beads (**D**)
- 1 gram opaque mauve cylinder beads (**E**)

Patterns

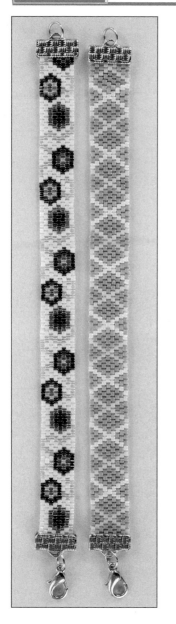

Even-Count Bracelet
Pattern

☐ = A   ■ = C
■ = B   ■ = D

Odd-Count Bracelet
Pattern

☐ = A ■ = C ■ = E
■ = B ☐ = D

TIP

Minimize Thread Changes by Starting at the Center of a Pattern

With both of these patterns, you can minimize the number of times that you need to begin a new thread by starting at the middle of the bracelet. Prepare a length of thread that is twice as long as you would normally feel comfortable working with, and place the bead stop at the center of the thread. Stitch the pattern until the thread begins to run out, and then return the needle to the extra-long tail (after removing the bead stop). Begin stitching rows in the opposite direction to build the second half of the bracelet.

Flat Peyote Stitch Bracelet with Picots

In this basic project, you use even-count peyote and two sizes of seed beads to create a textured flat band with picots along the edges.

Techniques and Materials

TECHNIQUES

In addition to the general techniques covered in Chapter 2, this project uses techniques from the following chapters and sections.

Chapter 3:

- "Weave Flat Peyote Stitch"

Chapter 9:

- "Make Beaded Picots, Fringe, and Drops"
- "Make End Loops and Attach Findings"

SUPPLIES AND FINDINGS

The items below are in addition to those listed under "Essential Tools and Supplies" in Chapter 1 (see page 16).

- Size 10 beading needle
- Size D Nymo beading thread in black
- 1 four-strand box clasp $^{15}/_{16}$-inch long with 3mm OD (outside diameter) jump rings (the example uses a sterling silver clasp with a floral design)

BEADS

This project uses Japanese seed and drop beads. Weights are rounded up to the nearest 0.5 gram and estimated based on an average-length bracelet.

- 5 grams size 11/0 opaque black seed beads (**A**)
- 4.5 grams size 8/0 opaque black seed beads (**B**)
- 1.5 grams size 14/0 or 15/0 opaque black seed beads (**C**)
- 4.5 grams 3.4mm opaque luster beige drop beads (**D**)

Directions

The sequence of beads in this project is shown with a diagram, rather than a graph pattern, so that you can see where to stitch the A beads in relation to the B beads and where and how to stitch the picots. Notice that every other column is made up of alternating A and B, and the remaining columns are all A. Until you get a feel for this motif, you can use a straight edge to keep your place in the diagram.

1 Using a prepared length of thread with the needle threaded, pick up 2A, 1B, 2A, 1B, 2A, 1B, 2A, 1B, and 2A, for a total of 14 beads. These will make up the first two rows. Position them, and your bead stop, so that you leave a tail approximately 9 inches long. (Do not weave-in this tail; use it later to attach the clasp.)

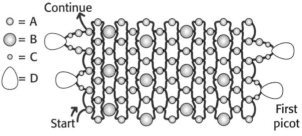

2 Use flat even-count peyote to stitch the third row (which is all A) according to the diagram. Recall from Chapter 3 that this also pulls the beads in the first and second rows into alignment. Keep the thread tension as taut as possible (see the FAQ on the next page for help).

3 Stitch the fourth row.

4 At the end of the fourth row, create a picot (see page 170) by picking up 1C, 1D, and 1C, before picking up 1A to begin the fifth row.

5 Stitch the fifth row according to the diagram, ending with the same picot that you created in Step 3.

6 Stitch the sixth, seventh, and eighth rows.

7 At the end of the eighth row, create a slightly longer picot by picking up 1A, 1C, 1D, 1C, and 1A, and then pick up another 1A to begin the eighth row.

8 Continue the pattern, alternating between sets of two rows that end without picots and sets of two rows that end with picots.

CONTINUED ON NEXT PAGE

TIP

Keep Track of High Beads and Low Beads

In Chapter 3, you learned that the high beads are the beads that you pass through in each peyote-stitch row, and the low beads are the ones that you skip over. When you stitch with the same size of bead, the high beads normally protrude beyond the low beads, making them easy to identify. However, when some beads are larger than others, like B in this project, you need to pay close attention to which beads are the actual high and low beads. In this case, a B that is a low bead (one that you should skip rather than pass through), may protrude farther outward than the adjacent A simply because it is taller than the A—not because it is a true high bead. You may find it helpful to work under a magnifier so that you can more easily identify the high and low beads.

9 Continue stitching to approximately your desired finished-bracelet length, less about ¼ inch plus the width of the box clasp. Then stitch the last six rows to match the first six rows, in reverse order. (The final two picots are short and the last two rows have no picots.)

10 To attach one half of the clasp, weave through the final row to create four small, simple loops, with each loop passing through a jump ring on the clasp. Make each loop by picking up 3C, then passing through a jump ring, and then picking up another 3C, for a total of 6C per loop.

Note: You may find it helpful to keep the clasp on a flat surface as you pass through its loops, to ensure that you pass through them in the proper direction.

11 Repeat Step 10 to attach the second half of the clasp to the other end of the bracelet, using the long tail. Take care to stitch-on this clasp piece so that it will latch properly with the first clasp piece.

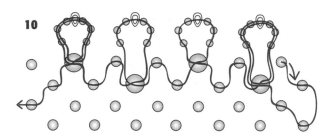

10

FAQ

How can I control thread tension while stitching the first few rows?

It is more difficult to keep thread tension tight when you use round seed beads rather than cylinder beads with the peyote stitch. Tension is even more challenging when you use two sizes of beads, like the A and B in this project. To keep the thread tight and the beads aligned properly for the first few rows, hold down the thread tail with the free fingers of your hand that is holding the beadwork, as shown here. If you keep the tail held tight, and gently tug on the needle-end of the thread after each stitch, you should be able to maintain the correct tension and stitch more comfortably.

Use even-count tubular peyote and graduating bead sizes to create dense, undulating ropes of beadwork. Zip-up the ends to create continuous rings that are perfect for adorning the napkins in your most stylish place settings.

Techniques and Materials

TECHNIQUES

In addition to the general techniques covered in Chapter 2, this project uses techniques from the following chapters and sections.

Chapter 3:

- "Create Tubular Peyote"
- "Zip-Up Peyote Stitch"

SUPPLIES AND FINDINGS

The items below are in addition to those listed under "Essential Tools and Supplies" in Chapter 1 (see page 16).

- Size 11 or 12 beading needle
- Size D C-Lon beading thread in chartreuse

BEADS

This project uses Japanese seed beads. The quantities below are for one napkin ring (multiply by the number of rings that you plan to make), and weights are rounded up to the nearest 0.5 gram.

- 1.5 grams size 11/0 crystal soft-blue lined seed beads (**A**)
- 4 grams size 8/0 silver-lined chartreuse seed beads (**B**)
- 1.5 grams size 11/0 transparent matte gold yellow seed beads (**C**)
- 1 gram size14/0 or 15/0 opaque light cream seed beads (**D**)

CONTINUED ON NEXT PAGE

Tubular Peyote
Napkin Rings *(continued)*

Directions

This approach to tubular peyote creates a relatively stiff beaded tube. It is important to keep the thread tension even, especially where you end an old thread and begin a new one (review the tip "Avoid Tension Problems in Thread Transition Zones" on page 38 in Chapter 2). Because this tube maintains its shape well, you probably do not need to use a form after the first few rounds.

1. Using a prepared length of thread with the needle threaded, pick up 1A, 2B, 2C, 2D, 2A, 2B, 2C, 2D, and 1A.

2. Pass through the first A again and pull the thread taut to create the initial ring of beads for even-count tubular peyote.

3. Begin stitching even-count tubular peyote, picking up the same color of bead that the needle exits after each stitch. The first bead in each new round is an A (numbered by round in the diagram). Notice that these A beads are also the beads that you pass through to step up at the end of each round.

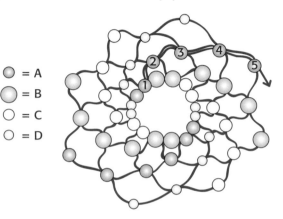

= A
= B
= C
= D

4. Continue stitching even-count tubular peyote, keeping the thread tension tight, until you have a tube that measures 5¾ inches long, bringing the needle out of the first 1A in the last round (the place where you would normally step up to begin another round).

5. Go back and weave-in the initial thread tail from your first length of thread, if you have not already done so. Again, take care to keep the thread tension relatively tight.

6. Inspect the entire tube for any areas of uneven tension. If you find an area of loose tension, weave-in a new thread and use it to reinforce that area by passing through beads (following the path of the existing thread as much as possible) and pulling the thread taut. Then, weave-in the end of this reinforcement thread.

7. Slowly and gently bend the tube into a circular shape, as shown.

7

8. Slightly flatten the circle in the area where the ends come together and then check the alignment of the beads. Recall from Chapter 3 that you must have an even number of rows or rounds to zip-up the peyote stitch. If your tube has an even number of rounds, the ends will fit together without altering the spiral pattern; if they do not fit together properly, go back and stitch one more full round at the end of the tube.

9 Align the ends for zipping-up and carefully stitch through one high bead at a time, alternating between one end of the tube and the other. Notice that you stitch sets of two high beads of the same color; from a high A on one end through a high A on the other end, then through a high B on one end and through a high B on the other end, and so on.

Note: *It's more challenging to zip up the inside of the napkin ring than the outside. Work slowly and carefully, and consider using a magnifier to help you see the beads.*

10 Pull the thread tight and then weave-in with knots, taking care to keep the tension even. The zipped tube ends should be seamless.

TIP

Knot Between the Largest Beads When Weaving-In

When you weave-in thread in a project that involves dense beadwork and varying bead sizes, like this one, it is often easiest to make knots only between the largest beads. Here, you can pass through two or three B at a time, making knots between these sets. You can also weave-in by passing through a large number of the smallest beads (D) without knots.

Netting and Right-Angle Weave Earrings

These colorful earrings begin with right-angle weave tops that serve as decorative bases for fans of vertical netting. You need to keep a close eye on the patterns as you work to make sure that you pick up beads in the proper number and sequence. If the multicolor pattern seems daunting, try them in a single color first for practice.

TECHNIQUES

In addition to the general techniques covered in Chapter 2, this project uses techniques from the following chapters and sections.

Chapter 4:

- "Create Vertical Netting"

Chapter 7:

- "Create Flat Right-Angle Weave"

SUPPLIES AND FINDINGS

The items below are in addition to those listed under "Essential Tools and Supplies" in Chapter 1 (see page 16).

- Size 13 beading needle
- Size D Nymo beading thread in olive
- 1 pair gold-filled French hook earring findings

BEADS

This project uses Japanese seed beads. Weights are rounded up to the nearest 0.5 gram and are per pair of earrings.

- 1 gram size 15/0 opaque luster medium orange seed beads (**A**)
- 1 gram size 15/0 transparent matte tourmaline seed beads (**B**)
- 1 gram size 15/0 opaque luster dark orange seed beads (**C**)
- 0.5 gram 11/0 opaque medium green seed beads (**D**)
- 0.5 gram size 15/0 shimmering icy green seed beads (**E**)

Directions and Patterns

MAKE THE EARRING TOPS

Stitch the top of each earring using flat right-angle weave. With this project, do *not* pass through each unit extra times for reinforcement.

1 Prepare a length of thread that is about 1½ arms' span long, without a bead stop.

2 After threading the needle, pick up all four beads for the first unit of flat right-angle weave, reading the pattern (a) from the bottom-left corner and moving in a clockwise direction around the first unit. (The first bead to pick up is labeled "1" in the pattern.)

3 Position the beads about 2 feet from the needle-end of the thread. (The extra-long tail is used later for the netting.)

4 Follow the pattern to stitch the first two unit rows of beadwork. Notice that the first unit row is regular right-angle weave, and the second is multiple-bead right-angle weave (the tops and bottoms of each unit contain one bead each, and the sides contain sets of the three beads each).

5 Begin the third unit row with an outside decrease. You should not need to weave through the beadwork to change the location of the thread; simply pass back through the second from last high bead in the previous row, which is marked with an asterisk in the pattern. (The first three beads that you pick up for the first unit of the third row are labeled "1," "2," and "3," respectively in the diagram [b].)

6 Complete the third unit row with an outside decrease by stopping one unit earlier than the end of the previous row.

7 You can now create the top loop: Following the path shown in the diagram (b), pass through the lower three beads in the last unit of the third unit row again, and then back through the second from last high bead in the third unit row.

CONTINUED ON NEXT PAGE

a

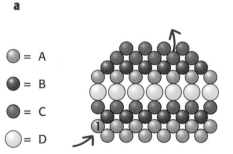

○ = A
● = B
● = C
○ = D

b

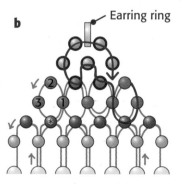

Earring ring

8. Pick up 1A and pass back through the third from last high bead in the third unit row, following the path shown in diagram (b) on the previous page.

9. Pull the thread taut and then pick up 2A.

10. Pass the needle through the bottom ring on the earring finding and then pick up another 2A.

11. Pass through all seven beads (outlined in diagram [b]) that make up the loop one more time.

12. Pull the thread taut and remove the needle from the thread. (You can weave-in and end the tail within the netting later.)

A completed earring without the loop is shown here (c).

A completed earring top with the loop completed is shown here (d).

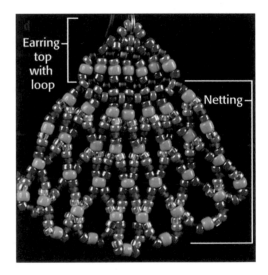

MAKE THE NETTING

1. Thread the needle onto the other end of the thread.

2. Begin the vertical-netting pattern on the next page by picking up 1B, 1C, and 1D.

3. Following the pattern, stitch the first column of netting, turn, and stitch the second column of netting.

4. At the top of the second column, pass back through the 1D, 1C, and 1B that you picked up in Step 2.

5. Pull the thread taut and then pass back through the bead in the earring top that the thread initially exited.

6. Moving clockwise, pass through the next two beads in that right-angle weave unit and pull the thread taut.

7. Following the pattern, stitch the next two columns of vertical netting. Begin by picking up 1B, 1C, and 1D. Pass back through those beads when you arrive back at the top of the netting.

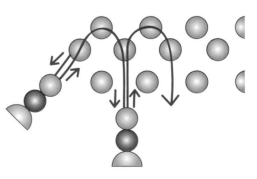

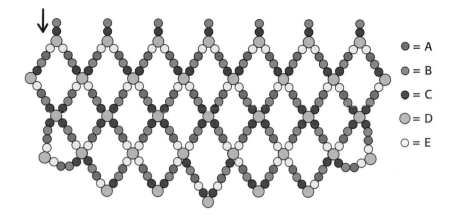

- = A
- = B
- = C
- = D
- = E

⑧ Using this same process, and following the pattern, stitch all of the vertical netting.

⑨ When the netting is complete, pass back into the earring top, reverse direction, and then pass down into the netting.

⑩ End the thread within a column of netting by weaving-in with knots.

⑪ Go back to the first thread tail and weave it through the earring top toward the netting.

⑫ End the second tail by weaving into one of the netting columns. Be sure to select a different column than the one you used to weave-in the first thread tail.

TIP

Tension and Reinforcement with Vertical Netting

It takes practice to stitch vertical netting with proper tension. The goal is to produce beadwork that is loose enough not to curl or twist, but tight enough that no more thread than necessary shows between beads. Do not get discouraged if your tension isn't perfect in your first netting project; it will become more even with every project that you complete.

In this project, the lower loops intentionally ruffle because they are larger than the upper loops. Even if you keep tight thread tension, the ruffles are relatively soft. To make them stiffer, you can weave back through all of the netting (following the path of existing thread), using size B or size 0 thread. Be sure to end this reinforcement thread within the netting, rather than within the earring top, which is already passed-through many times.

Tubular Brick Stitch Slider Necklace

The focal piece for this simple necklace is a hollow brass tube covered with tubular brick stitch. This beaded slider floats on a sturdy leather cord adorned with coordinating metal beads.

Techniques and Materials

TECHNIQUES

In addition to the general techniques covered in Chapter 2, this project uses techniques from the following chapters and sections.

Chapter 5:

- "Create Tubular Brick Stitch"

Chapter 9 tip:

- "Opening and Closing Jump Rings"

SUPPLIES AND FINDINGS

The items below are in addition to those listed under "Essential Tools and Supplies" in Chapter 1 (see page 16).

- Size 12 beading needle
- Size D Nymo beading thread in cream
- 2¾-inch curved brass tube in antiqued brass finish
- About 16–20 inches of brown 1.8mm Greek leather cord
- Household scissors or snips for cutting the leather cord
- 2 gold-tone fold-over crimp ends for cord
- E6000 (or similar) glue
- 2 gold-tone twisted-wire 6mm OD (outside diameter) jump rings
- 1 gold-tone 12mm lobster clasp
- Pliers for opening and closing jump rings

BEADS

This project uses Japanese seed beads. Weights are rounded up to the nearest 0.5 gram.

- 1 gram size 11/0 transparent yellow seed beads (**A**)
- 1 gram size 11/0 transparent light orange seed beads (**B**)
- 1 gram size 11/0 transparent medium orange seed beads (**C**)
- 2 gold-plated 7mm pewter Bali-style rondelle beads with 2mm holes

Directions

MAKE THE BEADED SLIDER

1 Beginning with an arms'-span length of conditioned thread, use 10A to stitch a ladder row.

2 Reinforce the ladder (see page 117), and then connect the ends to create the first round of tubular brick stitch.

3 Slip the ring onto the curved brass tube and position it about ¼ inch from one end of the tube, with the needle-end of the thread exiting toward that same end.

4 Using the tube as a form, stitch 42 more full rounds of tubular brick stitch following the sequence shown below. Slide the beadwork down the curved brass tube as you work so that you can cover the entire tube with beads.

- 6 rounds of 10A
- 9 rounds of 10B
- 11 rounds of 10C
- 9 rounds of 10B
- 7 rounds of 10A

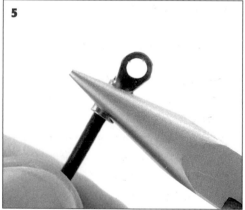

5

5 After ending the final thread and weaving-in all of the thread tails, use your fingers to center the beadwork on the curved brass tube. The beadwork should cover nearly all of the tube with only a very small area of metal visible at either end.

ASSEMBLE THE NECKLACE

1 Use household scissors or snips to cut the leather cord to your desired necklace length less about 1 inch (for the clasp).

2 Apply a small drop of glue to the inside of one fold-over crimp end.

3 Place one end of the cord inside of the crimp end.

4 Use chain nose pliers to gently squeeze down one side, or "wing," of the crimp end against the leather cord.

5 Use the pliers to gently press down the other side of the crimp, which may slightly overlap the first.

6 String one gold-plated bead onto the cord.

7 Slide the beaded slider tube onto the cord.

8 String the second gold-plated bead onto the cord.

9 Repeat Steps 2–5 to attach the second fold-over crimp end to the other end of the leather cord.

10 Attach the clasp to the crimp ends using jump rings.

To clasp the necklace, open the lobster clasp and clip it onto the jump ring on the opposite end of the necklace.

Flat Square Stitch Finger Ring

This modern finger ring features a square-stitch panel that incorporates three sizes and shapes of beads. The band, or *ring shank*, is made up of simple strands of size 14/0 seed beads. This design works well with many different combinations of colors. Select your own and let your creativity flow.

Techniques and Materials

TECHNIQUES
In addition to the general techniques covered in Chapter 2, this project uses techniques from the following chapters and sections.

Chapter 5:

- "Transition into Flat Brick Stitch"
- "Perform Brick Stitch Increases and Decreases"

Chapter 6:

- "Create Flat Square Stitch"

BASIC SUPPLIES AND FINDINGS
The items below are in addition to those listed under "Essential Tools and Supplies" in Chapter 1 (see page 16).

- Size 11 or 12 beading needle
- Size 13 beading needle
- Size D Nymo beading thread in a neutral or coordinating color

BEADS
All of the beads used in this project are manufactured in Japan. Weights are rounded up to the nearest 0.5 gram.

- 12 cube beads (3mm) in the color of your choice (**A**)
- 13 size 11/0 seed beads in the color of your choice (**B**)
- 3 drop beads (3.4mm) in the color of your choice (**C**)
- 0.5 gram size 14/0 seed beads in the color of your choice (**D**)

STITCH THE FRONT PANEL

1 Begin with a prepared length of thread that is about 1½ arms'-span long, with the size 12 needle attached and a bead stop secured about 12 inches from the loose end of the thread.

2 Pick up 1A, 1B, 1A, 1B, 1A, 1B, and 1A, and slide them against the bead stop. These make up the first row of square stitch.

3 For the second row, individually square-stitch each of the following: 1A, 1C, 1A, 1C, 1A, 1C, and 1A. Treat the C as if they were regular seed beads with centered holes. The tension may seem loose; keep it as tight as you can for now to make stitching easier. As you increase the tension, the beadwork should begin to curve.

4 Reinforce by passing through all of the beads in the first row, then the second row, and pulling the thread taut. Be careful not to skip over a B or C between pairs of A.

5 Pull the thread taut, and stitch the third row of square stitch, using the sequence of beads from Step 2. Make sure that all of the C in the second row face the same direction (toward you) as you stitch each B.

6 Reinforce by passing through all of the beads in the second and third rows again.

7 Pull the thread taut so that the last row of beadwork curves further into an arc.

8 Make a half-hitch knot over the first bridge of thread on the edge of the beadwork to preserve the tension and the arc shape.

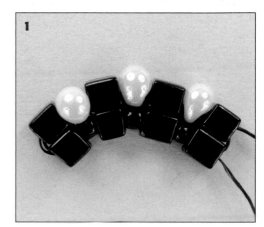

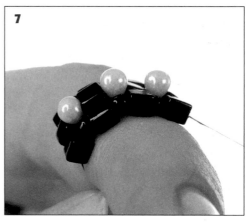

9 Pick up 2B and brick-stitch them onto the same bridge of thread that you knotted over in Step 8. Stitch through both beads using the technique you normally use to begin a row of brick stitch. (Because you stitch two beads onto the same bridge of thread, this is an outside increase.)

10 Pick up 1B and brick-stitch it onto the next bridge of thread.

11 Pick up 1B and brick-stitch it as an outside increase at the end of the row (see page 107), treating the last column of square stitch as if it were the previous row of brick stitch.

12 Pick up 2D and brick-stitch them to begin the second actual row of brick stitch. Allow the automatic, beginning-of-row decrease to occur (that is, do not make an increase).

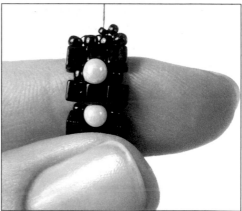

CONTINUED ON NEXT PAGE

⓭ Stitch 1D onto the next bridge of thread.

⓮ Remove the needle from the thread.

⓯ Remove the bead stop from the other end of the thread and thread the needle there.

⓰ Pull the thread taut so that the first row of square stitch curves into an arc, matching the tension of the last row of square stitch.

⓱ Make a half-hitch knot over the first bridge of thread on this edge of the beadwork to preserve the tension.

⓲ Repeat Steps 9–13.

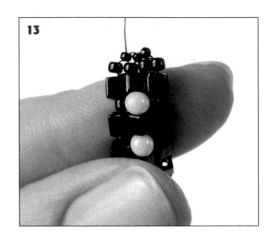

MAKE THE RING SHANK

Create the ring shank by stringing three strands of beads that each connect to both ends of the front panel.

① Thread the size 13 needle onto the other (longer) thread tail.

② Pick up enough B to reach all the way around the widest part of your finger (on which you plan to wear the ring) and to the other edge of the front panel. Hold the front portion of the ring against the underside of your finger when you do this, as shown. (The example uses 35B.)

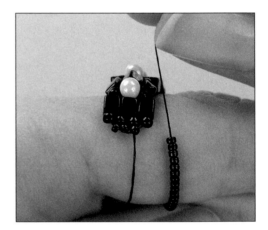

TIP

Design and Care for Beaded Finger Rings to Make Them Last Longer

When you design bead-woven rings, make them as durable as possible by using multiple passes of thread through the ring shank (as in this project) and by using a dense stitch (like square stitch or brick stitch). Optionally, you can use an extra-strong beading thread, like Power Pro (see page 13). Additionally, make sure that your rings do not fit too tightly, which increases wear, and do not allow them to get wet—especially if you use nylon thread, like Nymo. Water removes conditioner and causes nylon thread to stretch.

③ Weave into the front panel to reverse direction. If the needle sticks inside of a bead here, it should be safe to use chain nose pliers to gently tug it through.

④ Pull the thread taut and then pass back through all of the beads that you picked up in Step 2, going through several beads at a time.

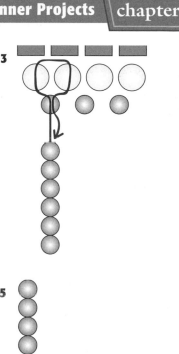

⑤ Pull the thread taut again and then weave through the front panel to change direction again, this time bringing the thread out through the next B on the edge.

⑥ Pick up the same number of B that you picked up in Step 2.

⑦ Repeat Steps 3–5 to attach this strand to the ring.

⑧ Begin one more ring-shank strand by repeating Step 6.

⑨ Repeat Steps 3–5 to attach this strand to the ring.

⑩ Change direction again (as you did in Step 3), and then pass back through several beads in the final shank strand.

⑪ Weave-in with knots within this strand to end the thread. Take care to ensure that each knot tightens down between two beads and not on top of a bead.

⑫ Weave-in and end the other thread tail in a different strand of the shank.

Flat Herringbone Bracelet

Bold stripes accentuate the distinctive pattern of herringbone stitch in this stylish band bracelet.

Techniques and Materials

TECHNIQUES

In addition to the general techniques covered in Chapter 2, this project uses techniques from the following chapters and sections.

Chapter 8:

- "Weave Flat Herringbone Stitch"

Chapter 9:

- "Make End Loops and Attach Findings"

BASIC SUPPLIES AND FINDINGS

The items below are in addition to those listed under "Essential Tools and Supplies" in Chapter 1 (see page 16). To attach these clamp ends, use the "Attach a Clamp End by Sliding" technique on page 176.

- Size 11 beading needle
- Size D Nymo beading thread in black
- Pair of 1-inch pewter-finish clamp ends
- 2 pewter-finish 6mm x 4mm oval jump rings
- Pewter-finish ball-and-socket clasp
- Pliers for jump rings and clamp ends
- E6000 (or similar) glue

BEADS

All of the beads used in this project are manufactured in Japan. Weights are rounded up to the nearest 0.5 gram and are approximate, based on an average-length bracelet.

- 2.5 grams size 11/0 white-lined transparent light brown seed beads (**A**)
- 2.5 grams size 11/0 opaque turquoise green seed beads (**B**)
- 2 grams size 11/0 matte transparent orange seed beads (**C**)
- 2 grams size 11/0 grape-lined amethyst seed beads (**D**)
- 2 grams size 11/0 silver-lined matte peridot seed beads (**E**)

Directions

1. Using a prepared length of thread with the needle attached, stitch and reinforce a 12-bead ladder row using 1A, 1B, 1C, 1D, 1E, 1A, 1B, 1C, 1D, 1E, 1A, and 1B.

2. Turn, and stitch the first row of flat herringbone from a base row, matching the color of each bead with that of the bead directly beneath it in the ladder row (this is the reverse order of beads in Step 1). Optionally, use the alternative turn described in the tip on page 160 to avoid exposing thread along the edges.

3. Continue the flat herringbone stitch, completing one row at a time and extending the vertical stripes until the beadwork is about ⅞ inch shorter than your desired bracelet length, including the clasp.

4. After weaving-in and ending all thread tails, attach a clamp end to each end of the band.

5. Attach the clasp pieces using the jump rings, making sure that both parts of the clasp face the proper direction.

TIP

Working with Tension and Reinforcing Herringbone Stitch

When you use true seed beads with herringbone stitch, as in this project, you have the option to use either gentle thread tension or tight tension. Gentle tension results in softer, more fluid beadwork that is more prone to showing "holes" or inconsistently sized spaces between beads. When you keep the tension tight (gently tugging after each stitch), the beadwork is stiffer, but the beads align more regularly. In this photo, the beadwork on the right is stitched with gentle tension, and the beadwork on the left with tight tension.

If unwanted spaces do occur between beads as you work, you can close them by reinforcing columns. When you reach the place in a row that is above the area with the space, pass down through that column until the space closes, then reverse direction and pass back up to the current row through an adjacent column. As always, follow the path of existing thread as much as possible.

chapter 11

Intermediate Projects

These intermediate-level projects are slightly more complex than those in Chapter 10, but after a little practice with the basic stitches, you should be ready to give them a try. Be sure to read and follow each step carefully, and take your time stitching each piece. Just like with the beginner projects, feel free to use different bead colors and experiment with your own variations and details.

Circular Peyote Briolette Cap Earrings

This project is an example of how you can use a circular stitch to cover the top of a curved object—in this case, a large briolette drop. Varying bead sizes and a transition from regular to two-drop peyote allows the beadwork to conform to the shape of the briolette. Multiple passes of thread add tension to maintain the shape of the beadwork caps.

Techniques and Materials

TECHNIQUES

In addition to the general techniques covered in Chapter 2, this project uses techniques from the following chapters and sections.

Chapter 3:

- "Make Circular Peyote"

Chapter 9:

- "Make End Loops and Attach Findings"

SUPPLIES AND FINDINGS

The items below are in addition to those listed under "Essential Tools and Supplies" in Chapter 1 (see page 16).

- Size 10 or 11 beading needle
- Size D Nymo beading thread in baby pink or dark rose
- Pair of gold-filled lever-back earring findings
- 2 gold-filled 4mm OD (outside diameter) jump rings
- Clear nail polish
- Pliers for opening and closing jump rings

BEADS

This project uses Japanese seed beads and a glass briolette made in China. Weights are rounded up to the nearest 0.5 gram.

- 2 large (25mm x 17mm x 8mm), clear glass ("glass quartz"), faceted briolette drops
- 1 gram size 11/0 dark rose-lined crystal seed beads (**A**)
- 8 size 15/0 transparent rainbow crystal seed beads (**B**)
- 12 size 11/0 transparent luster crystal seed beads (**C**)
- 24 size 8/0 magenta-lined crystal seed beads (**D**)

Directions and Pattern

MAKE THE TOP LOOP

1 Begin with a prepared length of conditioned thread that is about 2½ feet long, with the needle threaded. Take the time to pre-stretch the thread especially well.

2 String the briolette and position it about 6 inches from the loose end of the thread.

3 Tie a surgeon's knot against the narrow edge of the briolette. The thread should be taut so that the knot rests directly against the briolette.

4 Apply a small drop of clear nail polish to the knot.

5 Pass through the hole in the briolette and gently pull the knot into the hole.

6 Trim the short tail of thread near the briolette hole.

7 Pick up 1A, 2B, one closed jump ring, and another 2B. (The 1A is the base bead for the loop.)

8 Pass back down through the 1A while centering it against the top of the briolette and pull the thread taut. (A good way to do this is to rest the briolette against your work surface and hold the beads and jump ring against the top of the briolette with one hand while you pull the thread taut with the other.)

9 Pass through the briolette again.

10 Pass beneath both strands of thread that are against the edge of the briolette, next to the base of the beaded loop, and make a half-hitch knot over those threads. This secures the thread tension and helps to keep the beaded loop centered.

11 Pass back up through the 1A, through all of the beads in the loop again (passing through one or two beads at a time), and then back down through the 1A.

12 Pull the thread taut.

STITCH THE CIRCULAR PEYOTE CAP

1 Pick up 3A and then pass through all of the beads in the loop again, as shown in the diagram.

CONTINUED ON NEXT PAGE

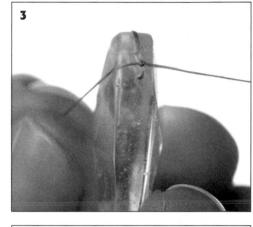

3

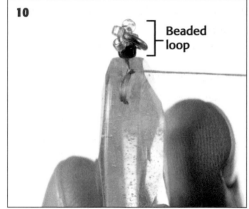

10

Beaded loop

Jump ring

● = A

○ = B

First 3A

Second 3A

Briolette

2 Pass through all of the 3A again.

3 Pull the thread taut and pick up another 3A (see the diagram on the previous page).

4 Bring the 3A from Step 3 all the way around the base of the beaded loop and then pass through the nearest (and last) A that you picked up in Step 1.

5 Pull the thread taut. You now effectively have a ring of 6A surrounding the center loop.

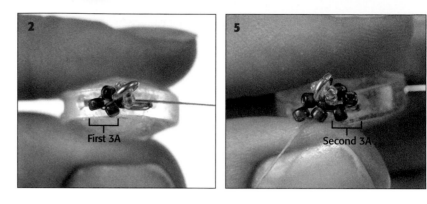

6 Keeping the thread pulled taut, tie a half-hitch knot over the existing thread between beads to secure the tension.

7 Pick up 1C to begin stitching circular peyote, treating the ring of the 6 beads (see Step 5) as the central ring of the beadwork.

8 Follow the pattern, on the next page, to complete the next three rounds. The bead marked with an asterisk is the first bead that you pick up.

9 Pass through all of the beads in the last two of those three rounds again (passing from a high bead, to the next low bead, to the next high, and so on.) These are the two rounds of size 8/0 beads, and reinforcing them bulks up the thread within their larger holes. (This second pass is not shown in the pattern.)

10 Bring the needle out of the beadwork on one narrow edge of the briolette, near its hole.

11 Pass through the hole in the briolette.

⑫ Weave into the beadwork on the other side of the briolette and bring the needle out of a high bead in the last round. (The beadwork is now better secured to the briolette and should not spin.)

CONTINUED ON NEXT PAGE

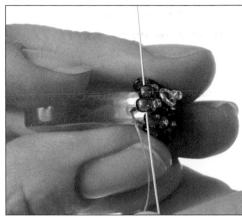

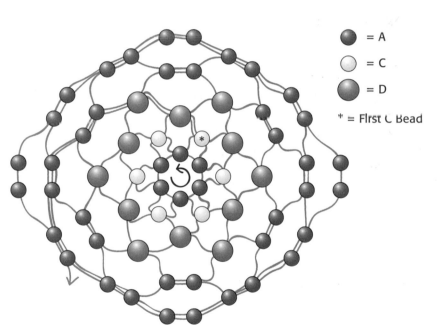

● = A

○ = C

🔵 = D

* = First C Bead

⑬ Pick up 2A and begin stitching two-drop circular peyote (stitching two beads at a time instead of one).

⑭ Following the pattern, complete three full rounds of two-drop peyote with A.

⑮ Weave through the last two rounds as necessary to reposition the needle and bring the needle out of the next high drop that is nearest the narrow edge of the briolette.

⑯ Pick up 2A and pass through the next high drop in the last round.

⑰ Weave through the last two rounds and bring the needle out after the next high drop that is nearest the narrow edge on the other side of the briolette.

⑱ Pull the thread taut and repeat Step 16.

⑲ End the thread by weaving-in with knots.

⑳ To attach the earring finding, use chain nose pliers to gently position the jump ring so that its opening faces upward and away from the beadwork.

㉑ Open the jump ring, slide it through the bottom ring on the earring finding, and then close the jump ring.

㉒ Complete all of the steps again to make a matching earring for your pair.

This long, lacy anklet is a wide band of flat horizontal netting with turning-bead edges. The loops gradually increase in size from one side of the beadwork to the other, giving this piece its elegant, expanding drape. Pairs of side-by-side link beads add a subtle flourish.

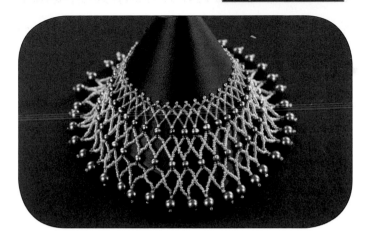

Techniques and Materials

TECHNIQUES

In addition to the general techniques covered in Chapter 2, this project uses techniques from the following chapters and sections.

Chapter 4:

- "Create Flat Horizontal Netting"

Chapter 9:

- "Make End Loops and Attach Findings"

MATERIALS

The items below are in addition to those listed under "Essential Tools and Supplies" in Chapter 1 (see page 16).

- Size 12 beading needle
- Size B Nymo beading thread in white
- 4 oval antique-brass-finish 5mm x 3mm jump rings
- 2 antique-brass-finish ball-in-loop clasps

BEADS

This project uses Japanese seed beads. Weights are rounded up to the nearest 0.5 gram, and based on an average-sized anklet.

- 2 grams size 15/0 transparent matte teal seed beads (**A**)
- 7.5 grams size 15/0 shimmering teal seed beads (**B**)
- 0.5 gram size 11/0 white-lined teal seed beads (**C**)
- 0.5 gram size 11/0 white-lined golden yellow seed beads (**D**)
- 68 light bronze round 4mm natural seed-pearl beads (**E**)
- 0.5 gram size 15/0 transparent teal seed beads (**F**)
- 34 bronze Swarovski glass round 6mm pearl beads (**G**)

CONTINUED ON NEXT PAGE

Directions and Pattern

As you stitch the horizontal netting in this project, do your best to keep the thread tension taut and even. You may find it easier to stitch the larger loops with the beadwork lying on your work surface, rather than held up in your hands.

1. Prepare a length of thread with the bead stop positioned about 16 inches from the loose end. (When you come back to weave-in this tail, use it to reinforce the tension in the first row by passing through all of the beads in that row again.)

2. Begin stitching horizontal netting, following the pattern below. Keep in mind that the number of beads varies from loop to loop within each row.

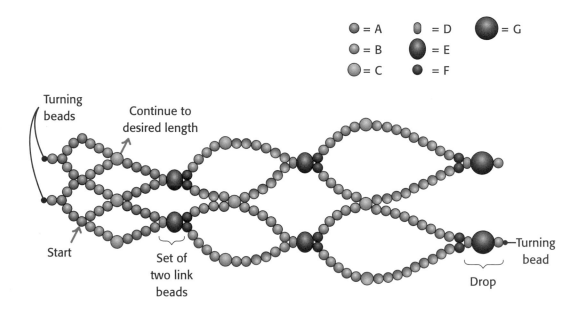

3 Continue stitching, repeating the pattern, until the beadwork reaches comfortably around your ankle, *less* about ¾ inch (for the clasp).

4 Begin a final row, but only stitch the first loop of netting (shown in the upper-left portion of the pattern).

5 If you have not yet woven-in the original thread tail at the beginning of the beadwork, move the needle and do so now. Remember to use that tail to reinforce the first row (see Step 1).

6 Return the needle to the thread exiting the last row of beadwork and reinforce the last full row by passing through it again.

7 Weave-in to end the thread.

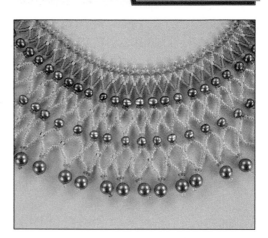

8 Use jump rings to attach the clasps to the first and second loops on both ends of beadwork. Make sure that both clasps face the proper direction.

TIP

Weaving-In to Begin and End Thread in Horizontal Netting
Recall from Chapter 2 that you should weave-in following the path of existing thread whenever possible. With horizontal netting, this limits you to passing through beads that make up the same horizontal row, and never changing direction mid-row. If you need to change direction in order to make more knots, or to position a new thread properly to begin where the old thread left off, always weave all the way to the end of the row before changing direction. In this project, pass through the turning bead or beads, following the path of the original thread.

Tubular Netting and Peyote Bezel Necklace

This project is an introduction to beaded-bezel making. It features a round cabochon surrounded by circular peyote beadwork, and suspended by a brick stitch bail. The supple rope is made entirely with three-bead tubular netting. Because this design uses tiny size 14/0 beads, it's a good idea to work under a magnifier. You also need to hold the beadwork in the very tips of your fingers, especially when stitching the bail.

Techniques and Materials

TECHNIQUES

In addition to the general techniques covered in Chapter 2, this project uses techniques from the following chapters and sections.

Chapter 3:
- "Make Circular Peyote"

Chapter 4:
- "Make Tubular Netting"

Chapter 5:
- "Perform Brick Stitch Increases and Decreases"

SUPPLIES

The items below are in addition to those listed under "Essential Tools and Supplies" in Chapter 1 (see page 16).

- Size 12 beading needle
- Size 13 beading needle
- Size D Nymo beading thread in ash
- Size B Nymo beading thread in ash
- 20mm round cabochon (the example uses a peach and orange speckled composite stone; alternatives include rhyolite, unakite, ocean jasper, crazy lace agate, or vintage glass)
- 10mm gold-filled lobster clasp
- 2 gold-filled 5mm OD (outside diameter) jump rings

BEADS

This project uses Japanese seed beads. Weights are rounded to the nearest 0.5 gram and are estimated based on an average-length necklace.

- 4 grams size 14/0 silver-lined rainbow orange seed beads (**A**)
- 4.5 grams size 14/0 transparent rainbow medium pale peach seed beads (**B**)
- 4 grams size 14/0 white-lined light olive seed beads (**C**)
- 4.5 grams size 14/0 crystal luster yellow seed beads (**D**)

Directions and Patterns

MAKE THE ROPE

In this three-bead tubular netting, the A beads serve as link beads. Because the completed rope needs to support the weight of a pendant, it is especially important to pre-stretch and condition the thread well to keep it from stretching over time.

1. Beginning with a conditioned, arms'-span length of size D thread with the size 12 needle threaded, pick up 1A, 1B, 1A, 1C, 1A, 1B, 1A, 1C, 1A, 1B, 1A, and 1C.

2. Position the beads about 10 inches from the loose end of the thread. (Do not weave-in this tail until you are ready to attach the clasp.)

3. **Optional:** Bring the first 1A and the last 1C toward each other and tie a square knot to create the initial ring of beads.

4. Pass through the first 1A and again and pull the thread taut.

5. Stitch three-bead tubular netting, picking up three beads at a time in colors matching the underlying three beads in the previous round. This creates vertical stripes along the tube. Try to keep the thread tension relatively tight, and remember to step up at the end of each round.

6. When the rope measures about 12–13 inches long when laid out on your work surface, hold it up around your neck in front of a mirror, with the ends spaced about 1 inch apart at the back. Because the rope slightly lengthens when held up, this allows you to check its actual length. If it needs to be longer, continue stitching, periodically checking its length in front of a mirror.

7. When you reach your desired length, pick up 2A, 1C, and 6A.

8. Pass back through the 1C (a base bead for the loop) again and pull the thread taut.

9. Pick up another 2A and then pass into the beadwork on the opposite side of the final round to complete this end loop.

10. Weave-in and end this thread.

11. Repeat Steps 7–9 on the other end of the rope, using the initial thread tail to create the other end loop, and then weave-in and end this thread.

12. Attach one jump ring to one of the end loops and attach the clasp to the other end loop using the other jump ring.

CONTINUED ON NEXT PAGE

MAKE THE BEZEL

Begin with the back of the bezel, stitching until the rounds reach the edges of the cabochon. Then add more rounds to conform the bezel to the sides of the cabochon and hold it in place. Remember to step up at the end of each round of circular peyote stitch before you begin the next round.

① Beginning with a prepared length of size D thread with the size 12 needle threaded, pick up 24B.

② Pass through the first B again and pull the thread taut to bring the beads into a ring. This is the initial ring of circular peyote stitch.

③ Begin the next round by picking up 1B (marked with an asterisk in the pattern below on this page), skipping a B in the ring, and then passing through the next B in the ring.

④ Following the pattern, pick up 2B, skip 1B, and pass through the next B in the ring. Alternate between picking up 1B and 2B for each stitch for the entire round. This completes the third round of beadwork.

Note: *Keep gentle, but not tight, tension on the thread as you stitch each round so that the beadwork remains flat.*

⑤ Stitch the fourth and fifth rounds by picking up 1A and skipping one bead in the previous round for each stitch.

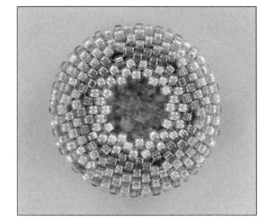

Back of completed bezel

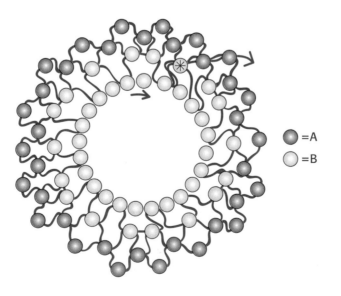

◯ = A
◯ = B

6 Stitch the sixth round by repeating this sequence until you arrive back at the beginning of the round: Pick up 1D and skip one bead in the previous round, pick up 2D and skip one bead in the previous round, and pick up 1D and skip one bead in the previous round. (Pick up another 1D to begin the sequence again.)

7 Stitch the seventh and eighth rounds by picking up 1D and skipping one bead in the previous round for each stitch.

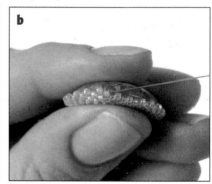

= A
= B
= D

8 At this point, check to see whether the bead-work reaches the edges of the back of the cab-ochon. If it does not, stitch one or more rounds like those in Step 7 until the beadwork covers the entire back of the cabochon (excluding the hole at the center of the bead-work) and overlaps the cabochon by the width of about one bead all the way around (a).

9 Stitch one more round by picking up 1D and skipping one bead in the previous round for each stitch.

10 Place the cabochon, back side down, onto the beadwork and hold it there with your thumb as you stitch the remaining rounds (b).

a   b

11 Stitch the next round by picking up 1B and skipping one bead in the previous round for each stitch.

12 Stitch another round by picking up 1A and skipping one bead in the previous round for each stitch.

13 Repeat Step 12 one or two more times, keeping the thread pulled tight, until there is just enough beadwork along the edges of the cabochon to keep the cabochon from falling out.

14 Pass through the last two rounds again (from a high bead, to a low bead, to a high bead, and so on) for reinforcement. Keep the thread pulled tight.

15 Weave-in using knots and end the thread.

16 Go back and weave-in the tail on the back of the bezel, if you have not already done so.
CONTINUED ON NEXT PAGE

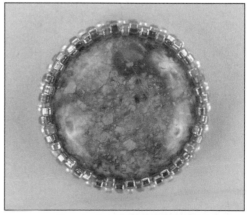

Front of completed bezel

STITCH THE BAIL

The bail is easiest to stitch in two separate halves, which you then join together.

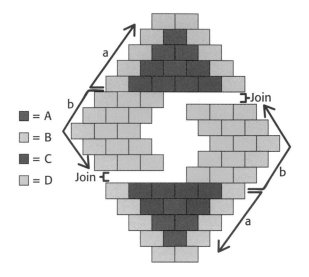

= A
= B
= C
= D

1 Beginning with a 2-foot length of prepared size B thread with the size 13 needle threaded, stitch and reinforce a ladder row at the center point of the thread (that is, leave a tail of about half the thread length), using 1B, 4C, and 1B. This is the longest row in the first half of the bail.

2 Following the pattern, stitch four rows of brick stitch (a), allowing each row to automatically decrease, until you complete the final row of 2B. However, in that final row, do not pass through both beads as you normally would at the beginning a row. Instead, pick up both beads, pass beneath the second bridge of thread, pass back through the second bead again, and stop. (This leaves more space in the bead holes for passing through them again when you later attach the bail to the bezel.)

3 Remove the needle and thread it onto the long thread tail exiting the first row.

4 Brick-stitch the next five rows (b), making outside increases and decreases as indicated in the pattern, and bringing the needle out through the middle bead in the last row.

5 Set this first half of the bail aside and repeat Steps 1–4 to create the second half.

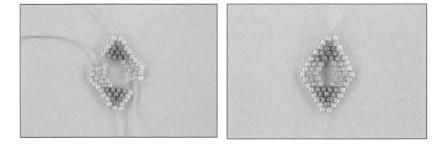

6 Holding the two halves together, use existing thread tails to join them on both sides where indicated in the above pattern. The best way to do this is to stitch over bridges of thread, as shown in the diagram on the right. Then pass through the outermost beads (B beads), and end the thread by weaving-in. Because the beadwork is dense, you can weave-in by passing through the diagonal line of B on the edge, and you only need to make one or two knots before trimming the thread.

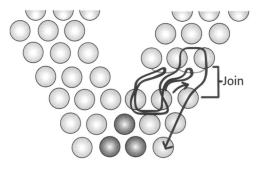

CONNECT THE ROPE, BAIL, AND BEZEL

Complete the necklace by stitching the bail to the edge of the bezel while wrapping the bezel around the rope.

 Thread the size 13 needle onto the tail at one end of the bail.

2 Pass through 1B on the edge of the bezel, as shown. Use the part of the bezel that you would like to be the top of the pendant.

3 Pass through the 2B that make up the last row of brick stitch on the end of the bail, beginning on the opposite side of the row from which the thread exits. Because the beads lie vertically in brick stitch, this action pulls them into a different, horizontal alignment.

4 Pass through the 1B on the bezel again and pull the thread tight.

5 Pass through the 2B on the bail again and pull the thread tight. Try to eliminate any space between the 1B on the bezel and the 2B on the bail.

6 Pass through the 1B on the bezel one more time and then weave into the bezel to end the thread.

End of bail

= A

= B

Bead in bezel

7 Bend the bail backward into a curve over the center of the rope.

8 Use the same technique that you used in Steps 2–6, using the tail on the other end of the bail, to stitch this end to the bezel, but pass through a D on the top edge of the bezel that is in the *same column* as the B that you passed through in Step 2.

The necklace is now complete.

Spiral Rope and Herringbone Pendant Necklace

This frilly yet contemporary necklace features a basic spiral rope chain and a ruffled herringbone stitch pendant. The pendant is stitched without a base row and accented with Czech fire-polished glass beads.

Techniques and Materials

TECHNIQUES

In addition to the general techniques covered in Chapter 2, this project uses techniques from the following chapters and sections.

Chapter 6:

- "Stitch Spiral Rope"

Chapter 8:

- "Flat Herringbone Without-a-Base Row"

Chapter 9:

- "Loops with Base Beads"

SUPPLIES

The items below are in addition to those listed under "Essential Tools and Supplies" in Chapter 1 (see page 16).

- Size 15 beading needle
- Size B Nymo beading thread in dark rose
- 1 pewter tone ball and socket clasp
- 1 pewter tone 4mm jump rings
- Chain nose pliers for opening and closing jump rings

BEADS

This project uses Miyuki Delica cylinder beads and Czech fire-polished glass beads. Weights are rounded up to the nearest 0.5 gram.

- 1 gram salmon satin cylinder beads (**A**)
- 2.5 grams dark rose silver-lined semi matte dark rose cylinder beads (**B**)
- 0.5 grams light peach satin cylinder bead (**C**)
- 5 Czech peach/pear fire-polished 4mm glass beads (**D**)

Directions and Pattern

MAKE THE ROPE

Stitch the necklace rope using a basic spiral rope technique. Finish the ends with end loops, as illustrated in the diagram on the right.

1. Begin with a prepared length of conditioned thread that is the longest you feel comfortable working with.

2. Begin spiral rope by picking up 3A (the core beads) and 2B (the loop beads). Leave a thread tail about 8 inches long to make an end loop later.

3. Pass through all 3A again, and pull the thread taut.

4. Pick 1A and 2B.

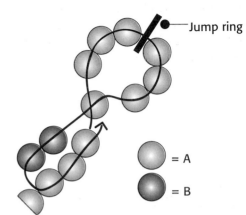

Jump ring

= A

= B

5. Continue spiral rope by passing through the last 3A in the core and through the 1A you just picked up and then pulling the thread taut.

6. Stitch to your desired finished necklace length, less about ¾ inch.

7. Pick 7A and a jump ring that is attached to one part of the clasp.

8. Pass back through the first A that you picked up in Step 7, and pull the thread taut to complete an end loop with a base bead.

9. Pass through the last two B in the spiral rope, and then back up through the last 3A and the entire end loop one more time for reinforcement.

10. Weave into the spiral rope to end the thread.

11. Repeat Steps 7–10 on the other end of the rope, using the initial thread tail.

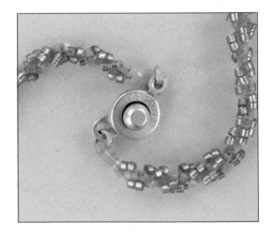

MAKE THE PENDANT

Use the pattern on the next page along with these directions to complete the pendant.

1. Using a new length of thread that is about an arms'-span long, pick up 20B for the first two rounds of herringbone without-a-base row (see page 150).

2. Stitch the third row (and pull the first and second rows into alignment) using 10C.

3. Complete the next three rows (rows 4–6) by stitching 10B for each row.

4. Stitch the spines in row 7 using a total of 10B and making mid-row increases of 1C between spines (see page 161).

5. Stitch row 8 the same way you stitched row 7, but this time make mid-row between-spine increases of 2C each.

CONTINUED ON NEXT PAGE

6 At the end of row 8 pick up the last bead in the row but *not* the first bead for row 9 (as you normally would). Instead, pick up 1D before passing into the first bead in the next spine.

7 Pull the thread taut, and pick up 1C before passing down into the second bead in that spine.

8 Continue stitching 1D between spines and 1C within spines to the end of the row. End the row by passing down through the last bead in the previous row so that the thread points toward the first row of beadwork (see the upper-left arrow in the pattern).

9 Go back and weave-in the original thread tail, if you haven't already done so.

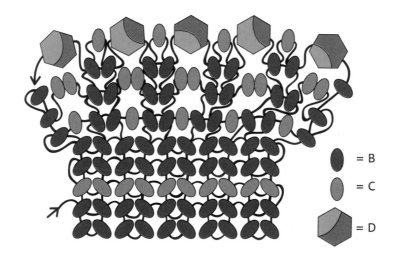

= B

= C

= D

🔟 Using the remaining thread, pass through all of the beads in the outside column of the beadwork and bring the thread out of the first bead in the first row. This positions the thread to make the first bail loop.

⓫ Pick up 12B for the first loop, and slide them down against the edge of the beadwork.

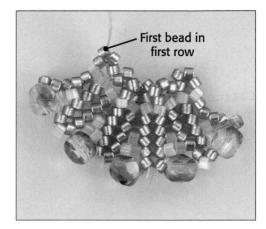

First bead in first row

⓬ Place the completed rope on top of the 12B, with the pendant centered along the rope, as shown.

⓭ Bringing the needle over the rope, pass back through the first B that you picked up in Step 11, and pull the thread taut to complete a loop with a base bead around the rope.

⓮ Pass through the second bead in the first row of beadwork, and then up through the first bead and the loop one more time for reinforcement.

⓯ Weave through the first row of beadwork, following the path of existing thread as much as possible, and bring the needle out through the second from last bead in the first row.

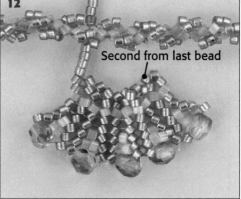

12

Second from last bead

⓰ Repeat Steps 11–14 to create the second bail loop.

⓱ Weave-in to end the thread within the herringbone beadwork.

Embellished Right-Angle Weave Bracelet

You can give right-angle weave bead-work a more substantial feel and ornate look by stitching beads into the open spaces inside of units. This elegant bracelet features drop beads and metallic-gold seed beads stitched into units that are slightly wider than they are long. The result is a thick, slinky band reminiscent of a jewel-encrusted cuff.

Techniques and Materials

TECHNIQUES

In addition to the general techniques covered in Chapter 2, this project uses techniques from the following chapters and sections.

Chapter 7:

- "Create Flat Right-Angle Weave"

Chapter 9:

- "Make End Loops and Attach Findings"

SUPPLIES

The items below are in addition to those listed under "Essential Tools and Supplies" in Chapter 1 (see page 16).

- Size 13 beading needle
- Size B beading thread in golden yellow

BEADS

This project uses Japanese seed beads and fire polished beads made in the Czech Republic. Weights are rounded to the nearest 0.5 gram and are estimated based on an average-length bracelet.

- 3 grams size 11/0 galvanized gold seed beads (**A**)
- 4.5 grams size 11/0 gold luster carnelian seed beads (**B**)
- 7 grams 3.4mm white-lined ruby red drop beads (**C**)
- 7 grams 3.4mm gold-lined crystal drop beads (**D**)
- 3 Czech fire polished 6mm ruby red glass beads (**E**)

Directions and Pattern

MAKE THE RIGHT-ANGLE WEAVE BASE

1 Beginning with a prepared length of thread with the needle threaded, begin stitching flat right-angle weave following the pattern on the right, leaving a 12-inch thread tail to use later for the clasp.

2 Repeat the pattern until the beadwork is about ½ inch shorter than your desired bracelet length (including the clasp). Do not weave-in the thread tails

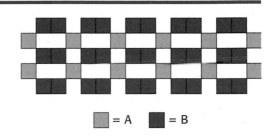

☐ = A ■ = B

In this pattern, each row contains five units. Each side of each unit contains a single A, and the top and bottom of each unit each contains a set of two B.

CONTINUED ON NEXT PAGE

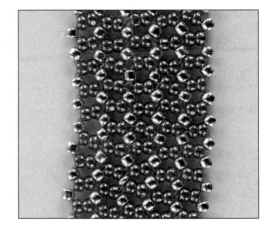

TIP

Using Galvanized Beads with the Right-Angle Weave Stitch

Galvanized seed beads, like A, tend to have smaller and less consistently sized holes than other beads. This makes them more challenging to use with right-angle weave, where the thread passes through many beads multiple times. To avoid problems, do not use any bead that sticks on the needle when you pick it up. Set the smaller-hole beads aside for a different project, and only use beads that slide easily over the needle. If the needle sticks inside of an A while you're stitching, you can use chain nose pliers to carefully attempt to pull it through. (If a bead breaks, replace it with a new one.)

Additionally, when you weave-in to end a thread or begin a new one, place each knot before or within a set of 2B—rather than immediately before an A. It is easier to hide knots within the larger B holes.

STITCH THE EMBELLISHMENTS

1 After completing the right-angle weave base, weave through the beadwork and bring the needle out at the top of the last unit in the second from last unit row (see the arrow in the upper-right corner of the diagram below).

2 Pick up 1C and then pass through both beads at the bottom of that unit, moving in the opposite direction, as shown.

3 Repeat Step 2 for each unit in this column, ending with the second from first unit row (shown at the bottom of the diagram).

4 To move to the next column, weave through the beadwork taking the path shown in the lower-right corner of the diagram. (Notice that this does not entirely follow the path of existing thread, which is the general rule; however, the thread in this location will be hidden by drop beads.)

5 For the next four columns, follow the diagram to pick up sets of three beads, or single beads, as indicated for each unit. Be sure to keep the first and last unit rows of the base unembellished.

 = A

 = B

= C

= D

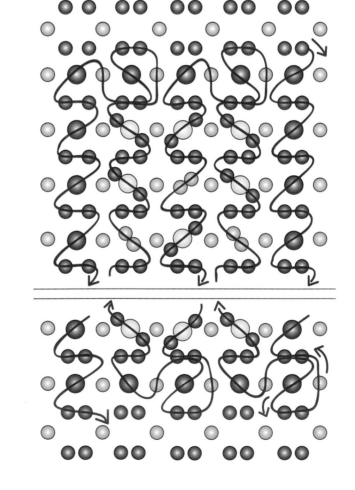

CREATE THE CLASPS

Finish the bracelet with a set of three bead-and-loop clasps spaced evenly along each end of the band, as shown in the diagram below. Each loop contains 16B, including its base bead. Although it's not shown in the diagram (for clarity), it's a good idea to pass back through each unit after adding its loop, and then passing through the entire loop again for reinforcement, before passing through the beadwork to create the next loop or weave-in.

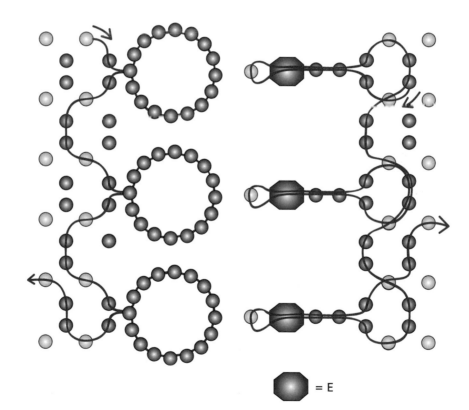

= E

Circular Brick Stitch Fringe Earrings

The rich colors in these fringy, "shoulder duster" earrings are inspired by peacock feathers. The domed top panel, which is a variation of circular brick stitch, supports the weight of the extra-long fringe below. The gold-filled earring posts add subtle elegance but not unnecessary length.

Techniques and Materials

TECHNIQUES

In addition to the general techniques covered in Chapter 2, this project uses techniques from the following chapters and sections.

Chapter 5:

- "Create Circular Brick Stitch"

Chapter 9:

- "Make End Loops and Attach Findings"

SUPPLIES AND FINDINGS

The items below are in addition to those listed under "Essential Tools and Supplies" in Chapter 1 (see page 16).

- Size 12 beading needle
- Size D Nymo beading thread in olive
- Pair of gold-filled 4mm ball-post earring findings
- Clear nail polish
- **Optional:** Size 15 beading needle to use temporarily in any areas where the size 12 needle fits too snugly

BEADS

This project uses Japanese seed, bugle, and drop beads. Weights are rounded up to the nearest 0.5 gram.

- 1 sapphire tortoise 4mm Czech fire polished glass bead
- 0.5 gram size 15/0 opaque black seed beads (**A**)
- 0.5 gram size 15/0 metallic purple iris seed beads (**B**)
- 0.5 gram size 15/0 metallic dark blue iris seed beads (**C**)
- 0.5 gram size 15/0 opaque luster light denim seed beads (**D**)
- 2 grams size 15/0 silver-lined rainbow peridot seed beads (**E**)
- 3 grams size 15/0 metallic blue-green iris seed beads (**F**)
- 0.5 gram size 15/0 silver-lined matte dark topaz seed beads (**G**)
- 32 silver-lined dark topaz twisted 12mm bugle beads (**H**)
- 32 gold luster olive 3.4mm drops (**I**)

Directions and Pattern

MAKE THE EARRING TOPS

Stitch the circular brick stitch tops in a counterclockwise direction around the central bead. After the first few rounds, the beadwork becomes slightly domed, and you can use the tip of your finger to support it from underneath.

1 Beginning with a prepared length of thread with the needle threaded, pick up the 4mm Czech glass bead and position it about 6 inches from the loose end of the thread.

2 Bring both ends of the thread together and make a surgeon's knot against the side of the bead.

3 Pass the needle through the hole in the bead and gently pull the thread until the knot is positioned against the edge of the bead hole.

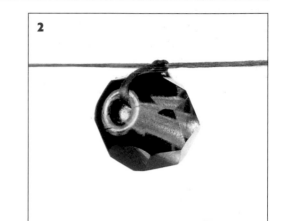

4 Apply a small drop of clear nail polish to the knot.

5 Gently pull the thread again until the knot disappears inside of the bead, and then trim the thread tail near the bead hole.

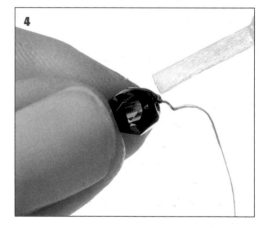

6 Pass through the bead in the same direction and pull the thread gently to remove any slack. There are now two wraps of thread on the outside surface of the bead. Push them apart so that they are on opposite sides and snug against the bead.

CONTINUED ON NEXT PAGE

7 Hold the thread tail and the 4mm bead with the fingers of your non-dominant hand and use your other hand to pick up 2A.

8 Position the 2A against one of the wraps of thread on the side of the 4mm bead and pass the needle beneath that wrap (as if it were a bridge of thread running between two brick-stitched beads). Be sure to hold the 2A against the 4mm bead as you do this, making sure that the 2A do not slip beneath the wrap of thread.

9 Using the same technique that you use to begin the second round of basic circular brick stitch (see page 110), pass back up through the second bead that you picked up in Step 7 and pull the thread taut.

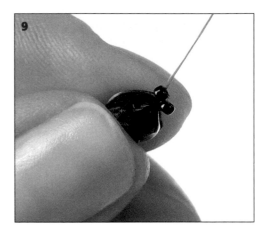

10 Pick up 1A and brick-stitch it to the same wrap of thread. Use a finger to hold this bead as you pull the thread through, to keep it from slipping beneath the thread.

11 Individually brick-stitch 1B, 1B, 1C, and 1C onto the same wrap of thread.

12 Skip the hole at the end of the 4mm bead, and then individually brick-stitch 1C, 1C, 1B, 1B, 1A, 1A, and 1A.

13 Pass down through the first A that you picked up in Step 7 and up through the last A that you stitched in Step 12 and pull the thread taut. This completes the first round of beadwork.

TIP

Weave-In Without Knots in Dense Beadwork
Because the beadwork is very dense in the top panel of these earrings, always weave-in to end or begin a thread without using knots. When you weave into the fringe, however, use half-hitch knots.

⑭ Find your location in the pattern below, and stitch the next six rounds of circular brick stitch (The central oval represents the 4mm bead). The pairs of beads marked with pink "Xs" in the diagram represent beads that you stitch onto the *same* bridge of thread (as mid-row increases). Stitch all of the other beads onto bridges of thread individually.

CONTINUED ON NEXT PAGE

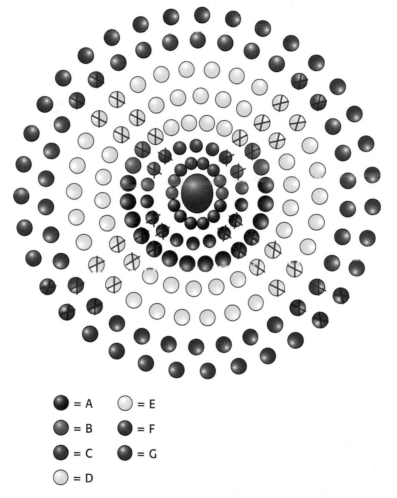

⬤ = A	◯ = E
⬤ = B	⬤ = F
⬤ = C	⬤ = G
◯ = D	

⑮ If the bare thread is more than 6–8 inches long, trim it down to that length now and remove the needle. (Do not weave-in this tail yet; you can weave it into the fringe later.)

⑯ Prepare a new length of thread that is about 2 feet long (be sure to pre-stretch it well), and begin it by weaving-in toward the upper edge of the top panel, starting at the location shown here. (The red bead is the stop bead on the new thread.)

⑰ Bring the thread out through the fourth F from the left side.

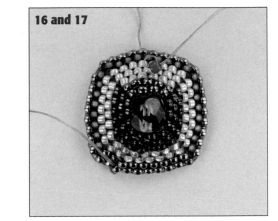

16 and 17

⑱ Pick up 3F and position them against the edge of the beadwork.

⑲ String on one earring post by passing the needle through the bottom ring on the post, and slide the post down against the 3F that you picked up in Step 18. Make sure that the post is positioned properly; its ring should point downward toward the beadwork and the front of the post should point forward.

⑳ Pick up 2F and slide them against the earring post.

㉑ Pass back through the first F that you picked up in Step 18 and slowly pull the thread taut while holding the F beads and earring post against the edge of the beadwork. This creates an end loop with a base bead.

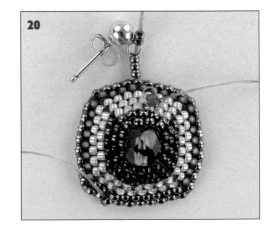

20

㉒ Pass down through the next bead at the edge of the beadwork and then up through the previous bead again, and all the way through the loop of beads (including the earring-post ring), one more time.

㉓ Before passing back into the panel again, pull the thread taut and make a half-hitch knot around the existing thread. (The thread should be very taut in the loop; the beads are spaced in the diagram to better show the path of the thread.)

㉔ Pass back into the panel as shown, pulling the knot into a bead.

㉕ Weave-in to end the thread. (See the previous tip on page 230.)

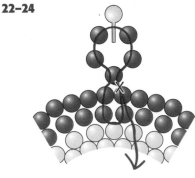

22–24

X = Knot

MAKE THE FRINGE

Because the fringe uses about one typical arms'-span length of thread, it's a good idea to prepare a slightly longer piece to ensure that you don't run out before you finish.

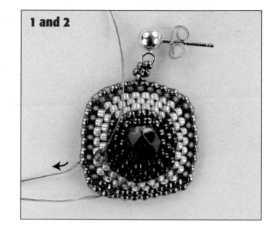

1 Prepare a new length of thread with the needle threaded, and begin it by weaving-in from the inside of the top panel, moving toward the edge, starting at or near the location shown here. (The red bead is a stop bead.)

2 Bring the thread out through the third from bottom F on the edge of the panel.

3 Pick up all of the beads for the first piece of fringe in this order: 4F, 1C, 1H, 1G, 12E, 13F, and 1I.

4 Skip the last *three* beads that you picked up in Step 3 and pass back through all of the remaining beads in the fringe piece. This creates a turning picot containing two true seed beads and one drop bead at the end of the fringe.

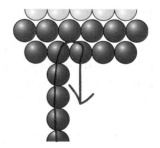

5 When you arrive back at the top of the fringe piece, pass back through the same bead at the edge of the beadwork that the thread exited in Step 2. Adjust the thread so that the fringe piece has proper tension (review fringe in Chapter 9).

6 To position the thread to make the next piece of fringe, bring the thread out through the next bead on the edge of the beadwork.

CONTINUED ON NEXT PAGE

Circular Brick Stitch
Fringe Earrings *(continued)*

7 Use the same technique to create all 16 pieces of fringe. Follow the instructions below to pick up the beads for each piece.

Note: When you reach the panel bead from which the tail of the old thread exits, leave that tail in place for now. Hold it to the side so that it does not entangle with your working thread.

Fringe 2: 4F, 1C, 1H, 1G, 12E, 13F, 1I
Fringes 3 and 4: 4F, 1C, 1H, 2G, 12E, 13F, 1I
Fringe 5: 4F, 2C, 1H, 3G, 12E, 13F, 1I
Fringe 6: 5F, 2C, 1H, 3G, 12E, 13F, 1I
Fringe 7: 5F, 3C, 1H, 4G, 12E, 13F, 1I
Fringes 8 and 9: 6F, 3C, 1H, 5G, 12E, 13F, 1I
Fringe 10: Same as Fringe 7
Fringe 11: Same as Fringe 6
Fringe 12: Same as Fringe 5
Fringes 13 and 14: Same as Fringes 3 and 4
Fringes 15 and 16: Same as Fringe 2

8 End the thread by changing direction within the panel, and then weaving-in with knots within the second from last fringe piece.

9 Go back and weave the remaining tail of old thread into the fringe.

You have now completed one earring. Perform all of the steps again to complete the matching pair.

8

X = Possible locations
of knots over
existing thread

This necklace features a beaded pendant made with a special type of diagonal peyote called *Russian leaf*, which—as its name implies—creates beadwork in the organic shape of a leaf. In this project, a faceted glass teardrop is stitched behind an open "window" in the upper portion of the leaf. The pendant hangs from a narrow, twisted-herringbone rope.

Techniques and Materials

TECHNIQUES

In addition to the general techniques covered in Chapter 2, this project uses techniques from the following chapters and sections.

Chapter 3:

- "Weave Flat Peyote Stitch"
- "Perform Peyote Stitch Increases and Decreases"

Chapter 8:

- "Create Tubular Herringbone"

Chapter 9:

- "Create Loop Clasps"

MATERIALS AND FINDINGS

The items below are in addition to those listed under "Essential Tools and Supplies" in Chapter 1 (see page 16).

- Size 12 beading needle
- Size D Nymo beading thread in ash
- Glass button with a shank (the example uses a 12mm clear-glass vintage button)

BEADS

This project uses Japanese seed beads, Miyuki Delica cylinder beads, and a faceted glass teardrop made in India. Weights are rounded up to the nearest 0.5 gram, and are estimates based on an average-length necklace.

- 3 grams size 11/0 white-lined teal seed beads (**A**)
- 3 grams size 11/0 transparent luster hint-of-celery cylinder beads (**B**)
- 3 grams size 14/0 silver-lined matte rainbow light gold seed beads (**C**)
- 3.5 grams size 11/0 opaque turquoise green cylinder beads (**D**)
- 17 size 11/0 metallic light bronze cylinder beads (**E**)
- 19 size 11/0 metallic bronze cylinder beads (**F**)
- 1 faceted "blue zircon quartz" 10mm glass teardrop

CONTINUED ON NEXT PAGE

Herringbone Rope and Peyote Leaf Necklace (continued)

Directions and Pattern

MAKE THE ROPE

The necklace rope is a narrow version of tubular herringbone with twisted columns. Because the beadwork only contains two spines, you need to remember to step up to stitch every other spine.

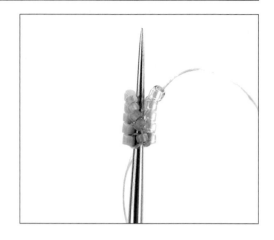

1. After preparing a length of thread and threading the needle, make an initial ring of ladder-stitched beads using 1A, 1B, 1C, and 1D, and leaving a tail about 12 inches long to use later for the clasp. The ring is too narrow to fit over a typical form, but if you need more support getting started, you can use a beading awl, as shown. (Once the rope begins to take shape, you can stitch without a form.)

2. Stitch each bead over a bead of the same color in the previous round. After stitching the first three rounds, transition into tubular herringbone with twisted columns (see page 154). When you weave-in to begin a new thread or end an old one, pass through and make knots between beads that are in the same twisted column (beads of the same color).

3. Continue stitching until the rope is about ½ inch shorter than your desired necklace length (including the clasp). The spirals may look slightly loose and uneven at this point; you can fix them later in Step 8.

4. Stitch the final three rounds of tubular herringbone (without twists).

5. To attach the button, pick up 1A and enough C to make a loop through and around the button shank.

6. Pick up the button shank and pass back through the 1A.

7. Pull the thread taut and pass back into one twisted bead-column of the beadwork.

8. Even out the tension in the spirals by passing back through *all* of the beads in the spiraled column that your thread currently exits. Do this by passing through 2 or 3 inches of beads of the same color, pulling the thread taut, making a half-hitch knot, and then repeating that sequence until you approach the other end of the rope.

9. Make one or two more half-hitch knots, then bring the thread out at the end of the rope and trim it.

10. Thread the needle onto the 12-inch tail of thread at this end of the rope.

11. Pick up 1A and enough C to create a loop (with a base bead) that fits over the button.

12. Pass back into the 1A and then weave-in to end the thread within one twisted bead-column in the rope (select a different column than the one you used to reinforce the rope).

MAKE THE PENDANT

With the Russian leaf diagonal-peyote technique, you do not need to weave back into the beadwork at the end of each row to make the turn. Instead, use a turning bead to change direction and create a soft-looking edge.

Begin stitching at the center of the pattern, which is labeled in diagram below, leaving an extra-long tail (as described in the steps below). Then stitch upward to complete the first half of the leaf before returning to the center to stitch the bottom half. You may find it helpful to keep your place by covering a portion of the diagram with a sheet of paper as you work.

1 Prepare about one arms'-span length of thread and thread the needle. (The pendant uses slightly less than one typical arms' span of thread.)

2 Pick up 1E, 2B, 2F, and 7D and position them at the center point of the thread. These beads will become the first two rows of peyote stitch (at the center of the pattern), plus one turn.

3 Locate those beads on the diagram below. The 1E, which is the first bead that you picked up, is marked with an asterisk, and the last D that you picked up is marked with a dot.

CONTINUED ON NEXT PAGE

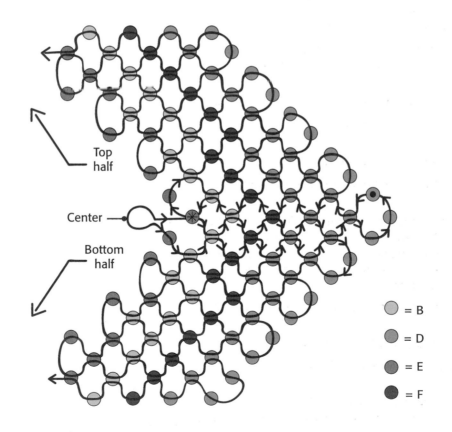

Top half

Center

Bottom half

○ = B

○ = D

○ = E

● = F

④ Follow the diagram (on the previous page) to stitch the third row.

⑤ At the end of the third row, pick up 1E (as shown) before picking up the B that is the first bead in the fourth row.

⑥ Stitch the fourth row, turn, and stitch the fifth row.

⑦ At the end of the fifth row, notice that you pick up three beads (1B and 2E) to make a two-column outside increase.

⑧ Continue stitching, following the diagram and using these same techniques, until you complete the final row at the top of the diagram. Do not weave-in the thread.

⑨ Thread the needle onto the other end of the thread.

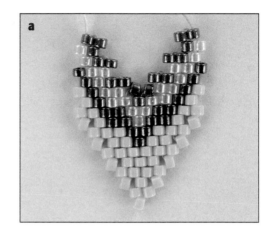

⑩ Continue peyote stitch, following the diagram on the previous page, downward from the center of the pattern.

⑪ Stop but do not weave-in the thread after completing the final row at the bottom of the diagram. The beadwork should look like this (a), and the thread should exit the last E in the second from last row.

⑫ Pick up the faceted teardrop and then pass into the matching E (see Step 11) on the opposite end of the beadwork.

⑬ Pull the thread tight so that the top edges of the leaf come together against the teardrop.

⑭ Make a half-hitch knot over the existing thread to secure the thread tension.

Note: If the thread still looks loose after you make the knot, weave through a few more beads and pull the thread tight again.

12–16

⬤ = B   ⬤ = E   ▲ = teardrop

✕ = Knot

⑮ Weave within the leaf to reverse direction and then pass through the E that is adjacent to the E that you passed into in Step 12.

⑯ Pick up 2 or 3E (however many you need to reach fully across the teardrop) and pass into the matching E on the other side. Position the 2 or 3E in front of (not behind) the top of the teardrop.

⑰ Pull the thread taut and make a half-hitch knot to preserve the tension.

⑱ Weave-in to end this thread within the leaf.

19 Thread the needle onto the other tail and pick up 5B.

20 Pass into the matching E the other side of the teardrop.

21 Pull the thread tight and make a half-hitch knot over the existing thread to preserve the tension.

22 Weave-in to end the thread within the leaf.

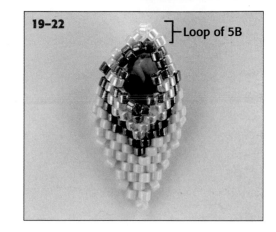

19–22 ⌐ Loop of 5B

23 Prepare a new length of thread that's about 12 inches long.

24 Thread the needle and pick up 20C for the beaded-ring bail.

25 Pass under the small loop of 5B at the top of the pendant, and then pass through all 20C in the bail again.

26 Weave into the ball ring, making knots, to end both of its thread tails.

26

27 To assemble the necklace, slide the bail over the loop-end of the rope and center it.

Index